THE TIMES

TOP 100

GRADUATE EMPLOYERS

The definitive guide to the leading employers
recruiting graduates during 2018-2019.

HIGH FLIERS

HIGH FLIERS PUBLICATIONS LTD
IN ASSOCIATION WITH THE TIMES

Published by High Fliers Publications Limited
The Gridiron Building, 1 Pancras Square, London, N1C 4AG
Telephone: 020 7428 9100   *Web:* www.Top100GraduateEmployers.com

Editor Martin Birchall
Publisher Gill Thomas
Production Manager Jeremy Brown
Portrait Photography Tatjana Panek
Guest Writer Simon Howard

The Times Top 100 Graduate Employers is based on research
results from *The UK Graduate Careers Survey 2018*,
produced by High Fliers Research Ltd.

The greatest care has been taken in compiling this book. However,
no responsibility can be accepted by the publishers or compilers for
the accuracy of the information presented.

Where opinion is expressed it is that of the author or advertiser and
does not necessarily coincide with the editorial views of High Fliers
Publications Limited or *The Times* newspaper.

Printed and bound in Italy by L.E.G.O. S.p.A.

A CIP catalogue record for this book
is available from the British Library.
ISBN 978-0-9559257-9-5

Contents

Foreword

By **Martin Birchall**
Editor, *The Times Top 100 Graduate Employers*

Welcome to the twentieth edition of *The Times Top 100 Graduate Employers*, your annual guide to the UK's most prestigious and sought-after graduate employers.

In the autumn of 1999, just as the first edition of a distinctive new red and black careers directory was being delivered to universities around the country, the London Eye was being lifted into place on London's South Bank in readiness for the Millenium celebrations.

In Europe, eleven countries were getting used to their new 'Euro' currency and, in the United States, President Bill Clinton was coming to the end of eight years in the White House.

Back in the UK, just 20 per cent of the population had access to the internet at home, and the first students to pay the £1,000-a-year tuition fees introduced by Tony Blair's New Labour Government had enrolled at university.

Britney Spears had the best-selling single of the year with 'Baby One More Time' and *Star Wars: The Phantom Menace* became the year's most-watched film at UK cinemas.

Graduates leaving university in 1999 emerged into a buoyant job market. Entry-level vacancies at the country's top employers had increased by an impressive 12 per cent the previous year: one of the largest annual increases in graduate recruitment since the late 1980s.

Starting salaries for new graduates were rising quickly too, by nearly twice the rate of inflation, as the UK's leading employers competed hard to recruit the best university-leavers for their organisations. The average graduate starting salary on offer for the 'Class of 1999' was £17,400, and just forty major employers paid their new recruits packages of £20,000 or more.

Now, as *The Times Top 100 Graduate Employers* celebrates its twentieth year, today's graduates are entering a very different employment market.

Average starting salaries at the top employers are now £30,000. But the great recession of 2008 and 2009 meant that graduate jobs at the leading employers were cut by almost a quarter and it took a further six years before graduate recruitment finally returned to pre-recession levels in 2015.

In the aftermath of the Brexit vote in 2016, the country's biggest private sector employers cut their graduate vacancies again last year, by an average of 10 per cent, with the biggest drops in recruitment at the top accounting & professional services firms, banking & financial companies, and the City's investment banks.

Over the last two decades, competition for places on employers' graduate programmes has intensified as the number of graduates leaving university has jumped from 237,400 in 1999 to

> *66 Most major employers are maintaining a 'business as usual' message for their graduate recruitment in 2018-2019. 99*

an expected 400,000 in 2019: an increase of more than 70 per cent. Employers featured in *The Times Top 100 Graduate Employers* received almost 40 applications per graduate vacancy during the 2017-2018 recruitment season.

With the UK set to leave the European Union in March 2019, the outlook for the next 12 months is inevitably uncertain, but most major employers are maintaining a 'business as usual' message for their graduate recruitment in 2018-2019.

Since the first edition of The Times Top 100 Graduate Employers was published in 1999, more than a million copies of have been produced to help students and graduates at universities across the UK research their career options and find their first job. Today's Top 100 continues to provide an unrivalled, independent assessment of the most sought-after graduate employers.

This year's rankings have been compiled from the results of face-to-face interviews with almost 20,000 final year students who graduated from universities across the UK in the summer of 2018. Students were asked to name the employer that they thought offered the best opportunities for new graduates. Between them, the 'Class of 2018'

named organisations in every major employment sector – from the top consulting firms, investment banks and technology companies, to the country's leading law firms, engineering companies, public sector employers, high street retailers, the Armed Forces, media groups, property companies, and accounting & professional services firms. The one hundred employers that were mentioned most often during the research form *The Times Top 100 Graduate Employers* for 2018-2019.

This book is therefore a celebration of the employers who are judged to offer the brightest prospects for new graduates. Whether through the perceived quality of their training programmes, the business success that they enjoy, the scale of their graduate recruitment, or by the impression that their on-campus promotions have made – these are the employers that were most attractive to graduate job hunters in 2018.

The Times Top 100 Graduate Employers won't necessarily identify which organisation you should join after graduation – only you can decide that. But it is an invaluable reference if you want to discover what the UK's leading employers are offering for new graduates in 2019.

THE TIMES TOP 100 GRADUATE EMPLOYERS — Finding out about the Top 100 Graduate Employers

IN PRINT

Each employer featured in this edition of the *Top 100* has their own **Employer Entry**, providing details of graduate vacancies for 2018, minimum academic requirements, starting salaries, and the universities employers will be visiting in 2018-2019.

ONLINE

Register now with the official *Top 100* website for full access to the very latest information about the UK's most sought-after graduate employers.

This includes details of employers' internships & work experience programmes, local campus recruitment events and application deadlines.

And get ready for your applications, interviews and assessment centres with up-to-the-minute business news about each of the organisations featured in this year's *Top 100*.

www.Top100GraduateEmployers.com

BY EMAIL

Once you've registered with the Top 100 website, you'll receive **weekly email bulletins** with news of the employers you're interested in, their careers events at your university, and their forthcoming application deadlines.

ALDI

It's been my biggest challenge.

And my greatest achievement.

Graduate Area Manager Programme

- **£44,000 starting salary (rising to £75,360 after four years)**
- **Pension • Healthcare • Audi A4 • All-year round recruitment but places fill quickly**

The Area Manager role gives graduates real responsibility and opportunities to progress. You'll need to combine intelligence and fresh ideas with a determined 'roll your sleeves up' attitude. But from day one I had a plan for the whole year. I was given world-class training from a global retailer and a dedicated mentor who helped me throughout. By the end of the year I knew I was making a real contribution to the success of one of the UK's fastest-growing supermarkets. Amazing when you think about it.

aldirecruitment.co.uk/graduates

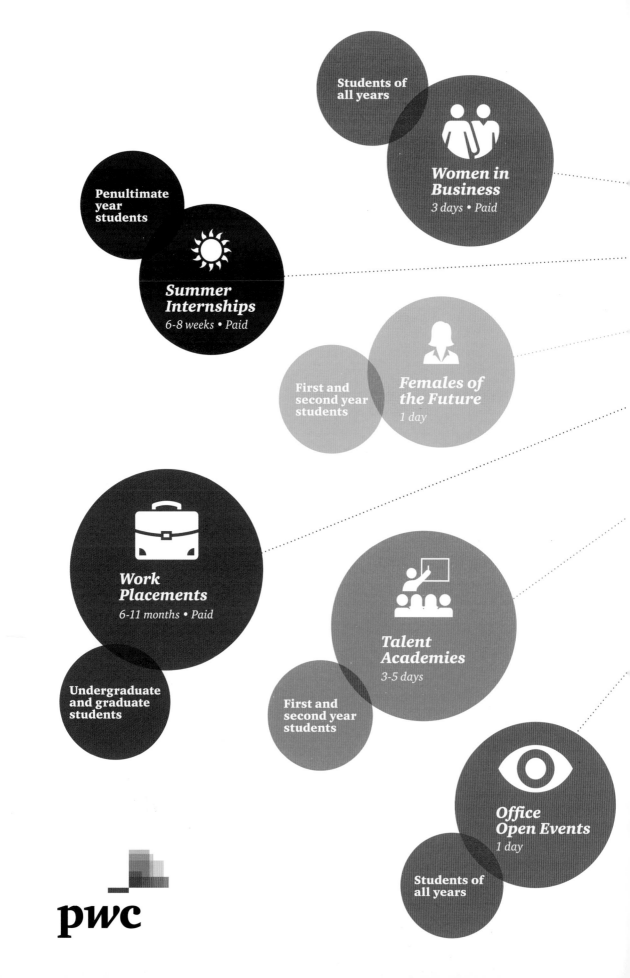

Students of all years

Women in Business
3 days • Paid

Penultimate year students

Summer Internships
6-8 weeks • Paid

First and second year students

Females of the Future
1 day

Work Placements
6-11 months • Paid

Undergraduate and graduate students

First and second year students

Talent Academies
3-5 days

Office Open Events
1 day

Students of all years

pwc

Boost your employability

The experience stays with you

We've got lots of different work experience programmes for every year of study, so you can learn more about our business and boost your employability. They'll help you make an informed decision about which of our career opportunities is best for you. If you do well you could even be fast-tracked to a graduate role.

Join us. We're focused on helping you reach your full potential.

Take the opportunity of a lifetime
pwc.co.uk/work-experience

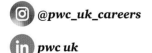 **@pwc_uk_careers**   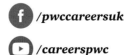 **/pwccareersuk**   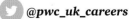 **@pwc_uk_careers**

in *pwc uk*   ▶ **/careerspwc**

Valuing difference. Driving inclusion.

THE TIMES

TOP 100 GRADUATE EMPLOYERS 2010-2011

TOP 100 GRADUATE EMPLOYERS 2011-2012

TOP 100 GRADUATE EMPLOYERS 2012-2013

TOP 100 GRADUATE EMPLOYERS 2013-2014

TOP 100 GRADUATE EMPLOYERS 2014-2015

TOP 100 GRADUATE EMPLOYERS 2015-2016

TOP 100 GRADUATE EMPLOYERS 2016-2017

TOP 100 GRADUATE EMPLOYERS 2017-2018

TOP 100 GRADUATE EMPLOYERS 2018-2019

Researching The Times Top 100 Graduate Employers

By **Gill Thomas**
Publisher, High Fliers Publications

When the first edition of *The Times Top 100 Graduate Employers* was published in 1999, there were an estimated five thousand employers, large and small, recruiting graduates from the UK's leading universities. Some offered formal management development programmes for new graduates, but many others were recruiting for entry-level vacancies requiring a particular degree of qualification.

With so many employers actively recruiting new graduates, the challenge for *The Times Top 100 Graduate Employers* was to identify the organisations that offered the best opportunities for university-leavers.

For students researching their career options, finding the 'right' graduate employer was often a daunting prospect. What basis could you use to evaluate such a large number of different organisations and the opportunities they offered for new graduates after university?

Twenty years on, the number of employers recruiting graduates has increased considerably and there are now an estimated 200,000 jobs available annually.

How then can anyone produce a meaningful league table of the UK's top graduate employers? Which criteria define whether one individual organisation is 'better' than another?

For the last two decades, *The Times Top 100 Graduate Employers* has been compiled annually by the independent market research company, High Fliers Research, through face-to-face on-campus interviews with final year students at the country's leading universities.

This latest edition is based on research with 19,147 new graduates who left universities across the UK in the summer of 2018.

The research examined students' experiences during their search for a first graduate job and asked them about their attitudes to employers.

Finalists from the 'Class of 2018' who took part in the study were selected at random to represent the full cross-section of final year students at their universities, not just those who had already secured graduate employment.

The question used to produce the *Top 100* rankings was "Which employer do you think offers the best opportunities for graduates?" The question was deliberately open-ended and students were not shown a list of employers to choose from or prompted in any way during the interview.

Within the full survey sample, final year students named more than 1,500 different organisations – from new start-up businesses and small local or regional employers, to some of the world's best-known companies. The responses were analysed

> **❝** *In an unparalleled achievement, PwC has been voted the country's leading graduate employer for the fifteenth time.* **❞**

THE TIMES
TOP 100 — The Times Top 100 Graduate Employers 2018
GRADUATE EMPLOYERS

	2017				2017	
1	1	PwC		51	54	AIRBUS
2	2	CIVIL SERVICE		52	NEW	ASOS
3	3	ALDI		53	77	PENGUIN RANDOM HOUSE
4	4	TEACH FIRST		54	70	BOOTS
5	5	GOOGLE		55	73	FACEBOOK
6	6	DELOITTE		56	55	SANTANDER
7	7	NHS		57	60	VIRGIN MEDIA
8	8	KPMG		58	64	DLA PIPER
9	9	EY		59	76	BLOOMBERG
10	10	GSK		60	49	SLAUGHTER AND MAY
11	12	UNILEVER		61	57	EXXONMOBIL
12	11	BBC		62	45	FRESHFIELDS
13	14	J.P. MORGAN		63	53	CANCER RESEARCH UK
14	17	HSBC		64	61	WPP
15	13	LIDL		65	58	BAKER McKENZIE
16	15	ROLLS-ROYCE		66	74	BAIN & COMPANY
17	18	GOLDMAN SACHS		67	81	WELLCOME
18	19	BARCLAYS		68	98	MCDONALD'S
19	20	JAGUAR LAND ROVER		69	59	CITI
20	16	ACCENTURE		70	67	BT
21	21	McKINSEY & COMPANY		71	78	BANK OF ENGLAND
22	23	BP		72	NEW	BLACKROCK
23	38	AMAZON		73	72	LOCAL GOVERNMENT
24	29	LLOYDS BANKING GROUP		74	85	DANONE
25	25	IBM		75	NEW	TPP
26	28	FRONTLINE		76	87	HOGAN LOVELLS
27	27	ARUP		77	NEW	JOHNSON & JOHNSON
28	35	BRITISH ARMY		78	63	ROYAL NAVY
29	26	SHELL		79	69	MI5 - THE SECURITY SERVICE
30	48	SKY		80	91	WHITE & CASE
31	34	RBS GROUP		81	66	NETWORK RAIL
32	33	PROCTER & GAMBLE		82	NEW	BRITISH AIRWAYS
33	22	JOHN LEWIS PARTNERSHIP		83	88	RAF
34	37	NEWTON		84	NEW	AON
35	50	MARKS & SPENCER		85	24	L'ORÉAL
36	43	CLIFFORD CHANCE		86	86	GRANT THORNTON
37	44	TESCO		87	75	BMW GROUP
38	30	ALLEN & OVERY		88	82	DEUTSCHE BANK
39	31	BAE SYSTEMS		89	99	CMS
40	46	LINKLATERS		90	NEW	POLICE NOW
41	36	MARS		91	56	SIEMENS
42	62	THINK AHEAD		92	83	SAVILLS
43	39	MORGAN STANLEY		93	NEW	MONDELEZ INTERNATIONAL
44	42	APPLE		94	68	NESTLE
45	41	ATKINS		95	97	IRWIN MITCHELL
46	51	ASTRAZENECA		96	71	CHARITYWORKS
47	40	THE BOSTON CONSULTING GROUP		97	94	LLOYD'S
48	47	HERBERT SMITH FREEHILLS		98	NEW	PFIZER
49	32	MICROSOFT		99	NEW	PINSENT MASONS
50	52	DYSON		100	80	AECOM

Source **High Fliers Research** 19,147 final year students leaving UK universities in the summer of 2018 were asked the open-ended question "Which employer do you think offers the best opportunities for graduates?" during interviews for *The UK Graduate Careers Survey 2018* and the one hundred organisations that were mentioned most often make up *The Times Top 100 Graduate Employers* for 2018.

Looking at the considerable selection of answers given by finalists from the 'Class of 2018', it is evident that students used several different criteria to determine which employer they considered offered the best opportunities for graduates. Many evaluated employers based on the information they had seen during their job search – the quality of on-campus recruitment promotions, the impression formed from meeting employers' representatives, or their experiences during the application and selection process.

Some focused on employers' general reputations and their public image, their business profile or commercial success. Finalists also considered the level of graduate vacancies available within individual organisations.

Other final year students, however, used the 'employment proposition' as their main guide – the quality of graduate training and development an employer offers, the starting salary and remuneration package available, and the practical aspects of a first graduate job, such as location or working hours.

Irrespective of the criteria that students used to arrive at their answer, the hardest part for many was just selecting a single organisation. To some extent, choosing two or three, or even half a dozen employers, would have been much easier. But the whole purpose of the exercise was to replicate the reality that everyone faces: you can only work for one organisation. And at each stage of the graduate job search there are choices to be made as to which direction to take and which employers to pursue.

The resulting *Top 100* is a dynamic league table of the UK's most exciting and well-respected graduate recruiters in 2018. In an unparalleled achievement, the accounting and professional services firm PwC has been voted the UK's leading graduate employer for the fifteenth time, with a total of 7.5 per cent of finalists' votes.

The Civil Service, best known for the prestigious Fast Stream programme, has increased its share of finalists' votes but remains in second place, its highest ranking for thirteen years. Aldi's popular trainee area manager programme has also attracted more votes year-on-year, but again appears in third place. Votes for the widely acclaimed Teach First scheme, currently the UK's

largest individual recruiter of graduates, have slipped year-on-year, but it continues in fourth place, just ahead of internet giant Google, which stays in fifth place for the third year running.

All of the 'Big Four' accounting & professional services firms appear within this year's top ten, with Deloitte in sixth place and KPMG in eighth place in the new *Top 100*. EY stays in ninth place for the third consecutive year. With the NHS in seventh place and pharmaceutical & consumer goods company GSK in 10th position – matching its best-ever ranking in 2017 – this means the whole of the top ten remains unchanged from last year, the first time this has happened in the twenty years since the launch of *The Times Top 100 Graduate Employers* in 1999.

There have been very mixed fortunes for the leading City banking and financial institutions in this year's *Top 100*. Just five of the top investment banks remain in the latest league table, and only J.P. Morgan and Goldman Sachs have improved their rankings year-on-year. Among the other eight banking or financial institutions listed in the top graduate employers, HSBC and Barclays have moved up into the top twenty, whilst Lloyds Banking Group has reached 24th place, its highest ranking yet. RBS has moved back up to 31st place, its best result for five years.

The highest climbers in the new *Top 100* are led by McDonald's, which has jumped back up thirty places to 68th place, following a large drop in 2017. Publishing group Penguin Random House and mental health charity Think Ahead have each climbed twenty places or more. And online retailer Amazon continues its rise up the rankings; having joined the *Top 100* in 81st place in 2015, it has now climbed an impressive fifty-eight places to reach 23rd place this year.

L'Oréal has had the biggest move of any employer this year, dropping sixty-one places from last year's 24th to 85th place in the new rankings, one of the largest falls ever recorded by *The Times Top 100 Graduate Employers* in a single year.

There are a total of ten new entries or re-entries in this year's *Top 100*, the highest being for online retailer Asos in 52nd place. Investment management company BlackRock reappears in the *Top 100* rankings in 72nd place. Technology firm TPP, medical & consumer goods company Johnson & Johnson and professional services firm Aon are new entries in 75th, 77th and 82nd places respectively. British Airways and Mondelēz

Get ahead of the curve.

Graduate and undergraduate opportunities

It's always good to get a head start. And thanks to Launch Pad, you could be starting your career journey in Audit, Consultancy, Technology, Tax, Deal Advisory or Business Services sooner than you think.

Launch Pad is an innovative approach to graduate recruitment. A one-day event at the final stage of the process, it could see you being offered a role within as little as two working days. An interactive experience, it will give you the opportunity to demonstrate your talents through assessment activities and interviews with senior members of our team. Plus, you'll gain new skills, meet lots of people and find out more about the many opportunities at KPMG in the UK. Apply now.

kpmgcareers.co.uk

Anticipate tomorrow. Deliver today.

International both return to the *Top 100* this year, along with pharmaceuticals company Pfizer, which re-enters in 98th place, its first time back in the league table since 2008. They are joined by the Police Now graduate scheme, which is a new entry in 90th place, and law firm Pinsent Masons in 99th place.

Employers leaving the *Top 100* in 2018 include drinks giant Diageo, GE, engineering firm Mott MacDonald, investment bank UBS, Oxfam, law firm Norton Rose Fulbright, GCHQ, and energy companies E.ON and Centrica.

In the twenty years since the original edition of *The Times Top 100 Graduate Employers* was published, just three organisations have made it to number one in the rankings. Andersen Consulting (now Accenture) held onto the top spot for the first four years and its success heralded a huge surge in popularity for careers in consulting; at its peak in 2001, almost one in six graduates applied for jobs in the sector.

In the year before the firm changed its name from Andersen Consulting to Accenture, it astutely introduced a new graduate package that included a £28,500 starting salary (a sky-high figure for graduates in 2000) and a much talked-about £10,000 bonus, helping to assure the firm's popularity, irrespective of its corporate branding.

In 2003, after two dismal years in graduate recruitment when vacancies for university-leavers dropped by more than a fifth following the terrorist attacks of 11th September 2001, the Civil Service was named Britain's leading graduate employer. Just a year later it was displaced by PricewaterhouseCoopers, the accounting and professional services firm formed from the merger of Price Waterhouse and Coopers & Lybrand in 1998. At the time, the firm was the largest private-sector recruiter of graduates, with an intake in 2004 of more than a thousand trainees.

Now known simply as PwC, the firm has remained at number one ever since, increasing its share of the student vote from five per cent in 2004 to more than 10 per cent in 2007, and fighting off the stiffest of competition from rivals Deloitte in 2008, when just seven votes separated the two employers.

PwC's reign as the UK's leading graduate employer represents a real renaissance for the entire accounting & professional services sector. Whereas, fifteen years ago, a career in accountancy was regarded as a safe, traditional employment choice, today's profession is viewed in a very different light. The training required to become a chartered accountant is now seen as a prized business qualification, and the sector's

THE TIMES TOP 100 — Number Ones, Movers & Shakers in the Top 100

NUMBER ONES		HIGHEST CLIMBING EMPLOYERS		HIGHEST NEW ENTRIES	
1999	ANDERSEN CONSULTING	1999	SCHLUMBERGER (UP 13 PLACES)	1999	PFIZER (31st)
2000	ANDERSEN CONSULTING	2000	CAPITAL ONE (UP 32 PLACES)	2000	MORGAN STANLEY (34th)
2001	ACCENTURE	2001	EUROPEAN COMMISSION (UP 36 PLACES)	2001	MARCONI (36th)
2002	ACCENTURE	2002	WPP (UP 36 PLACES)	2002	GUINNESS UDV (44th)
2003	CIVIL SERVICE	2003	ROLLS-ROYCE (UP 37 PLACES)	2003	ASDA (40th)
2004	PRICEWATERHOUSECOOPERS	2004	J.P. MORGAN (UP 29 PLACES)	2004	BAKER & MCKENZIE (61st)
2005	PRICEWATERHOUSECOOPERS	2005	TEACH FIRST (UP 22 PLACES)	2005	PENGUIN (70th)
2006	PRICEWATERHOUSECOOPERS	2006	GOOGLE (UP 32 PLACES)	2006	FUJITSU (81st)
2007	PRICEWATERHOUSECOOPERS	2007	PFIZER (UP 30 PLACES)	2007	BDO STOY HAYWARD (74th)
2008	PRICEWATERHOUSECOOPERS	2008	CO-OPERATIVE GROUP (UP 39 PLACES)	2008	SKY (76th)
2009	PRICEWATERHOUSECOOPERS	2009	CADBURY (UP 48 PLACES)	2009	BDO STOY HAYWARD (68th)
2010	PRICEWATERHOUSECOOPERS	2010	ASDA (UP 41 PLACES)	2010	SAATCHI & SAATCHI (49th)
2011	PWC	2011	CENTRICA (UP 41 PLACES)	2011	APPLE (53rd)
2012	PWC	2012	NESTLÉ (UP 44 PLACES)	2012	EUROPEAN COMMISSION (56th)
2013	PWC	2013	DFID (UP 40 PLACES)	2013	SIEMENS (70th)
2014	PWC	2014	TRANSPORT FOR LONDON (UP 36 PLACES)	2014	FRONTLINE (76th)
2015	PWC	2015	DIAGEO, NEWTON (UP 43 PLACES)	2015	DANONE (66th)
2016	PWC	2016	BANK OF ENGLAND (UP 34 PLACES)	2016	SANTANDER (63rd)
2017	PWC	2017	CANCER RESEARCH UK (UP 38 PLACES)	2017	DYSON (52nd)
2018	PWC	2018	MCDONALD'S (UP 30 PLACES)	2018	ASOS (52nd)

Source High Fliers Research

CHANGE YOUR LIFE
TRANSFORM THEIRS

Join a movement of leaders working to address social disadvantage through children's social work

FRONTLINE

The Frontline Organisation is a registered charity in England and Wales
Charity number: 1163194 Company number: 09605966

leading firms are regularly described as 'dynamic' and 'international' by undergraduates looking for their first job after university.

A total of 209 different organisations have now appeared within *The Times Top 100 Graduate Employers* since its inception, and forty of these have made it into the rankings every year since 1999. The most consistent performers have been PwC, KPMG and the Civil Service, each of which have never been lower than 9th place in the league table. The NHS has also had a formidable record, appearing in every top ten since 2003, and the BBC, Goldman Sachs and EY (formerly Ernst & Young) have all remained within the top twenty throughout the last decade.

Google is the highest-climbing employer within the *Top 100*, having risen over eighty places during the last decade, to reach the top three for the first

time in 2015. But car manufacturer Jaguar Land Rover holds the record for the fastest-moving employer, after jumping more than seventy places in just five years, between 2009 and 2014.

Other employers haven't been so successful though. British Airways, ranked in 6th place in 1999, dropped out of the *Top 100* altogether a decade later, and Ford, which was once rated as high as 14th, disappeared out of the list in 2006 after cancelling its graduate recruitment programme two years previously. The latest high-ranking casualty is retailer Sainsbury's, which – having reached 18th place in 200 – tumbled out of the *Top 100* in 2016.

Thirty graduate employers – including Nokia, Maersk, the Home Office, Cable & Wireless, United Biscuits, Nationwide, Capgemini and the Met Office – have the dubious record of having

THE TIMES TOP 100 — Winners & Losers in the Top 100
GRADUATE EMPLOYERS

MOST CONSISTENT EMPLOYERS	HIGHEST RANKING	LOWEST RANKING
ANDERSEN (FORMERLY ARTHUR ANDERSEN)	**2nd** (1999-2001)	**3rd** (2002)
PWC	**1st** (FROM 2004)	**3rd** (1999-2001, 2003)
KPMG	**3rd** (2006-2008, 2011-2012)	**9th** (2015)
CIVIL SERVICE	**1st** (2003)	**8th** (2011)
BBC	**5th** (2005-2007)	**14th** (1999)
GSK	**10th** (2017-2018)	**22nd** (2002-2003)
IBM	**13th** (2000)	**25th** (2017-2018)
EY (FORMERLY ERNST & YOUNG)	**7th** (2013)	**20th** (2001)
BP	**14th** (2013-2014)	**32nd** (2004)
ACCENTURE (FORMERLY ANDERSEN CONSULTING)	**1st** (1999-2002)	**20th** (2014)

EMPLOYERS CLIMBING HIGHEST	NEW ENTRY RANKING	HIGHEST RANKING
GOOGLE	**85th** (2005)	**3rd** (2015)
LIDL	**89th** (2009)	**13th** (2017)
JAGUAR LAND ROVER	**87th** (2009)	**16th** (2014)
ALDI	**65th** (2002)	**2nd** (2015-2016)
MI5 – THE SECURITY SERVICE	**96th** (2007)	**33rd** (2010)
TEACH FIRST	**63rd** (2004)	**2nd** (2014)
APPLE	**87th** (2009)	**27th** (2012)
NEWTON	**94th** (2013)	**34th** (2018)
AMAZON	**81st** (2015)	**23rd** (2018)
ATKINS	**94th** (2004)	**37th** (2009)

EMPLOYERS FALLING FURTHEST	HIGHEST RANKING	LOWEST RANKING
BRITISH AIRWAYS	**6th** (1999)	**Not ranked** (2010, 2011, 2017)
FORD	**11th** (1999)	**Not ranked** (FROM 2006)
UBS	**17th** (2002)	**Not ranked** (2018)
SAINSBURY'S	**18th** (2003)	**Not ranked** (FROM 2016)
THOMSON REUTERS	**22nd** (2001)	**Not ranked** (2009-2012, FROM 2014)
ASTRAZENECA	**24th** (2003)	**Not ranked** (2012-2014)
ASDA	**27th** (2004)	**Not ranked** (FROM 2016)
BANK OF AMERICA MERRILL LYNCH	**27th** (2000)	**Not ranked** (FROM 2017)
RAF	**32nd** (2005)	**Not ranked** (2015)
MINISTRY OF DEFENCE	**35th** (2003)	**Not ranked** (2007, FROM 2012)

Source High Fliers Research

only been ranked in the *Top 100* once during the last fifteen years. And Marconi had the unusual distinction of being one of the highest-ever new entries, in 36th place in 2001, only to vanish from the list entirely the following year.

One of the most spectacular ascendancies within the *Top 100* has been the rise of Aldi, which joined the list in 65th place in 2002, rose to 3rd place in 2009 – helped in part by its memorable remuneration package for new recruits (currently £44,000 plus an Audi A4 car) – and was ranked in 2nd place in both 2015 and 2016. Teach First, which appeared as a new entry in 63rd place in 2003, climbed the rankings in each of years following and reached 2nd place in the *Top 100* in 2014.

This year's edition of *The Times Top 100 Graduate Employers* has produced a number of significant changes within the rankings, and the results provide a unique insight into how graduates from the 'Class of 2018' rated the UK's leading employers. Most of these organisations are featured in the 'Employer Entry' section of this book – from page 84 onwards, you can see a two-page profile for each graduate employer, listed alphabetically for easy reference.

The editorial part of the entry includes a short description of what the organisation does, its opportunities for graduates and its recruitment programme for 2018-2019. A fact file for each employer gives details of the business functions that graduates are recruited for, the number of graduate vacancies on offer, likely starting salaries for 2019, their minimum academic requirements, application deadlines, the universities that the employer is intending to visit during the year, plus details of their graduate recruitment website and how to follow the employer on social media.

If you would like to find out more about any of the employers featured in *The Times Top 100 Graduate Employers*, then simply register with **www.Top100GraduateEmployers.com** – the official website showcasing the latest news and information about *Top 100* organisations.

Registration is entirely free and, as well as being able to access the website, you'll receive regular email updates about the employers you are most interested in – this includes details of the careers events they're holding at your university during the year, up-and-coming job application deadlines, and the very latest business news about the organisations.

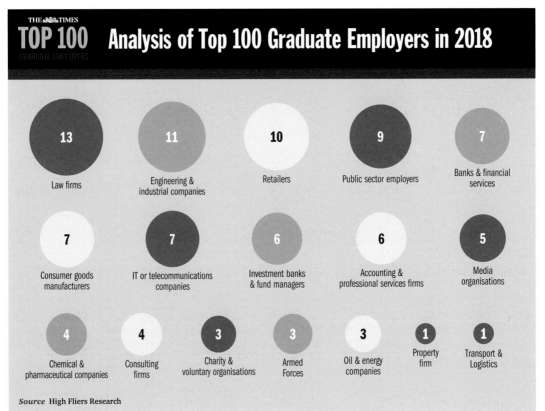

THE TIMES
TOP 100 Analysis of Top 100 Graduate Employers in 2018
GRADUATE EMPLOYERS

13	**11**	**10**	**9**	**7**
Law firms	Engineering & industrial companies	Retailers	Public sector employers	Banks & financial services
7	**7**	**6**	**6**	**5**
Consumer goods manufacturers	IT or telecommunications companies	Investment banks & fund managers	Accounting & professional services firms	Media organisations

4	**4**	**3**	**3**	**3**	**1**	**1**
Chemical & pharmaceutical companies	Consulting firms	Charity & voluntary organisations	Armed Forces	Oil & energy companies	Property firm	Transport & Logistics

Source **High Fliers Research**

Deloitte.

Can you hear the sound of ideas?

Welcome to the home of the ingenious.
A place for those who know that solutions
are often found where nobody is looking.
To those people we offer careers supported
by on-the-job learning, real challenges, real clients,
and global opportunities, wherever their location.
Those who can imagine the improbable and
add real value to everything they touch.

deloitte.co.uk/careers
What impact will you make?

THE TIMES TOP 100 GRADUATE EMPLOYERS
15 Years as the UK's Number 1 Graduate Employer

"It means a huge amount to us that PwC has been voted the country's top graduate employer in *The Times Top 100 Graduate Employers* for the last fifteen years. It's been a real annual celebration that so many university students believe that the firm offers the best opportunities for new graduates.

We've always worked very hard to be innovative with our recruitment campaigns and maintain a high profile at as many universities as we can across the UK. For each of the years that we've been number one, we've done something different to really bring to life the culture and opportunities at the firm.

Whether it's giving students guidance and advice on wellbeing and mental health, hosting skills workshops, teaching people to code, handing out free hot drinks on a cold winter's day, or showcasing our digital capability with an in-house built selfie/celebrity matching game using AI, we host more than 800 campus events each year to meet students and graduates who could be the future of PwC.

Laura Hinton, Chief People Officer, PwC

That powerful university presence has undoubtedly helped establish us as an attractive employer for the next generation of work experience students and graduate job hunters. Having so many opportunities to meet us in person helps potential applicants see for themselves that the thing that really distinguishes PwC from its competitors is the quality of its people.

Our recruitment is very different now compared with 2004: the first year that the firm was named the top graduate employer. Most of our entry-level roles then were in audit, assurance or tax roles – the more traditional accountancy roles – whereas now we have more than twenty different graduate programmes ranging from consulting and technology to corporate finance, forensic accounting and actuarial work. And the number of graduates has increased too, from around 1,000 annually fifteen years ago, to 1,500 graduates a year now, for our 24 UK offices.

Over the years, our graduate recruitment campaigns have used different straplines like 'it's the experience that stays with you' or 'the opportunity of a lifetime' to explain that the world-class business training and qualifications that PwC gives graduates will be the bedrock of their future career, irrespective of whether that's inside the firm or elsewhere.

We have more than 60,000 alumni of the firm, which is a phenomenal community to be part of. The ethos we're developing is that people may leave us and come back later in their careers, or they might work for us as an experienced consultant after a successful career in another industry.

In the fifteen years that PwC has been at the very top of the rankings in *The Times Top 100 Graduate Employers,* the firm has recruited, trained and developed more than 15,000 new graduates and provided work experience for more than 5,000 undergraduates. It's a legacy that we are very proud of. "

ICAEW

Chartered Accountants change the world

Over 9,000 ICAEW Chartered Accountants play a vital role in helping charities to raise and make the most of funds that can save lives. So if you want to make a difference while making a living, then you can use your skills to support the things you really care about.

More than you'd imagine
icaew.com/careers

Flight Lieutenant James "Hadders" Hadfield commands 'F' Flight on Tactical Communications Wing. He was sponsored by the RAF whilst studying his A-Levels at Welbeck Defence Sixth Form College and then at university where he read Electronic Engineering at the University of Birmingham.

James commands a Flight of 42 Cyberspace Communications Specialists whom are all experts on the systems that the RAF delivers. Be that Satellite Communications, Local Area Networks, Computer Systems, Applications and the defence of our networks from a diverse range of cyber threats.

"I could be deployed anywhere in the world as the lead communications specialist. I need to have an in depth understanding of the effect that the RAF is trying to achieve in order to deliver the communication systems that are required to support humanitarian aid and disaster relief; defence of the air; or the delivery of precision guided munitions from combat aircraft. Without communications you can't have air operations."

"The RAF is an organisation like no other because of our people and the world-class training that we receive. By investing in them, they always exceed our expectations, delivering in the most testing circumstances. No matter how big the challenge, the team always succeeds – that's why I love what I do."

ROYAL
AIR FORCE
REGULAR & RESERVE

Flight Lieutenant Nosheen Chaudry is an Aerosystems Engineering Officer who has worked on several Squadrons including a GR4 Tornado Sqn at RAF Marham and on the Royal Air Force Aerobatic Team (RAFAT), The Red Arrows.

From early childhood Nosheen had a fascination with aircraft and the idea of flight. She was offered a RAF scholarship to be sponsored through Birmingham University to study engineering and now works around the cutting-edge aircraft used by the RAF.

"I fulfil a variety of roles, with responsibility for the teams maintaining aircraft within our fleet. It's challenging work but I like the fact I get posted from one station to another every two years to work on other related and sometimes different projects."

"One of the big attractions for me about the Royal Air Force is the sports and adventurous training on offer. I am really keen on athletics and have competed for the RAF Athletics Team for the last eight years." The RAF requires its personnel to keep physically fit and actively encourages adventurous training.

"I knew from an early age that this is the kind of thing I wanted to do and my family were very supportive in my career choice. In fact, they encouraged me to apply for the University Bursary which certainly helps with the cost of getting a degree."

For information about all of the roles available in the RAF, as well as sponsorship opportunities, visit the RAF Recruitment website. Search online for RAF Recruitment.

Celebrating 20 Years of the UK's Top Graduates

Compiled by **Martin Birchall** and **Simon Howard**
Photographs by **Tatjana Panek**

Over the last twenty years, employers who've appeared in *The Times Top 100 Graduate Employers* have recruited a total of more than 400,000 new graduates for their organisations, providing world-class training and development in each of the UK's major industries and business sectors.

But behind this statistic are the lives of individual graduates who've left university during the past two decades and are now in the working world.

To celebrate the twentieth year of *The Times Top 100 Graduate Employers*, this edition features specially-commissioned interviews with twenty graduates, one from each year that the directory has been published.

They studied a wide variety of degree subjects at universities right across the UK, but what all twenty graduates have in common, is that they joined one of *The Times Top 100 Graduate Employers* and have remained there since.

What follows over the next twenty pages, are their life stories, in their own words, based on interviews they gave in the summer of 2018. They're not written by their employers or prepared as recruitment case studies – they are first-hand accounts of how a generation of new graduates made their way from university into successful careers in areas as diverse as engineering, law,

" Inspiring accounts of how individual undergraduates from the last twenty years seized different opportunities and experiences. "

teaching, retailing, consulting, the Armed Forces, healthcare, technology and advertising.

Only a handful of these graduates had any idea when they left school what they wanted to do for their careers. Many had opted to study a degree subject that they'd enjoyed at A-level and few remembered getting lasting careers advice while they were at school or college.

The graduate employers they decided to apply to were often influenced by the work experience they'd done at university or by recruitment events they'd taken part in on-campus. Few, if any, had any idea that the organisation they joined after graduation would offer them a long-term career.

The career paths that they have followed since are often a timely reminder that for around 70 per cent of graduate jobs in the UK, a specific degree subject is not required.

These graduates' stories do not provide a blueprint for how to become a qualified accountant, the partner of a law firm, or a chartered engineer, nor are they a practical recruitment guide to landing a place on a top employer's graduate programme.

Instead, they are an inspiring record of how individual graduates from the last twenty years seized different opportunities and experiences to follow their passions and find careers that have challenged, stretched and excited.

1999 **Ben Kay, WPP**

In the year *The Times Top 100 Graduate Employers* launched, Ben Kay joined WPP. His career since has led to roles in North America, Asia and the UK.

"I graduated from Edinburgh in 1999 with a degree in business studies, unsure of whether to pursue a career in advertising or management consultancy. Having gone through the milkround process with a number of employers, I discovered the WPP Fellowship, a three-year graduate programme for the world's biggest marketing communications business. The Fellowship promised to combine the creativity of advertising and strategic rigour of consultancy, and it felt like a natural fit.

The Fellowship's proposition was – and still is – 'ambidextrous brains required'. They were looking for people as interested by the emotional as the analytical side of business and communications. It was pretty tough to get in, with over 1,200 applications for just a handful of places, but thankfully things went my way and after a three-round process, I was offered the job.

I started my Fellowship at a brand consultancy in London and then, after a year, moved to Toronto and joined the advertising agency, Ogilvy. There I worked as a planner with clients such as FedEx and American Express. Planning is all about helping our clients to grow by understanding the relationship between the people, brands and businesses. We use that understanding to develop brand, communications and creative strategies for our clients.

From Canada I moved to Singapore to work in public relations with Burson Marsteller: a very different world to advertising planning. There I got to understand the fundamentals of consumer PR and crisis management – both critical parts of the client communications arsenal. As with all my placements, the year in Singapore was a steep learning curve, working with some exceptionally bright and talented people.

After these three placements I decided to return to advertising and moved to Y&R in New York where I enjoyed a fantastic four years, working with clients such as Sony and The Absolut Spirits Company. London and New York have historically been the two big centres for advertising and the opportunity to spend time at the heart of Madison Avenue in my mid-20s is one that I'll always look back on with great happiness, both professionally and personally.

I joined the Y&R New York team as a senior planner – still very much work in progress – and over those four years was able to go deep into the role and improve both my hard and soft skills across several different clients and sectors.

From New York I made the personal decision that it was time to come back to the UK and I became Planning Director with Y&R in London. Over the next few years I moved through various management positions to become Chief Strategy Officer, working across clients as diverse as Virgin Atlantic, Land Rover, Lloyds Banking Group and Bombay Sapphire.

I was appointed as Chief Executive Officer of Y&R in London when I was 35 years old and spent four years in that role. I learned a huge amount in that time about running a business, but ultimately I missed the side of the industry I most love, helping clients to tackle the challenges of growing their businesses, and so I decided to take what I'd learned and to apply it to a group planning role at WPP.

Effectively my role now is to work across multiple different disciplines and companies within WPP to piece together effective strategies for our clients, globally. Which, in its own way, reflects what the Fellowship is all about – breadth of knowledge and experiences being brought together in one place.

The marketing and communications business has changed immensely since I joined it in 1999, driven in part by a revolution in data and technology. Thanks to those changes, our clients have more ways to engage more meaningfully with their customers than ever before.

What hasn't changed, and keeps the industry as stimulating and exciting as my first day, is the privilege of working with some of the brightest, most creative and passionate people, day in, day out, on both the client and agency side.**"**

After nearly 20 years at IBM, Rob Sedman is now a senior leader, helping clients to tackle the challenges of cyber security and make the world a safer place.

❝Having studied a Masters in civil engineering at the University of Bristol, I had come to the conclusion that engineering wasn't for me and was looking for something that would inspire me. During my search, IBM stood out – it seemed to offer real choice and opportunity, and I immediately liked all the people I met there.

It was the 'dotcom' era and everything was moving really quickly. There was a lot of excitement about the developments in IT and communications and, having spent two years on the IBM Foundation programme, I took on my first role in sales in 2000, in what was then called e-business hosting. At that time it was considered the forefront of internet technology, working with everyone from dotcom start-ups to multi-nationals.

I stayed in that area of the business for the next four years. The deals got bigger and bigger, more complex, more transformational, and I was really driven by getting new clients on board.

My next move took me to our outsourced services business, which meant taking over and then running our clients' IT for them. Again, the deals increased in size and complexity, but it was about creating deals that helped transform our clients' businesses and improve their value. On a day-to-day basis, that meant setting the strategy, helping to build the solution and negotiate the contract, and bringing the team together to win the business.

It can be pretty intense when you're working on a deal – there are huge peaks and troughs, but it is fantastic fun. I was playing rugby fairly seriously at the time and that helped maintain a bit of balance within the demands of the role. It really was 'work hard, play hard', and I enjoyed it immensely.

In 2010 I took on my first real management role. That's one thing IBM is very good at – offering people the flexibility to alter career paths across the business. From a personal point of view, I had recently married and was hoping to have a family, so I wanted more influence over where and when I was working.

In that role I enjoyed the challenge of getting to know people – understanding their goals, strengths and what they were driven by so that I can could help them be successful. Management is an entirely different challenge to what I had been doing

2000 **Rob Sedman, IBM**

previously. Over three years it meant acquiring a lot of new skills and learning to adapt my style, so I could take on a sales director role.

At that level, there are new challenges to face and new frontiers to explore. Throughout a number of different roles, I had the opportunity to work with clients to help them change and transform their own businesses while also influencing and driving IBM's strategy in the UK and Ireland.

Today, I'm Director of Cyber Security for the UK and Ireland, and run a business which is at the forefront of all aspects of cyber security. We know attacks will come in many different forms, but – whether the rogue elements are criminal or geopolitical – it's our job to make sure that our clients are fully protected and that the world is a safer place as a result.

I hadn't anticipated when I joined IBM that I'd still be here nearly 20 years later. I think it's important to make informed decisions with your career; if you decide to do something, then throw yourself into it, and if you're enjoying it, keep doing it.

I don't know what my next role will be – IBM evolves very rapidly and changes, so it depends what opportunities are put in front of me. But what I do know is that I joined IBM because of the people I met during the recruitment process and the choice and opportunity on offer. That is still true today – our values and our people have been a constant throughout my career and there is still as much choice and opportunity as ever.**❞**

> *IBM stood out – it seemed to offer real choice and opportunity and I immediately liked all the the people I met there.*

2001 Luke Stephens, Morgan Stanley

Having graduated with a degree in zoology, Luke Stephens did a Masters conversion course in IT and joined Morgan Stanley for a career in technology.

❝My path into banking technology was probably different to anyone else – certainly very different to anyone else working in the Technology Division at Morgan Stanley. Having studied zoology at the University of Manchester, I did at one time harbour ambitions to be the next David Attenborough. But I quickly realised the job prospects for a zoologist were pretty limited. So, I decided to do a conversion MSc in information technology at Queen Mary University in London.

Part of that course was a three-month project in industry, so I applied to Morgan Stanley for an internship. I was lucky that they agreed that not only would they take me, but the internship could also be the project which I presented back at the end of my Masters. And from that day to this, I've not left Morgan Stanley.

My first step at the end of the internship was to do a pre-traineeship to enable me to stay and work at the firm until the start of the next graduate programme in February 2001. That meant going to New York for sixteen weeks to learn the ropes – which, at the time, as it does today, meant plenty of coding. The best thing about being based at our global HQ is that it allowed me to start building a network within the bank, and I got to know a number of people who I've remained close to – both professionally and personally – throughout the past seventeen years.

From New York I came back to London for my first 'proper job' in what was then the Bond Trading Technology Division, working with a team based throughout Europe. There I learned the importance of working closely with both traders and external clients. Being able to understand the issues which non-technical people face and being able to translate their needs has been fundamental to my career – as has been being able to translate technical issues for less technical people.

I was promoted to vice president in 2005 and moved to the eFX department at the very beginning the electronic trading division was set up. E-trading is incredibly real-time, and if stuff goes wrong its impact is immediate. So, we're all about preventing mishaps by properly managing operational and technology risk. Early in that role it was all about delivery and immediacy, but now, as a managing director, I'm making sure that we're correctly resourced, that we have the right skillsets in my team and that we are making the right strategic and investment decisions to enable increased revenue generation.

Hence, my job now is leading a multi-year strategy and making sure we position ourselves at the forefront of e-trading. 'Leading' means that I'm there to take the flack and remove the obstacles for my team so that they can deliver solutions to the business problems of clients.

But it's not just about delivering in a high-profile role. I have three daughters and my family is the number-one thing in my life – and at Morgan Stanley I've been able to balance that with the demands of the job. I believe that if the person at the top of the department demonstrates that sort of balance, it sets the right example.

My job now is leading a multi-year strategy and making sure we position ourselves at the forefront of e-trading.

I've found that Morgan Stanley is an organisation that consistently stretches and challenges you. The reason that I'm here after seventeen years is that I am passionate about what I do, and people only stay if they stay challenged, and only stay happy if they have the right work-life balance.

I'm now on the European Technology Graduate Recruiting Committee, and what we're looking for today is as true as it was when I joined. It involves finding candidates who have as much potential as proven technical excellence, and who can bring a wide set of problem-solving abilities and strong communication skills.❞

Ruth Doyle's sixteen-year career at Aldi has taken her from being a trainee area manager to become Regional Managing Director for the north west, responsible for one hundred of the company's stores.

"When choosing which university to go to I made the decision to stay local, so that I could carry on living at home. I come from a big family of teachers and was certain that I didn't want a career in education, so I studied for a BSc in quantitative business analysis at the University of Salford. It was a four-year course and I stayed on for an extra year as president of the Student Union.

During my course I'd done a year-long placement within the automotive industry. My first graduate job was for a motor manufacturer, but it wasn't what I'd hoped it would be. The graduate programme wasn't very established or structured and I decided to leave after just a few weeks.

I returned to the north west and remembered seeing Aldi at a graduate job fair that I'd been to. They stood out from the other graduate employers there because they were the only ones in suits and when I spoke to them they were so full of energy and enthusiasm. I applied to their graduate programme and started work as a trainee area manager in November 2002.

My training began as a store assistant and I learned very quickly how to deal with a fast-paced, customer-facing role that was non-stop all day: from how to run the tills to eventually managing a whole store. It was a tough experience but that's the way Aldi's training works – if you can't successfully do the role of the person who works for you, you won't be able to fulfil your role as a leader.

During the programme, I ran two stores, for a total of six months. In each store, you had a week's handover with the existing manager and needed to get to know your colleagues very quickly, to be able to run the store from there. I was very aware that I was jumping in at the deep end, but I'd been trained to do it.

I took six months maternity leave and returned as area manager for six stores in Cheshire, about an hour away from where I lived. Being given your own area feels like a real achievement after the twelve months of training. But at the age of 25, with more than seventy people to manage, I was aware of what a huge responsibility it was too. That's what I really loved about the role: you could directly impact so many people and help them to develop and achieve more.

Four years later, I was promoted to Store Operations Director to manage my region's team of

2002 **Ruth Doyle, Aldi**

area managers. It was a very natural move to make because you understand the role beneath you so well, but it was challenging for me because I was managing my former colleagues and overnight I'd become their boss. My job was to develop the area managers to be the best that they could be and get them ready for their future roles. Seeing them progress to become directors themselves is one of the things that I'm most proud of.

After seven years, my team of area managers had doubled and as the number of stores continued to increase rapidly, I was asked to set up the Aldi Academy, the company's first centralised department for human resources, recruitment and training.

It was a fascinating job and in just eighteen months we built a whole new department to make recruitment across the company as efficient as possible and to ensure that the training we provided was of the highest quality.

I'm now Regional Managing Director of the north west region that I worked in originally. It's a much bigger operation than it was when I joined Aldi sixteen years ago, with one hundred stores, a team of directors from different disciplines, a full Logistics department and a huge warehouse.

This is very much my dream job but, in many ways, my role now is similar to each of my previous ones. It's all about developing people, to enable my directors and their departments to be the very best that they can be."

2003 David Dignam, PwC

After joining PwC's 'Flying Start' scheme for a sponsored degree, David Dignam is now a director in the firm's Forensic Services Capital Projects team.

"I grew up in south London in a working class family and studied at a college in Clapham for my A-levels. I knew then that I was interested in business but wasn't sure what to study at university or what kind of career would be right for me. It was my form tutor who suggested I should look into the 'Flying Start' programme at PwC.

The scheme combined a sponsored accountancy degree at Newcastle University with four months paid work experience each year at the firm, alongside studying for the ACA exams needed to become a chartered accountant.

I applied, made it through the two-day assessment centre, joined the firm and started my degree in Newcastle in 2003. From the placements I did over the next four years in audit and financial accounting, I knew that I wanted to focus on supporting clients to solve their important problems, which I had really enjoyed.

Just at the beginning of the global financial downturn, I did a really interesting project on how charities could maintain their income as the recession took hold. It gave me a real taste for crisis

It was an exciting time and gave me some great experience of how PwC delivers really complex projects for its clients.

management, and so it was this that I decided to pursue when I qualified as a chartered accountant.

I transferred from Assurance to PwC's Deals business, working as a Senior Associate in the Forensic Services team for eighteen months. The projects were so varied – helping manage the recovery of a health trust, supporting the resolution of a multi-billion dollar legal case in Europe and Asia, and even three weeks in rural India investigating a late-running construction site on behalf of investors.

It was an exciting time and gave me great experience of how PwC delivers really complex projects for its clients. It was also a great opportunity for me to work closely with some of the firm's senior managers, directors and partners. They supported my personal and professional development, and continue to be close friends and mentors today.

I've been promoted three times since then and in 2017, ten years after leaving university, I became Director in the Forensic Services Capital Projects team. I'm now a leader in a team of sixty and support clients to successfully deliver major infrastructure projects all over the country and overseas. The firm is highly entrepreneurial and empowering – it brings together different multidisciplinary teams to collaborate on clients' problems, to make the most of the huge range of skills, backgrounds and experiences of our people.

As a Director, I divide my time between leading projects for clients and supporting and developing my team. Projects can be based anywhere in the UK or beyond, so they do inevitably mean working away from home, sometimes for extended periods. There can be some challenging deadlines and the nature of crisis resolutions means that they can be quite unpredictable.

But PwC encourages everyday flexibility and we always try to maintain a positive work-life balance. As an Arsenal season ticket holder, I always make it back to London for midweek football games, and this summer I've proactively managed my diary and commitments to make the most of the great weather.

I really enjoy the sheer breadth of the projects we're involved in. In the last eighteen months alone, I've introduced a cost management system for a new European metro line, transformed programme management practices at a nuclear development company, and supported the leadership team to restructure a large defence programme.

It continues to be a fascinating job that gives me the chance to make a real difference to the clients I'm working with. "

2004 Richard Mitchell, NHS

Having started his career as a graduate trainee, Richard Mitchell is now the Chief Executive of a major NHS trust, aged 36.

" I left the University of Southampton in the summer of 2002 with a degree in geography but without a clear idea as to what I wanted to do next, other than go travelling. To earn some money, I moved back to my parent's house in London and got temp jobs working as a receptionist at Lewisham Hospital and then in admin support at Guy's and St Thomas'.

It really opened my eyes as to what an interesting environment working in the NHS is – even without being a doctor or nurse, you could be part of a team that makes a big difference. I went travelling for six months and applied for a place on the NHS graduate management training scheme as soon as I got back.

I was accepted onto the programme in 2004 and after a six-week 'Cook's tour' of different parts of the NHS, my first placement was on the Isle of Wight, working as a junior manager in a team that ran the mental health service for three prisons on the island. I was there for 12 months and it was fascinating – I spent lots of time working with people who were caring for patients with incredibly complex needs.

For my second placement, I went to a large teaching hospital in southern Brazil, working with their infection prevention team. I was 24 and wanted to really challenge myself by working in a different culture where I didn't speak the language and didn't know anyone. It was an amazing six months and I came back from Brazil a different person.

When I got back to the UK, my final placement was in Kent with the part of the NHS that commissions healthcare services. I then moved back to London and got my first 'proper' job, working as a service manager

in the dental services unit at Guy's and St Thomas' Hospital NHS Foundation Trust. Over the next three years, I moved into different manager roles in trauma & orthopedics and then cancer care. It gave me the chance to understand how hospitals operate in far more detail than I'd been able to on the graduate programme. I felt like I was really responsible for a small part of a very busy hospital.

After spending a year as a divisional manager at an NHS trust in north-west London, I was appointed head of operations at Imperial College Healthcare NHS Trust, running a division with 1,800 people and an annual budget of £160 million. It was a very rapid promotion for someone who was just 29 years old and who had only moved out of his parent's house a couple of years before.

I learnt a great deal about myself and the type of leader I wanted to be during my two and a half years there, and felt ready to try for a job on a trust board. I left London and became Chief Operating Officer for Doncaster and Bassettlaw NHS Foundation Trust in Yorkshire. It was a smaller trust, but my new role meant I had day-to-day responsibility for running the hospital, which was a truly 24/7 experience. Chief Operating Officer (COO) jobs take huge commitment and if you do them properly they will absorb your energy, time and emotion – on a Saturday and Sunday, just as much as a Monday to Friday.

From there, I became Deputy Chief Executive and COO at the University Hospitals of Leicester NHS Trust. It's one of the biggest and busiest in the UK with an annual budget of almost £1 billion and more than 13,000 staff. I was in the role for over four years and, whilst it was a really tough job, it was a really important part of my life and hugely exciting.

I became Chief Executive of Sherwood Forest Hospitals NHS Foundation Trust in Nottinghamshire at the age of 36 and we provide care for half a million patients. I love my job and feel a huge responsibility to our patients, staff and volunteers.

For me there are two acid tests of whether a hospital is doing well. Do the patients who we care for get the same level of care that I'd want my Mum or wife to receive? And are we treating our colleagues in the way I want to be treated? All staff in the NHS do exceptional jobs. Whether they are clinical or not, they truly transform patients' lives, often in difficult circumstances, every day of the year. I'm very happy to be behind the scenes, hopefully supporting cultural growth and team work to ensure we deliver good, safe care to all patients.

I have changed massively as a human and a leader since I joined the NHS graduate scheme fourteen years ago. I believe I'm a much kinder person now and I recognise I have a long way still to go. **"**

It took law graduate Sally Wokes just ten years from starting as a trainee solicitor at Slaughter and May to becoming a partner of the firm.

❝I first came across Slaughter and May when I was studying law at University College London. At the outset it hadn't been my intention to become a solicitor, but I was impressed by the firm's presentation, so I applied for a summer placement, which I did in 2003 before going back to do my finals. I was lucky enough to get a couple of other placements and so was able to see these firms from the inside too.

After those experiences I decided I wanted to work for Slaughter and May and felt really fortunate to be offered a training contract at the beginning of my third year. I took the Legal Practice Course (LPC) the following year, before joining the firm in 2005 as a trainee.

One of the first things that struck me about Slaughters was its very flat structure: there are just three levels – trainee, associate and partner, which really encourages a culture of collegiality, as opposed to competitiveness. The lack of billable hours targets at all levels also really helps.

I imagined that I'd be working with stereotypical lawyers, but it couldn't be further from that, as there's a very broad mix of personalities here.

In the early days as a trainee you move around every three to six months, taking 'seats' with different partners and associates, and eventually I chose to work in the corporate practice and qualified as a solicitor in 2007.

That was a really demanding time as the global financial crisis was beginning to bite and I was working with multi-specialist teams on some very complex projects. One of the good things about Slaughters is that it's a true meritocracy and you are given work that suits your individual skillset. This keeps you interested, regardless of the level you're actually at, and allows you to develop more quickly as a lawyer.

Of course the hours can be tough, although when you're in a quieter period, you're not expected to sit here just for the sake of it – we don't have a face time culture. But it also helps if you love what you do!

By the time you hit years four and five post-qualification, you're beginning to lead transactions and, at that point, I was starting to be assessed for the promotion process to Partnership. That's a process which for me lasted a couple of years and involved being assessed not only by the partners I had worked

2005 **Sally Wokes, Slaughter and May**

with previously, but also those whom I hadn't. I was made partner in 2015.

Compared to other firms, the track to Partnership is significantly shorter and in many ways simpler, as it focuses on doing what you've already experienced. And people tell you if you're on track, you know how you're getting on, so if you're progressing well and you want Partnership, it's there for you to get it.

I now find myself working with a wide range of corporate clients and have been lucky enough to be involved in some really significant transactions. My clients are across a wide range of sectors – from retail to tech to oil and gas – and winning and developing new clients is becoming evermore key.

There are plenty of challenges ahead, not least Brexit, but if I think back to the global financial crisis of 2007 & 2008, one of the firm's biggest strengths is its ability to quickly adapt when necessary. I believe that this flexibility is critical to our ongoing success.

One of the major changes I've noticed over the years is that we've become far more diverse as a firm. We're working hard to develop diverse talent at all levels through to Partnership. We know that we have more to do in in this area, but I can see a real difference in the atmosphere and focus here.

I'm a big proponent of more diversity in general, not just in gender, but social and ethnic background too. And because Slaughters has such a track record of adaptability, I believe you'll see more change here than elsewhere, which is really positive.**❞**

> *There are just three levels, which really encourages a culture of collegiality, as opposed to competitiveness.*

2006 **Janet Murphy, Rolls-Royce**

A teenage visit to NASA inspired Janet Murphy to pursue a high-flying career as an engineer in the aerospace industry.

❝I got into engineering because of my Dad. He was a telephone engineer with BT and I did a lot of 'take your daughter to work' days. From my GCSEs onwards I knew that it was engineering that I wanted to do for my career. After a trip to NASA as a teenager I decided on aerospace because it's right at the cutting edge of technology.

I did a four-year Masters in aerospace engineering at the University of Liverpool and in my third year I saw a recruitment presentation about Rolls-Royce. During my degree, the parts I enjoyed most were learning about propulsion systems and gas turbine engines, which Rolls-Royce manufactures. So I decided it was the company for me, applied in my final year and was accepted for a place on the graduate programme.

The programme included three attachments in different areas of the company. My first was based in Derby, in development engineering, working on engine testing: proving they are suitable for flights and certifying them. The second placement was in the US, working in repair and overhaul in Texas. I was on the shop floor with the fitters on a continuous improvement program to reduce the time it took to strip and rebuild engines. It was really interesting to be very hands-on and driving improvements in tooling and repair of components.

I never expected to work with such a fantastic, multicultural group of people, and that's the thing that inspires me every day.

My final placement was back in Derby, in marine engineering, on a project looking at biomechanical propulsion. We were designing propellers that mimic the motion of whale tails, taking insights from nature to make them more efficient, working closely with our businesses in Norway and Sweden.

When the graduate programme came to an end, I joined Rolls-Royce's System Design department as a performance engineer. It's a great place in the company to understand the functionality of gas turbines and the thermodynamic cycle of an engine. My job was to perform calculations to analyse the cycle and to optimise the fuel-burn of the gas turbines.

After two years, I broadened into fluid systems engineering and took a role in the team designing the cooling air system, the oil system and the fuel system of the Trent XWB gas turbine engine. Over the next four years, I worked my way from being an analyst to a technical lead, then a team lead.

I did a secondment in Indianapolis in the US, leading a team of six engineers designing the new Trent 1000 engine. This felt like quite a leap for me, going from being an engineer who is responsible for my own task, to becoming a leader, and not only doing the analysis and design work myself.

My next move was to become an installations engineering manager in Rolls-Royce's supply chain business. I had a team of eighteen design engineers and was responsible for technical audit and review of the designs we produced. This was my first formal management role and included doing performance reviews, setting people's objectives and supervising them.

I'm now the capability manager for Thermo-Fluids, the department that delivers the fluid systems and thermal analysis for all Trent gas turbine engines. We have about ninety thermal and fluid engineers, and much of my time is spent doing staff recruitment, training and skills development, as well as making sure that project delivery is on track and my teams have the resources they need. My role also focuses on the development of new capability, such as analysis methods, tools and processes to ensure Rolls-Royce remains a world class engineering company.

Twelve years after joining on the graduate programme I'm still excited by my role as an engineer and the advances in pioneering technology I've been a part of. I never expected to work with such a fantastic, multicultural group of people and that's the thing that inspires me every day. The technology is really interesting but it's the people that make the difference.❞

Anthony Cockburn has enjoyed a wide-ranging technology career with one of the world's largest consumer goods companies.

❝ I'd always been interested in technology and so I suppose it was only natural that I studied information management & computing at Loughborough. The first two years gave me a good basic understanding, but it was during my industrial placement in the third year that I got to understand what IT truly was in the real world and understand the complexities that you have to deal with.

I applied to Unilever for my placement and was lucky enough to be accepted. It was a really massive leap for me – just coming to grips with the sheer scale of the organisation was challenge enough. I got to see a lot of the back-end technology, which gave me a really good grounding in understanding how the supply chain worked and how country operations differed.

Unilever is completely flextime and so an important learning point for me was self-management. This was helped by the fact that, throughout this time, I had a line manager and a coach who helped me navigate the challenges, but perhaps more importantly helped me think about what might be possible after graduation.

Because I had been on an industrial placement I didn't have to complete all aspects of the graduate selection process, but it wasn't in the bag either. I'd already created quite a strong network of other graduates I'd met during the placement and that definitely helped me with the recruitment process. After completing the final stage of the interview in my final year at Loughborough, I was offered and accepted a graduate position within Unilever.

At the time of joining, it was a two-year programme with four individual placements. I started in North Wales and ended up in the London area for the final three. In that time, I built up experience of how the company outsourced parts of its IT forecasting – which involved looking at future IT trends, security issues and exposure to our front line marketing.

My first management role came at the end of the programme. This was a fascinating project to discover how much of our country-based IT we should outsource and, if we did, how we might do it. This involved me travelling to fourteen countries and not only getting to understand their IT capabilities but also working with HR and, in some cases, works councils, to review the potential impact on IT staff.

I then moved to a global change role in IT innovation – which was even further away from hands-on tech. We were going through big organisational change at the time and not only did

2007 **Anthony Cockburn, Unilever**

we need to change the way we did things in IT, we needed to communicate that effectively with the rest of the organisation. Changing people's behaviour is one of the toughest things to achieve and we had about 3,000 people in our part of the company.

It was a role which stood me in good stead for the future as I got to work closely with members of the IT leadership team – it's great visibility when you work with people who are far above your normal pay grade. After that I requested a move to the supply chain side of the business, responsible for much of the IT in our factories and introducing SAP to streamline processes and upgrade capabilities.

Next I joined the marketing part of Unilever as a business partner responsible for how we can create IT tools which make the lives of our marketers easier and more effective – whether working with agency partners or communicating directly with our customers. Which today has led me to being the product owner for a tool which personalises our communications with customers and is used globally.

What I've learned in the past eleven years is that there's no standard day-to-day role and that I've had an enormous opportunity to progress through the organisation – an organisation that even today I'm still impressed by its sheer scale and capability. **❞**

2008 **Sinead Fox, Bain & Company**

Following a PhD at Oxford, Sinead Fox joined consulting firm Bain & Company and is now a partner in their London office.

"I studied in Ireland for my first degree, which was in biomedical science – majoring in anatomy and IT. Although the degree had been created based on feedback from industry, there wasn't an obvious career path.

So I became quite proactive, approaching different companies, and landed a job with a diagnostics company, working on next-generation pregnancy tests. It was a fun time, but when I looked around me I could see that if I wanted to progress I'd need a PhD and, anyway, perhaps more study would also help me decide what I really wanted to do. I got an opportunity to do a PhD at Oxford studying stem cell biology and that turned out to be a phenomenal experience.

Lincoln College was a real melting pot, both academically and socially. With more than forty nationalities there, I was myself mixing with lawyers, engineers and people in management, whereas before I'd just lived in a scientific world. This really opened my eyes to career possibilities outside the lab and I started attending presentations on campus.

I knew I wanted to do something different and had a friend who worked at a management consultancy. I spoke to her and she explained what she did each day and I thought: wow, that sounds fantastic and actually the approach is very similar to what I do as a scientist – you ask a question, you develop an hypothesis, you do the analysis to test or disprove the hypothesis, and then you communicate that as simply as possible.

I found the Bain selection process told me a lot about the firm. I went through two rounds of assessment and at no point did I feel that they were trying to test me or trick me – it was all very collaborative and very much 'let's explore' and 'let's be creative'.

And that's exactly what I found the firm to be, from the day I joined to this. There's been a huge breadth of work and I've worked across retail, financial services, consumer products telecommunications – a whole host of sectors, but I have also become something of a retail specialist.

The way you develop with Bain is very flexible and at the outset is based on the apprenticeship model, so after a short induction you learn on the job. There's a real vibrancy to that and because we work closely with clients we get to work at the coal face too.

As part of that apprenticeship model there's global training almost every year, and at every promotion point, so there's multiple opportunities to refresh and learn new skills. And one of the things about Bain is the feedback culture is structured and frequent and action-oriented. So you know very quickly what you're doing well and what you need to work on and you're given advice and support about how to do that. So you really can rapidly develop.

There are a lot of flexible models for career progression, and in my case I was able to take an 'externship' as part of my development, and spent time based in a major retailer. I really loved it, but it confirmed what I was really committed to and I missed the pace of Bain and its people.

Bain is a real meritocracy and the route to Partnership is not just about internal perceptions and performance, but as part of the promotion process partners will talk to your clients and ask them about how you've worked with their teams and what legacy you've left.

Today as partner I still work on projects across the world, with a focus on the retail and consumer goods sectors, as well as championing diversity issues in the firm, not least as I'm now a working mum.

As a core member of women@bain and having established parents@bain, I see that same supportive culture that I first witnessed back in Oxford – and there's still that same eagerness and passion to get the job done.**"**

We value your dedication.
Because we're just as dedicated.

At HSBC we like our employees to focus on doing the right thing – to strive forward
and reach for new heights. Because it's this sense of purpose and dedication that
enables us to best serve all our customers.

That's why we're looking for people who think, see and do things differently.
Regardless of your degree discipline, we have a variety of internship
and graduate opportunities just for you.

Visit hsbc.com/earlycareers

 HSBC

Together we thrive

2009 Beck Owen, Teach First

After completing the Teach First scheme, Beck Owen joined the founding team for a new free school in west London, and has just been appointed its headteacher.

❝ When I went to Cardiff in 2005 to study English literature, I thought I was going to be a lawyer. I went on a summer experience with one of the more prestigious firms and knew within three hours that it was totally the wrong thing for me. It didn't match my values at all and I absolutely hated it.

I was lucky that one of my friends told me about the Teach First scheme and I realised straightaway that it was the thing I wanted to do. Teach First's mission was to eradicate the educational disadvantage of being born in the 'wrong' postcode or having parents who didn't go to university.

I took a gap year and went through the selection process for Teach First. I was accepted and did my initial training in the summer of 2009, during six of the best, most intensive weeks of my life. The secondary school I was assigned to was in east Birmingham: it was 99 per cent Muslim and I was teaching English to pupils aged 11 up to their GCSEs.

Handling the workload at the beginning was hard. It might take you three hours to plan an hour-long lesson and then, if the behaviour wasn't good in the lesson, you'd wonder why you'd spent so long on it.

When you're alone in the classroom and there's thirty-two children staring at you, you have to solve the problem yourself.

There were plenty of times when I thought 'I really don't know how to solve this problem', but when you're alone in the classroom and there's thirty-two children staring at you, you have to solve the problem yourself.

By my second year I'd achieved my 'qualified teacher status' and was becoming more confident. The leadership training that Teach First provided was invaluable and reminded us about the wider goals of the programme to tackle educational disadvantage. In the daily cycle of marking, planning and giving feedback, you could sometimes lose sight of that.

At the end of the programme, I decided to stay on at the school for an another year. It was then that I heard about plans to open a brand new free school in Feltham, one of the most disadvantaged areas in west London. It sounded really exciting and an amazing opportunity to be part of something that could make a real difference to people's futures, so I applied to join the staff and became the school's first employee.

When I started, we didn't have a building or any pupils. We got our students by knocking on doors in Feltham and standing outside Asda with a big brochure for the school. We found a temporary building that we could use and, in September 2012, the Reach Academy Feltham opened its doors to sixty reception children and thirty in Year 7.

After a year I became the school's Head of English and then spent two years as assistant headteacher. As the staff and pupil numbers grew, the school moved to a new permanent site. I taught English to our original intake of Year 7 students, all the way through to their GCSEs. Their results were fantastic, the 15th best in the country for overall progress from Key Stage 2.

For the last two years I've been the school's deputy head and from September 2018, I'll be the headteacher of the whole school – we're now an all-through school, from reception classes all the way to Sixth Form.

To help children reach their full potential, our approach is to support the whole family, not just the child. We offer parenting workshops and do home visits for every child that joins us. It's a really important way to demonstrate to families that this is a team effort.

This is a job that I love and it's not just about a school or my career, it's the impact on individual children and their families that you can have. I never have 'Sunday night blues' because I've got a real sense of purpose. There's not many other 32-year-olds that I know who live and work in London who can say that. ❞

Flight Lieutenant Robyn Hackwell's career with the RAF began at university, and it has already taken her to the Middle East, the Falkands Islands and stations in the UK.

❝I've been obsessed with flying ever since my 10th birthday. We were flying home from a family holiday and, as a birthday treat, I got to go up into the cockpit – and that was it, I wanted to fly. By the time I was 15 I'd joined the Air Cadets and went to my local Armed Forces Careers Office to find out about the RAF. They suggested I train to become an Engineering Officer and, from then on, that was my goal.

The RAF sponsored me to study for a Masters in systems engineering at Loughborough University and, as part of the sponsorship, I became a member of the University Air Squadron. As well as regular weekend activities, I went on a two-week camp each summer at an operational base, shadowing engineering officers and experiencing life in the RAF. But the highlight for me was learning to fly – I did a hundred hours of flying while I was at university.

After graduating, I did my Initial Officer Training at RAF Cranwell. At the time, training lasted thirty weeks, and was delivered in three ten-week phases; this starts with learning the basics of being in the military – learning to iron a uniform, march, drill and shoot a weapon. Then you move on to developing your leadership ability in different scenarios.

On completion of Initial Officer Training, I began Engineer Officer Foundation Training, which was also a thirty-week training package. It's classroom-based and teaches you everything from radar and telecommunications principles to office management, leadership and how to ensure technical equipment is serviced correctly. The training culminates in a final test where you take on the role of a Flight Commander for a week and are assessed throughout.

On successful completion, I graduated as an Engineer Officer (Communications and Electronics) and was assigned to my first posting. My first role was at RAF Coningsby where I was responsible for a team of twenty people who delivered a variety of IT systems to over 3,000 users, including IT support to the Typhoon aircraft deploying all over the world. My Engineer Officer Foundation Training had prepared me really well for the job – many of the scenarios I'd thought had been so far-fetched during the training happened to me in the very first week in the real RAF.

Eighteen months later I was promoted from Flying Officer to Flight Lieutenant and went on a six-month detachment as a communications expert supporting bases in Bahrain, Oman, Al Udeid and Al Minhad, just outside Dubai. I absolutely loved it – the opportunity to travel and experience different cultures was one of

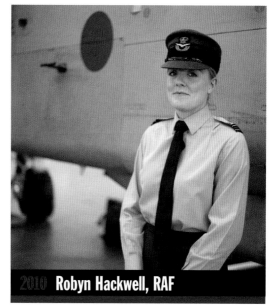

2010 **Robyn Hackwell, RAF**

the main reasons I joined the RAF. We were based alongside the US Air Force, but there were so many other nationalities to mix with and learn from.

Over the next two years, I worked in HQ Air Command at RAF High Wycombe within Information Security, and then went on another detachment, this time to the Falklands. I worked within Information Systems and Services as deputy to the Units Officer Commanding with a team of sixty people who delivered cable management, telephone systems, computers, radars and aerials. I loved the experience. The Falklands is a unique place with amazing wildlife and military history, and the base's sports facilities are second to none. Some people find being 8,000 miles away from home tough, but I was very lucky – I'm married and my wife was actually stationed there with me.

When I returned, I was deployed to Northwood in London as Officer Commanding Deployed Systems Group, leading a large tri-service team that ensured joint operations between the Army, Royal Navy and RAF had the communications they needed.

I'm now based at RAF Cosford as an instructor on Engineer Officer Foundation Training. It's a nice thing to come back and do because I can share the experiences I've had with our new Engineering Officers as they go through their training.

By being in the RAF, I'm constantly working with like-minded people and I've been to some fantastic places and done some amazing things. I've been able to gain fantastic qualifications and play a variety of sports, like rugby and nordic skiing. I was lucky to be supported by the RAF at university and, on my last flight with the University Air Squadron, I flew from RAF Cranwell to my home in Kent, to have lunch with my family. It was a once-in-a-lifetime experience.❞

2011 Michael Thompson, GSK

A scientist through and through, Michael Thompson is a research & development director who is committed to making a real difference.

❝I should say that early in my life I was very into science and wanting to understand the world around us. So I applied to do a Chemistry degree down south at Hull – I come from Durham, so Hull definitely wasn't in the north for me. Chemistry fascinated me because of its complexity and how it's linked to so many things in life.

Hull is very strong on physical chemistry and, in particular, colloid science – the science of emulsions which are present in so much of the world around us, everything from chocolate to paint. I enjoyed my first degree and decided I'd study a PhD in colloid science and soon discovered it's a big leap forward from a taught degree to a project-driven one.

There were a few industry-linked PhDs at Hull and I chose one sponsored by GSK, which meant that I had quite a tight connection between the industrial world and academia throughout. I also realised that if I wanted to make the kind of difference that I did, then industry was the quickest way to do that.

A year and a half in, and I started to learn about the different graduate schemes at GSK and used some of my contacts from the PhD to get a better understanding. It was a pretty tough selection process and the multiple-day selection centre covering personality and behavioural traits was very different from anything I'd experienced within academia.

Luckily they were looking for colloid scientists and I was offered a role as a material scientist. As part of GSK's Future Leaders Programme there's a lot of core training that all graduates do, but you also get to set your own development, based on the direction you want to go. There are three rotations on the programme which get progressively shorter – the first one is normally eighteen months, followed by twelve months, then eight months.

My first rotation was a role in the supply chain in the new product introduction team based back up north in Barnard Castle. It was a really varied role working at all levels in the factory, which involved learning a lot of new things.

The second rotation was in Leichlingen near Cologne at a company that GSK had recently acquired. That was an exciting period, working in a small R&D team in a German-speaking company that had some products which were to become really important for GSK. And then my final rotation was back in London where I worked in new product development and was responsible for creating completely new lab facilities.

Then in September 2014 I was offered the role of senior scientist at the New Product Research facility in North Carolina. Moving to the US was huge step for me – both professionally and personally – as it involved my wife leaving her job in the UK to come with me. We were only in North Carolina for a year before we moved up to New Jersey where I became Principal Scientist working on the innovation of new skin health products in a new joint venture GSK had established with Novartis.

The work while I was over there was hugely rewarding as it involved developing a gel to stop infection of the umbilical cord in new-born babies, especially for sub-Saharan Africa. We worked very closely with Save the Children and the WHO and I had the chance to visit Kenya and meet babies who would otherwise have died had we not developed this life-saving gel.

It was at this stage, that as part of my development plan, I started to take on more leadership of projects and a more senior role in the team. I'm still a scientist at heart but leadership can have a big impact on how we bring innovations into the real world.

So we left the US at the beginning of 2018 and I'm now based in Weybridge as R&D Director, leading both a team and new product development. I'm only seven years out of academia, but I've worked in six locations, travelled the world and have a leadership role. It's been quite a whirlwind.❞

When Emily Csizmazia began studying for her psychology degree, she never imagined it would become the starting point for an ambitious career in banking.

❝At the beginning of my second year studying at the University of Kent, I applied for work experience with Lloyds Banking Group. Although I'd never seen myself going into banking, I'd heard such good things about Lloyds through friends who'd worked there, so I applied for one of their summer internships.

It was an incredible experience as I was working for one of the most inspiring senior directors in human resources, who was also responsible for the graduate scheme. I was delighted that, at the end of the summer, Lloyds offered me a place on their graduate programme, starting the following year. My final year was bliss. While my housemates were stressing about life after graduation, I was able to focus on my dissertation and enjoy my last summer before work.

I joined what was then the HR graduate scheme, a two-year programme with a generalist placement and graduate projects like our charity challenge. This gave me a well-rounded view of the whole organisation. Lloyds also sponsored me for my CIPD Level 7 and MSc in professional HR. This investment in me really made me feel valued.

My first placement was an HR Manager in TSB during the move out of Lloyds and into Banco Sabadell. It was a brilliant opportunity to get out in the branch network and experience the challenges faced by our customers and front line colleagues. My second placement was in our Wealth Division, and nothing to do with HR at all. In that role, I got to help set up a feedback group for our high net worth clients and was lucky enough to run one of our events in Spain. In Spanish!

My final placement was back in HR which involved meeting with very senior directors and identifying specific courses and events to help with their development. I kept thinking to myself: 'I'm a grad, I can't believe I'm doing this!' I thought I'd be making the tea, but here I am leading big projects and working with senior people!

After completing my three placements for the graduate programme, I had to find a permanent role. I jumped at the chance to join a new team as a consultant in 'activity value analysis'. This was outside of HR and I was pleased that Lloyds allowed me to be flexible with my career and experience other parts of the company.

We were trained by McKinsey for three months

2012 Emily Csizmazia, Lloyds Banking Group

I was delighted that, at the end of the summer, Lloyds offered me a place on their graduate programme, starting the following year.

on how to identify process improvements, and I travelled across the UK, as well as to Amsterdam and Berlin. I was one of two graduates appointed into a team of very experienced consultants, which made me realise again that at Lloyds if you're enthusiastic and willing to learn, they'll give you the opportunities to develop and progress your career.

I then took on a brief executive assistant role before leading our 'Negative Into A Positive' programme, which took an innovative approach to how we handle and reduce customer complaints. I was overwhelmed with the support I received from people across all parts and levels of the bank. Although we've been around for 250 years, we're very forward-thinking – which is why the programme has been a success.

Since then I've had two more jobs: first I led the Senior Managers Certification Regime, and now I work within our Transformation Division. One of our mottos is "doing well by doing good." We get involved in a variety of activities from driving digital inclusion and working with communities to supporting our vulnerable customers and promoting inclusion and diversity.

I've learnt that Lloyds is a very open and supportive environment. If you're talented and enthusiastic you'll get the right support to do well.

It's hard to imagine that it was just seven years ago that I completed my summer internship and six since I joined the graduate programme, but I can honestly say that I've never looked back since and would highly recommend both.❞

Deloitte.

Do you expect the unexpected?

Welcome to the home of the imaginative.
A place for those who can ride the wave of constant change and even better, influence it. To those people we offer swift career progression, the support of smart leaders and caring colleagues, and a solid balance between personal interests and work.
Those who can empathise with teams and clients with the purpose of leaving a legacy behind.

deloitte.co.uk/careers
What impact will you make?

2013 **Anneka Shah, BlackRock**

A career in technology with global asset management firm BlackRock was not the future Anneka Shah thought was mapped out for her.

❝When I was younger, I was kind of pushed in the direction of going into something medical. But after my A- and AS-levels, I knew I wanted to concentrate more on maths, as that was the subject that came most naturally to me.

So I went to King's College London to study maths, management and finance. I thought that choice would keep my career options fairly open for the future. I only came across BlackRock when a friend who studied computer science told me about them and their internship. It sounded interesting and so I applied and was really impressed by the way they assessed me.

Lots of other internship applications involved endless tests, but BlackRock invited me to a day to get to know them and explain more about the internship. I was always interested in technology and had been working part-time for Apple, so the summer internship really appealed to me. After all, I thought, why not try it out; it was a good opportunity and I had nothing to lose and could dabble in it – and

in essence, it's not too far from maths in terms of logic and problem solving.

During the internship, I got to work on a few projects and connect with a lot of different teams, but what really struck me was the culture – more than anything else I really enjoyed working there. So when I was offered a place on the graduate programme just after the end of the internship, it wasn't a difficult decision to make.

I joined BlackRock after graduating in 2013 and had four placements as part of the graduate programme. These covered portfolio management technology – which is the core of our business – client systems, securities lending tech and the last one on our own Aladdin system, which I work on now. This meant that, by the end of these placements, I had a really good understanding of all aspects of the BlackRock business and a deeper understanding of the culture.

It also meant that I got to see different management styles and the dynamics of how different teams work. So by the time I had my first proper job I had some really valuable applied knowledge and I could figure out what was the ideal job for me.

My first role was as an analyst and then I got promoted to associate in 2014. An important part of the culture here are the principles of the firm – especially 'One BlackRock' which is about how diversity strengthens us and how we can all contribute to creating innovative solutions. This means that, as an associate in technology, I am accountable and must take more responsibility for my performance and work at a higher level.

I am now a software developer working on the Aladdin system, which has over three thousand users around the world. I am responsible for specific apps within the system, so I have responsibility for their design and architecture, as well as their implementation. Communication with end users is critical and will often involve me leading webinar training sessions with several hundred users around the world.

What I really appreciate in this environment is that I have the flexibility to choose what it is that I work on. I have had a focus on managing people in the past, but right now I'm concentrating on my technical expertise and streamlining projects within the tools.

I've got a pretty clear career path in management and my next promotion would be to Vice President. I still think sometimes, 'wow, that's five years already', but it doesn't feel like it.

The reason that I joined in the first place was not just the technology but that I was really impressed by the culture, and it's the reason I'm still here with a future at BlackRock ahead of me.❞

2014 **Alice McCullagh, Dyson**

The past four years have been a whirlwind for Alice McCullagh as she's travelled across the globe, being based in Hong Kong, Dubai – and Wiltshire.

❝I studied German and European politics at the University of Manchester, which included a year working in Munich, as a marketing intern. I was excited when I heard about Dyson's International Commercial Executive programme through my university careers office. Throughout my childhood, our big yellow Dyson vacuum cleaner had been a part of the family and I'd always seen James Dyson as an inspirational leader.

Having applied for the graduate scheme, I'd gone off travelling to South America, and my first telephone interview was out in Lake Titicaca in Bolivia. They asked if I could attend an assessment centre as soon as I got back. I ended up starting within a month of returning, which is pretty much the pace at which things happen around here.

I went straight into a commercial role working on the launch of a new product in Japan. It was a massive leap for me. Suddenly I'm thinking that here I am, a young girl from Yorkshire, working with Dyson engineers and a team in Japan on the marketing for one of our most innovative vacuum technologies. But you have got to be a self-starter to get on here. I'm quite laid back and can work well under pressure and I like being thrown in at the deep end.

I think that's one of the key things at Dyson, you've got to be pro-active about what you do and who you are meeting, and you have conversations with people knowing where you want to go. That approach took me next to Hong Kong to work on the launch of the Dyson Supersonic hair dryer, which at the time was a top secret project.

I arrived there in 2016 and it was an amazing experience. The culture in Hong Kong is very much 'work hard, play hard' and within six weeks I had visited all the key markets in the region to introduce our new technology to new Dyson stylists. I was leading the marketing strategy for a completely new concept in beauty technology, which was radically different and better than anything else in the market. Following a successful launch across Asia, my role changed and I stepped up to lead the marketing plans, launches and delivery across all Dyson categories for the Hong Kong market.

The placement was a real rollercoaster experience, but the senior leadership team in the region were there to give me the support I needed and made sure I was always learning, as well as being pushed out of my comfort zone.

But, as well as working, during my time in Hong Kong I managed to visit twelve countries across Asia, from Japan to the Philippines. When I wasn't travelling, most weekends involved exploring the incredible hiking that the island has to offer. My evenings were spent at Happy Valley racecourse and I could even start many days with a morning run up Victoria Peak. This was one of those once-in-a-lifetime opportunities, so you give it your all.

The pace is so rapid at Dyson that the next opportunity – to launch our second Dyson global flagship retail store in Dubai – came up, and within six weeks I'd left Hong Kong and was in the UAE.

Creating Dyson stores so customers can try our products and understand the engineering behind them is an important part of our growth strategy, as is the Middle East market, so we had to get this right.

It was a mammoth task, not just hiring the team (we ended up with eleven different nationalities in the team), but ensuring they understood Dyson's values and technologies, adhered to regulations and had the correct permits, as well as managing our suppliers. It was a very different experience to my time in Hong Kong.

At the beginning of 2018, I progressed off the graduate scheme and came back to our headquarters in the UK to start a management role, leading the strategic side of our commercial activities across Europe and the Middle East.

What I've found at Dyson, as we have accelerated into becoming a leading global technology enterprise, is that it has been crucial to think like an engineer, have an international mindset and maximise every opportunity you have. I can be a bit of a workaholic, but there's so much going on and coming into Dyson has been such an incredible experience.❞

Lottie Dunham originally saw herself working as a hospital pharmacist in the NHS, but joining AstraZeneca opened up a whole world of opportunities.

❝I studied pharmacy at Keele because at the time I thought I wanted to be a ward-based clinical pharmacist. At school I'd always been good at maths and science and wanted to do something medical, but rather than just do science and maths as a degree I wanted to do something a bit more applied – hence choosing pharmacy.

But during my first year I met some people who worked for a small pharmaceutical company and I realised there were other things out there for pharmacists. Pharmacy is a four year course and, at the end of my third year, I did a summer placement with AstraZeneca. It was quite competitive to get in, but over those ten weeks I met lots of people around the company and what particularly struck me was that there were pharmacists working in all sorts of roles.

As part of the qualification process to become a pharmacist, you have to do a fifth 'pre-reg' year: either in the NHS or split with some time in industry. I decided to do a year in hospital, but kept in touch with AstraZeneca and applied for the graduate programme. I think it helped enormously that I'd done the summer placement and had left a positive impression after those ten weeks, and I started on the programme in 2015.

The graduate programme has three eight-month placements and my first was in the supply chain for clinical trials. This meant working closely with hospitals around the world, making sure that oncology patients who were part of the trials were getting the right drugs, in the right place, at the right time – and that everything was done to the strict regulatory regime. It was a really good place to start.

I then did a lab-based role, which was working with a team of scientists on drug formulations for children and young adults. It was a really innovative project where the team were looking at more effective ways of administering drugs rather then just reducing the adult dosage. It was very different to the first placement, but it also helped me realise that I would probably prefer working outside the lab environment.

Your third placement tends to be one that matches your education and skills and I went back to the supply chain area, but working in a different group on planning and capability. This time, instead of having responsibility for a specific project, we were looking more strategically about how we distribute our

2015 Lottie Dunham, AstraZeneca

clinical trials drugs across the whole global portfolio.

As this placement was coming to an end I applied for a permanent role in the team and got offered a role. So I stayed with the project, but with more responsibility, to ensure it was successfully delivered.

Once that was completed, I went into a new role at the start of this year. I'm leading a piece of work looking at how we design our clinical trials, which involves me working with AstraZeneca teams around the world. It's a transformation project, so that means it's not straightforward – much of it is about changing the way people work. I'm an inherently positive person and very energetic, and I think you have to be for these big change projects because much of it is about people and their perceptions and willingness to change.

At the site I'm based at, we have the Peak District right on our doorstep, so I see people going off cycling and running in our breaks.

I'm a working mum and I've found that this is a fantastic place to work. I can work flexibly and achieve a good work life balance, and at the site I'm based at, we have the Peak District right on our doorstep, so I see people going off cycling and running in our breaks.

Being part of the graduate programme meant that I got to meet a lot of senior people and build up a network of contacts across the company. That, together with my mentors, means that I can see my route forward. I never dreamed I would be working in clinical trials, but I don't regret for one minute changing my mind about hospital pharmacy.❞

2016 **Laura Steedman, BP**

From a university scholarship, to working on a North Sea oil rig, Laura Steedman is relishing life with BP.

❝When I was at school, I came across engineering by chance. I had to do a residential course for my Duke of Edinburgh Gold Award and so spent a week at the University of Strathclyde doing their 'Headstart' introductory course about engineering. I ended up loving it and decided I would apply to do an engineering degree.

I chose Robert Gordon University in Aberdeen because they had plenty of practical and lab-based course content, as well as strong links with industry. It was a five-year Masters course and, during my second year, I was awarded a BP scholarship which gave me financial support for my course, annual mentors and work experience each summer.

My first placement with BP was at the end of my third year, based at the Grangemouth site. I was working on a 'turnaround' where a plant or facility is shut down for critical maintenance and was given responsibility for removing 144 valves and taking them to the workshops to be overhauled. I got a real buzz from seeing how engineers, contractors and workshops came together to deliver a successful turnaround.

A year later, my next placement was in a completely different role, in BP's Aberdeen office, in the discipline engineering team. It was a more technical role, investigating difficulties our engineers were having with heat exchangers. I knew very little about them when I started the placement but spent time working with our suppliers to really understand the problem and recommend ways to improve the safety of repairs to the exchangers.

Having completed two successful placements, I entered the final part of the assessment process for BP's graduate programme and was offered a job during my last year at university.

After graduating in the summer of 2016, I returned to the Aberdeen office to work on a project looking into improving the reliability and efficiency of gas turbines. It was an industry-first, using new technology that hadn't been proven or used before. I had to draw up a business case and then worked with our suppliers from the development of the technology, to factory acceptance-testing, and then its implementation.

It was a huge project that was delivered successfully two months ahead of schedule, delivering cost savings and efficiencies for the company. For me personally, it was a very steep learning curve and a big challenge, but one that I really enjoyed. I knew when I chose BP that I wanted to do something that made a real difference.

For my second year on the graduate programme, it was time to learn more about BP's operations. So, for the last ten months I've been on an offshore rotation, working on a platform in the North Sea, about 150 miles east of Aberdeen. We work three weeks on the platform, then have three weeks back at home.

I'm the only Production Support Engineer on the platform but I'm part of a wider team of more than a hundred and fifty people. It's my job to look at which oil wells are producing, optimise the production and try to rectify any deferrals or delays.

For the last ten months, I've been on an offshore rotation, working on a platform in the North Sea, 150 miles east of Aberdeen.

I've absolutely loved working offshore, although it can be long hours. I was nervous at the start and wasn't sure I'd be able to last three weeks away from my family, but there's a great atmosphere here and I genuinely feel like I'm part of a team that cares about me.

BP works really hard to recognise its people and it was a huge honour for me to win the 'Young Professional of the Year' award at the recent SPE Offshore Achievements Awards.

Next year will be my final year on the graduate programme and I'm expecting to go back to the Aberdeen office. In the longer term I'd like to join a project team and gain experience further afield because I'm really keen to learn about new cultures and find out how the business works globally.❞

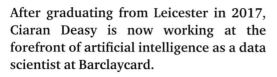

After graduating from Leicester in 2017, Ciaran Deasy is now working at the forefront of artificial intelligence as a data scientist at Barclaycard.

" I've always had a fascination for technology and, the more I researched it, the more I thought computer science was the degree I wanted to study. As I'm from London I wanted to go somewhere else in the country and decided on Leicester. Originally it was going to be a three-year course but after my second year I took a year-long placement in industry, so it ended up being four years.

That third year turned out to be quite manic. It started with a summer internship at Barclays which was then immediately followed by the industrial placement at IBM, and then back to Barclays for another summer internship.

The University of Leicester has got a really good careers service and they helped me pull together my résumé and prepare for interviews and assessment centres. I applied for the internships as soon as I could because I knew that I wanted get as much experience as I could before I graduated.

I was torn between whether I wanted a financial career or a technology one, so I applied to both – and by doing a technology placement at Barclays it meant that I could see which path might be right for me.

What I discovered was a diversity of hugely different cultures in Barclays. In the first summer internship I worked in the corporate part of the bank as a business analyst, whilst for the second internship I worked in the investment bank as a software developer. There, I got to work with Python (a leading-edge programming language) which was something that helped with my dissertation in my final year.

Before that second summer experience had finished I was offered a place on the Barclays Graduate Programme, and so over the course of that final year in Leicester, we were able to talk about where I could start my career, and I opted for Barclaycard based in Canary Wharf.

This is quite unlike any other area of the bank that I've experienced. In some ways it's got more of the feel of a tech start-up, and we do have an offshoot in Shoreditch where I spend part of my time.

We're working on advanced data science projects which means looking at how we can improve and automate processes – hence, as a team, we get to work with some of the latest AI and machine learning techniques.

2017 **Ciaran Deasy, Barclays**

I've enjoyed being part of the graduate programme and have developed a really good network. I do think there's a perception out there that banks are a bit 'establishment', but while we might not have the cool factor of tech start-ups or Google or Facebook, I do think that Barclays is an exception.

I was very fortunate to be placed in a team which had been newly formed just a couple of months before I joined, so I've seen the team grow and had the chance to work on projects from their inception.

At the outset, we had hardly any projects but now we're working on over twenty, which are all focused on cutting edge machine learning.

Something I enjoy too is being able to work flexibly – be it from home or at our accelerator space in Shoreditch where I'm based a couple of days a week. That's home to numerous fin-tech start-ups and I get the chance to network with them and provide support as they grow.

In terms of the future, I do know that I'm working at the forefront of data science and machine learning and building up invaluable knowledge and experience. I look forward to the potential opportunities that might arise here at Barclays. **"**

> *I'm working at the forefront of data science and machine learning, and building up invaluable knowledge and experience.*

2018 Salewudin Ibrahim, White & Case

A television courtroom drama from the 1970s helped inspire Salewudin Ibrahim to study law at university and train to become a qualified solicitor.

❝I knew when I was still at school that I wanted to be a lawyer. I'd spent hours one summer watching an old ITV programme called *Crown Court* and I got really interested in the legal system.

So when it came to applying for university, I selected politics and law courses as my options. I got offers for both but thought that law would be the more intellectually-demanding choice, so accepted a place on the undergraduate law degree course at the University of Lincoln.

It was a challenging course but I enjoyed it and went on to graduate with a first class degree. I got involved in street law and law clinic, which helped me understand how the law impacts people in real life situations.

It was during the second year of my degree that I had my first experience of White & Case. I did an introductory week-long taster which was a great way to find out about the firm and at the end of it, they encouraged me that I should apply for a training contract after graduation.

Instead of going straight to law school, I opted to do a Masters course at Warwick University and studied for an LLM in international corporate governance and financial regulation. It was something that I'd been really interested in during the financial crisis, with banks going down and all the various regulatory issues, so it was great to have the opportunity to study this in-depth.

At the end of my year in Warwick I did a vacation placement back at White & Case. It was a nice way to get to know people at the firm, try some of the work, and especially to be able to see what life would be as a solicitor in a practice. It was a busy two weeks doing research tasks, checking case law and writing memos to advise the firm's clients on their options and the right course of action.

On the fun side, we were put into groups for a game where you ran your own business and could see how much money you'd make after each decision you took. It made you really think about the business world and how to do things commercially.

My placement was a success and White & Case offered me a training contract. I started at the BPP law school later that autumn. A family bereavement meant I did the legal practice course (LPC) in two halves and worked for a few months as a paralegal in between.

I joined White & Case in March 2018 and began the first of my four six-month training placements, known as 'seats', in the firm's private equity team. You don't really know what to expect or what your responsibilities will be, but it's been great. My supervisor trusted me from the start to draft documents for him, so it's been quite challenging learning on the job how to do that. Private equity is very fast-paced and it's hard for someone to explain all the intricate details, so there's been lots to learn along the way.

I'm not sure what my next training placement will be but for the final six months of the training contract, the firm gives everyone the chance to go abroad to do an international seat.

One of the reasons I chose White & Case was the mix of graduates they recruit. In my intake, there were three graduates from Oxbridge, but all the others had graduated from other universities around the country. The firm has a real focus on recruiting people from different backgrounds and experiences because of how diverse their clients are.

I hope I'll have the opportunity to work towards becoming a partner of the firm in the future. So in addition to my regular work, I've been trying to do some networking with my friends at banks and other institutions, because one day they'll become the senior people in their organisations too.❞

Institute and Faculty of Actuaries

ACTUARIES
MORE
THAN MATHS

If you love maths and have big ambitions, becoming an actuary could be an exciting and rewarding career for you. You'll use your mathematical skills to solve business problems by measuring and evaluating the probability and risk of future events and work on projects across a fascinating range of sectors, from artificial intelligence (AI) and big data to healthcare and banking.

MORE rewarding, **MORE** prestigious, **MORE** challenging and much **MORE** at:

www.actuaries.org.uk/become-actuary

The thing is, My homework in my pencil

Grace Wilcox,
Assistant Headteacher

When you're a teacher, nothing can live up to the funny things that children will say. With every new day in school, there's a new comment from a pupil that's worth its weight in comedy gold. That's one of my favourite things about the job: I love the variety, no two days are really the same.

My own experience of school had a big impact on me deciding to teach. I very much got my place at university because of two specific teachers. Without their willingness to give me that extra time and show me that I could do it, I wouldn't have been able to achieve the things I did. Having someone to say, *'we believe in you, so you should do it'* was invaluable.

Ultimately, it's a teacher that helps to unleash a child's potential. All the hard work pays off in the end and regardless of how your day's gone, there's always a point that you can pick out where you know you've made a real difference. There aren't many careers you can say that for.

Department
for Education

Miss...
x's still

To find out more about a career in teaching,
search **Get Into Teaching**

THE ✦ TIMES
THE SUNDAY TIMES
Know your times

Students pay £26 per year, which is a saving of 90%

Get life ready

Students know more. Students get more. Students save more.

Considered journalism
We provide diverse opinion along with in-depth insight on all the stories that matter.

\+

Global news
With 36 correspondents across six continents, read in-depth analysis, anywhere in the world.

\+

Exclusive benefits
Enjoy up to 25% off at 2,000 restaurants nationwide and enjoy 2-for-1 cinema tickets every weekend.

THE TIMES
TOP 100
GRADUATE EMPLOYERS

Sector Guide to the UK's Top Graduate Employers

1999-2018

20 YEARS

BE INSPIRED TO
DO GREAT WORK

BDO is one of the UK's largest accountancy and business advisory firms providing services to ambitious businesses within the UK and worldwide. We provide integrated advice and solutions to help businesses succeed in a changing world. Our clients are Britain's economic engine – ambitious, entrepreneurially spirited and high-growth businesses that fuel the economy.

We offer graduate programmes specialising in:

▶ Audit

▶ Tax

▶ Advisory

▶ Business Services & Outsourcing

Find your inspiration at

bdoearlyincareer.co.uk
twitter.com/BDO_trainees_uk
facebook.com/BDOTraineesUK

Accounting & Professional Services

The accounting & professional services sector has long been dominated by the 'Big Four' firms. Together, Deloitte, EY, KPMG and PwC audit the accounts of 99% of the UK's largest companies, and all four have appeared in every edition of *The Times Top 100 Graduate Employers* over the last twenty years.

Since 2009, each of the 'Big Four' firms has been ranked within the top ten graduate employers, with a combined graduate intake of more than 4,000 new trainees annually. Around half the firms' entry-level vacancies are accountancy roles within audit, assurance or tax, but there are a wide range of other opportunities for graduates in areas such as consulting, actuarial and technology.

According to Dan Richards, Recruiting Leader for EY in the UK & Ireland, the Big Four work hard on campus to promote their graduate and undergraduate programmes, helping students to understand the wide variety of careers and programmes available.

"As a firm we visit over 75 universities each year and hire graduates from about 120 different institutions," he says. "We look to attract students from any degree backgrounds; only half of our intake have studied a relevant degree as we actively seek diversity of thinking in our teams. We run an extensive programme of campus events, taster schemes, internships and employability workshops to help students better understand the careers we offer."

EY is growing its 21 regional offices and over half its student vacancies are now outside of London.

Becoming a chartered accountant typically takes three years and although the cost of graduates' training is paid by the firms they

Dan Richards, Recruiting Leader in UK and Ireland, EY

join, the combination of working full-time, classroom-based learning, and studying for several rounds of professional exams can be tough.

EY is one of a number of major employers that has removed academic requirements from its upfront screening of applications, instead focusing the selection process on a candidate's strengths and future potential.

"We used to have a minimum entry requirement of a 2.1 degree and 300 UCAS points," says Richards. "But our data showed that there

was very little correlation between job performance and academic qualifications, so we removed that academic screening filter in 2015."

He is proud of the increased diversity that this has brought to the firm's graduate recruitment and is helping to widen access to the profession. "It's opened us up to a huge range of new talent, because 18 per cent of our current intake at graduate level wouldn't have had their applications considered previously."

The firm has a reputation for being particularly people-orientated, and this is a strong focus for its graduate recruitment. "EY is a great place to work because of the diversity of our teams, who are focused on solving complex problems for our clients around the world", explains Richards.

"The graduates who are successful here are those who collaborate, love complexity, have emotional intelligence and a passion to learn," he concludes. "We look for the best and brightest talent, but they need to be open-minded, with plenty of empathy and self-awareness."

THE TIMES

TOP 100
GRADUATE EMPLOYERS

ACCOUNTING & PROFESSIONAL SERVICES

1. **PWC**
2. **KPMG**
3. **DELOITTE** (FORMERLY DELOITTE & TOUCHE)
4. **EY** (FORMERLY ERNST & YOUNG)
5. **GRANT THORNTON**
6. **BDO** (FORMERLY BDO STOY HAYWARD)

Source **High Fliers Research**
Top accounting & professional services firms of the last 20 years, based on rankings in *The Times Top 100 Graduate Employers* 1999-2018.

The latest thinking?
Time to out-think it.

At Barclays, we believe opportunities are created by those who like to challenge convention, explore new possibilities and run with bold ideas.

Whether the result is a product that makes our customers' and clients' lives easier, a deal that helps to ensure a company's future success, or a wider initiative that benefits the communities we serve, that's what makes this an inspiring place to build a career.

But that's just our thoughts. It's yours we're interested in.

So tell us, what do you think?

joinus.barclays

Banking & Finance

Over the last twenty years, a dozen of the UK's best-known banking groups, insurance companies and financial institutions have been ranked in *The Times Top 100 Graduate Employers*.

Barclays and Lloyds Banking Group have both featured in the rankings every year since 1999, but the sector's leading employer, HSBC, achieved a place in the top ten employers for five years running between 2003 and 2007, and has appeared in the top twenty a total of sixteen times.

"HSBC is a truly international organisation which plays an important role in the world's economy, covering more than 90% of global trade," explains Priya Chandra-Rogers, Global Head of Emerging Talent. "Our values of being open, dependable and connected are at the core of how we hire as HSBC. We believe success comes from recruiting great people, treating them well and making sure they develop throughout their career."

The bank's annual intake of new graduates includes roles in retail and commercial banking, global banking and markets, wealth management and global private banking.

"The range of opportunities is tremendous and HSBC is very proud of the important role its graduates play," says Chandra-Rogers. "Our graduate and intern programmes genuinely matter to the bank's senior leaders, with several of them – including our Group Chief Executive – having joined as graduates. They understand first-hand the value of graduates as a source of diverse, capable talent."

Graduates joining HSBC have the opportunity to move into different parts of the organisation as their careers develop. "There's a huge

Priya Chandra-Rogers, Global Head of Emerging Talent, HSBC

wave of digital innovation within HSBC, which brings opportunities to work in more specialist areas of finance and in other functions too," Chandra-Rogers says.

"Graduates can join us on a programme within one of our global business lines, but their career path can become very diverse from that point onwards," she continues. "We have an International Manager Programme that takes some of our

THE TIMES
TOP 100
GRADUATE EMPLOYERS

BANKING & FINANCE
1. **HSBC**
2. **BARCLAYS**
3. **RBS** (FORMERLY ROYAL BANK OF SCOTLAND, NATWEST)
4. **LLOYDS BANKING GROUP**
5. **SANTANDER** (FORMERLY ABBEY NATIONAL)
6. **BANK OF ENGLAND**
7. **CAPITAL ONE**
8. **LLOYD'S**
9. **FINANCIAL SERVICES AUTHORITY**
10. **NATIONWIDE**

Source **High Fliers Research**
Top banking & finance employers of the last 20 years, based on their annual rankings in *The Times Top 100 Graduate Employers* 1999-2018.

most ambitious graduate alumni all around the world on a series of fast-track rotations in different countries."

Students applying for HSBC's graduate programmes don't need previous experience of banking or finance in order to be successful.

"By the time you make your application, it's important to know exactly why you want to work in financial services and why HSBC in particular," says Chandra-Rogers. "But our training will provide all the in-depth banking and technical knowledge once you've joined us. We take the view that financial services is a people business, rather than a money business, so we're looking for graduates who can articulate why they have a passion for people too."

Speaking at a recent global graduate induction, Group Chief Executive John Flint outlined what he thinks defines a successful HSBC graduate. "Be that colleague that everybody else wants to work with," he said. "It's not about competing with each other, it's about being part of a system that exists to serve other human beings – our customers."

Consulting

Twenty years ago, management consulting was the number one career destination for the UK's top graduates, but in the aftermath of the recession of 2002 it was overtaken by jobs in marketing or the media.

During the last four years, the sector has enjoyed an impressive resurgence and more than one in six of the finalists leaving university in 2018 applied for graduate jobs in consulting.

A total of twelve consulting firms have featured in *The Times Top 100 Graduate Employers* over the last twenty years but just one – McKinsey & Company – has appeared in the rankings every year since 1999.

For new graduates, the appeal of a career in consulting lies in the diverse range of projects on offer. "Consultancy is a great career if you're ambitious and excited by intellectual challenge but want to keep your options open and experience a variety of different industries," says Nick South, Partner & Managing Director at The Boston Consulting Group.

"We offer the chance to do interesting, meaningful work with some very senior clients, tackling complex problems and taking real responsibility from day one. It's all about having an impact and making a difference," he says.

Competition for entry-level places at the top firms is fierce and, to be successful, graduates need a range of skills and abilities. "As well as a level of academic achievement, we're looking for people with initiative who have shown leadership and can take personal responsibility," explains South. "The ability to structure problems, work collaboratively and communicate effectively is important too."

Graduates join the leading

Nick South, Partner & Managing Director, The Boston Consulting Group

consulting firms as Associates, working as junior members of project teams.

"Our teams use a combination of skills and capabilities – from partners who have deep expertise in an industry and project leaders who work closely with that particular client or sector, to new graduates who can bring fresh thinking and new ideas," says South. "At BCG we

THE TIMES
TOP 100
GRADUATE EMPLOYERS

CONSULTING

1. MCKINSEY & COMPANY
2. BAIN & COMPANY
3. THE BOSTON CONSULTING GROUP
4. NEWTON
5. METASWITCH NETWORKS
6. PA CONSULTING
7. MERCER
8. OLIVER WYMAN
9. MARAKON ASSOCIATES
10. MITCHELL MADISON GROUP

Source **High Fliers Research**
Top consulting firms of the last 20 years, based on their annual rankings in *The Times Top 100 Graduate Employers* 1999-2018.

have an intellectual curiosity which means we always think about what is at the core of a problem and what its root causes may be."

Progression within consulting firms can be rapid and most of the leading firms offer a well-defined career path. "After two years as an Associate, you have the chance to do a sponsored MBA or some people opt for an external secondment," explains South. "You return to the firm ready to take on the role of Consultant, and then Project Leader."

For those who are successful, the next step is to work as a Principal, leading bigger projects and teams, before becoming a Partner. "Our firm has doubled in the past seven years and it's this strong growth that I think enables you to continue to develop personally and professionally," he says.

At every level, a career in consulting is a demanding one. "I won't pretend that this is an easy '9 to 5' job," warns South. "It requires a lot of commitment and resilience, but the people who join us thrive on that."

CHANGE LED BY YOU

A BETTER BUSINESS. A BETTER WORLD. A BETTER YOU.

JOIN NOW **UNILEVER.CO.UK/CAREERS/GRADUATES**

Consumer Goods

Although their company names may not always be familiar, the brands produced by the leading consumer goods manufacturers are known the world over.

P&G, Unilever, L'Oréal and Mars have each been listed in *The Times Top 100 Graduate Employers* every year since its launch in 1999, and a further eleven employers from the consumer goods sector have appeared in the rankings over the last two decades.

Graduate programmes at the leading employers are heavily oversubscribed, with more than 200 university-leavers competing for each entry-level vacancy in the sector in 2018.

"For us, everything starts with great recruitment," enthuses Ian Morley, Group Sales Director at P&G – the company that produces Fairy, Ariel, Gillette, Pampers, Olay and Always. "We have a 'build-from-within' culture and we only really hire graduates who will want to stay with us for multi-year careers. That's our business model and, if you get it right, the backbone of your business is supported for decades to come."

This approach permeates across the whole company. "Everybody who works in P&G is involved with recruitment, from new graduates up to the senior management team who go out on campus every year," Morley explains. "We're working with universities to build P&G case studies into their business courses, to help demystify what the consumer goods industry is all about."

Most graduates join P&G having done either a nine-week summer placement or a three-day 'career academy' that the company runs each Christmas. "When we bring people in for these experiences, it's a mutual trial and a two-way

Ian Morley, Group Sales Director for Northern Europe, P&G

assessment," says Morley. "I want them to see what we do, feel what we do and smell the culture, so they know exactly the types of career we are offering."

There's no requirement to do the placement whilst at university. "We hire very good people who have decided to concentrate on their studies and then apply after graduation," Morley says. "And there are others who want to take a

year off before they start, which is something we're very open to. What we're after is great talent, whenever people choose to come to us."

P&G recruits graduates into more than a dozen different areas within the company, including marketing, sales, engineering, R&D and finance.

Morley believes one of the biggest differences between P&G and its competitors is the level of responsibility it gives new graduates. "We have a very clear and stated policy of providing meaningful work from day one," he explains. "In sales, this means handling multi-million pound portfolios, with real money, real budgets and real customers. Our training gives the highest level of coaching and support to enable new graduates to become account managers for our major customers like Tesco, Boots or Superdrug."

Graduate retention at P&G is high, but according to Morley it is continuing to increase. "We're very proud that five years after joining, 80 per cent of graduates are still with us. It's something we work incredibly hard on, to create an environment where people really want to stay."

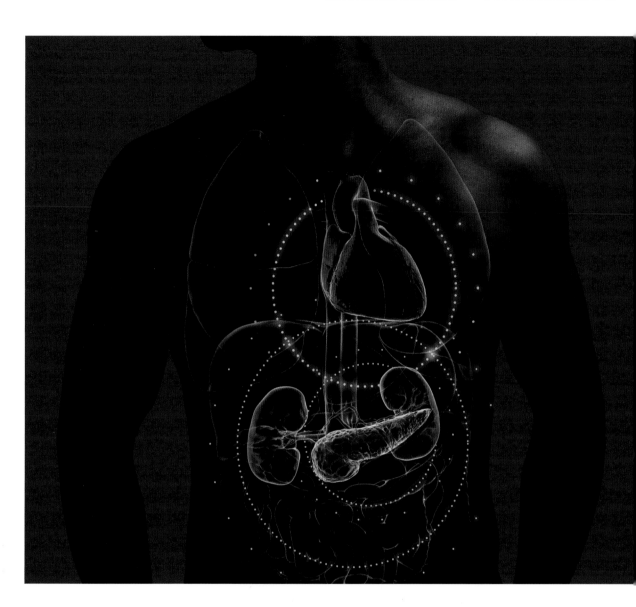

Exciting challenges on a global scale.
How will you make a difference?

At AstraZeneca we believe in the potential of our people and you'll develop beyond what you thought possible. We make the most of your skills and passion by actively supporting you to see what you can achieve on our Global Graduate Programmes.

Find out more at
careers.astrazeneca.com/students

Engineering & Industrial

Jacqueline Castle, Head of A350 & A380 Landing Gear Engineering, Airbus

During the last twenty years, more companies from the engineering & industrial sector have featured in *The Times Top 100 Graduate Employers* than any other type of employer.

Ranging from steel producers and motor manufacturers to industrial conglomerates, defence contractors and engineering design firms, a total of twenty-four major employers from the engineering & industrial sector have appeared in the rankings over the last two decades.

Airbus is one of three companies from the aerospace industry that has been regularly listed among the UK's top graduate employers since 1999. The company produces commercial aircraft, such as the iconic A380 double-decker airliner, as well as helicopters, military aircraft, and space technology.

"Graduates are attracted to Airbus because we're at the very forefront of the aerospace industry," says Jacqueline Castle, Head of A350 & A380 Landing Gear Engineering at Airbus. "We're known as an engineering pinnacle, leading in the design, manufacture and delivery of aerospace products and services. People are really excited by the aircraft we produce and the cutting-edge technologies behind them."

Airbus recruits over a hundred graduates annually for a broad range of engineering, technical and commercial roles. "We've always been a major engineering employer," Castle says. "But in addition to the more traditional skills like electrical or mechanical engineering, today we need more computing and avionics engineers, and people to work on emerging technologies like artificial intelligence."

The company's graduate scheme lasts two years and includes a series of placements in different parts of the organisation. "The thing that differentiates Airbus' graduate programme is that it is truly global and includes some amazing placements," Castle enthuses.

"We can guarantee an overseas placement for those who want it and most of our graduates also do an external placement, typically with an airline, a supplier or a customer," she says. "They get to see how our products effect the end-user and can then bring that knowledge and experience back into the business."

For engineering graduates, Airbus offers a choice of different career paths. "Some of our engineers become highly-technical skilled specialists, experts in their field," says Castle. "But equally, we need graduates who will go on to do broader technical management, leading big teams or the overall management of projects. You don't need to decide these things in the early stages of your career, that evolves once you realise where your talents and interests lie."

Aerospace remains a highly competitive sector, and Castle sees graduate recruitment as a key part of Airbus's future.

"Our industry is changing and we need talented graduates with a broad variety of skills to enable Airbus to continue innovating. We've got traditional competition within our industry but there is a new wave of competition too," she says. "Start-up companies have a very different approach and the rise of individual urban mobility aircraft means that Airbus graduates have many exciting challenges ahead!"

THE TIMES TOP 100 GRADUATE EMPLOYERS

ENGINEERING & INDUSTRIAL

1. **ROLLS-ROYCE**
2. **BAE SYSTEMS**
3. **ARUP** (FORMERLY OVE ARUP)
4. **ATKINS**
5. **JAGUAR LAND ROVER**
6. **AIRBUS**
7. **FORD**
8. **QINETIQ**
9. **SIEMENS**
10. **SCHLUMBERGER**

Source **High Fliers Research**
Top engineering & industrial employers of the last 20 years, based on rankings in *The Times Top 100 Graduate Employers* 1999-2018.

Together

That's how we do things.

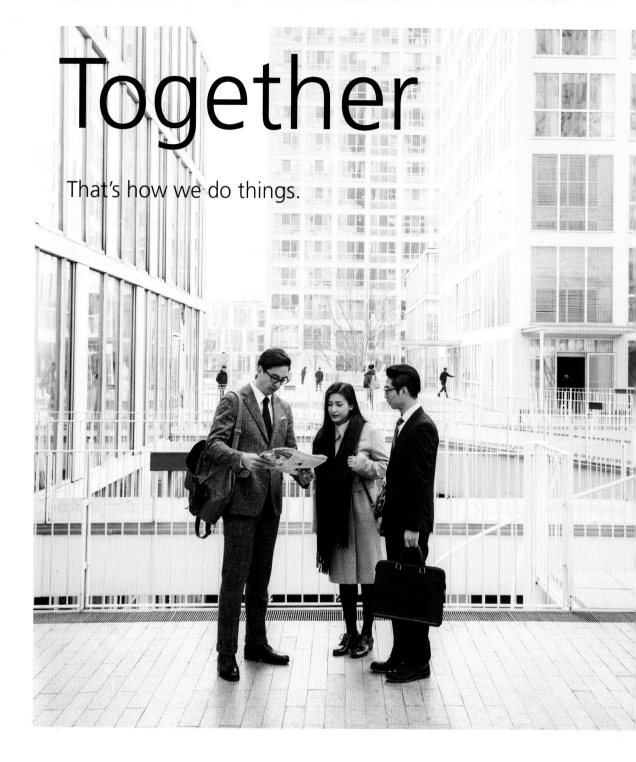

Are you truly collaborative? We offer a supportive, challenging and inclusive working environment. We value passion and commitment. And reward performance. Want to join our team?
ubs.com/careers

Investment Banking

Janine Glasenberg, Head of EMEA Graduate Recruitment, Goldman Sachs

Market-leading salaries and bonuses, the buzz of working in global finance and the promise of one of the world's most rewarding careers means that investment banking has remained a highly sought-after destination for ambitious new graduates over the last two decades.

Seventeen top investment banks and asset management companies have been featured in *The Times Top 100 Graduate Employers* since 1999. The highest-ranked bank, Goldman Sachs, was listed among the UK's top ten graduate employers for four years running, and two other leading banks, J.P. Morgan and Citi, have appeared in all twenty editions of the *Top 100*.

For penultimate year students, the competition for the top banks' annual summer internships is fierce, as this is often the main entry route onto the top graduate programmes. At least three-quarters of graduate vacancies within the sector were filled via internships in 2018.

"We always encourage students not to worry about how many other people are applying and to focus on putting in the best application they can," says Janine Glasenberg, Head of EMEA Graduate Recruitment at Goldman Sachs. "Our ten-week internships are the best way to peek behind the curtain and see what life would be like at the firm. Even if you don't make it onto the internship, keep in touch with us and you can re-apply later for the graduate programme."

Like several other banks, Goldman Sachs has replaced its first round face-to-face interviews with pre-recorded video interviews. "It means we can see far more people because we're not limited by how many bankers are available at a particular time to do the interviews," explains Glasenberg. "And it gives people a much better chance to showcase who they are, beyond what's on the pages of their CV."

Internships are a good way to find out about the working culture of a bank and its different divisions. "There's no doubt that working at Goldman Sachs is rewarding," says Glasenburg, "and our people are working on interesting projects and real-life transactions that they want to be a part of."

The bank takes a deliberately personal approach to its graduate recruitment and works hard to send recent recruits and former interns back to their old universities to share their experiences.

"When we're on campus, we always encourage our speakers to talk about themselves as people and what it's like to work at the firm, rather than the awards we've won and where we are in league tables," Glasenberg says. "People outside the firm often think of us as being really competitive, but everything inside the building is actually very collaborative and teamwork-orientated."

Every graduate that joins the bank goes to New York for global training within their division. "We're proud that it's one of the ways that we differentiate our graduate programme," says Glasenberg. "As well as the training, the connectivity that this experience brings ensures our graduates build a global network which will help them throughout their career."

THE TIMES

TOP 100
GRADUATE EMPLOYERS

INVESTMENT BANKING

1. **GOLDMAN SACHS**
2. **J.P. MORGAN**
3. **MORGAN STANLEY**
4. **CITI** (FORMERLY CITIBANK)
5. **DEUTSCHE BANK**
6. **UBS**
7. **BANK OF AMERICA MERRILL LYNCH**
8. **CREDIT SUISSE**
9. **STANDARD LIFE** (NOW ABERDEEN STANDARD)
10. **LEHMAN BROTHERS**

Source **High Fliers Research**
Top investment banks of the last 20 years, based on their annual rankings in *The Times Top 100 Graduate Employers* 1999-2018.

ALLEN & OVERY

MADE
FOR
MORE
____

IT'S TIME

The world around us is changing. New ways of working create new opportunities, and we're looking for people who are ready to make an impact. With our world-class development programme and industry leading experts behind you, you can become a lawyer of the future. If you're made for more, we want to hear from you. Visit our website to find out more.

A career in Law
aograduate.com

@AllenOveryGrads   /allenoverygrads   AllenOveryGrads

Law

With starting salaries now averaging £44,000, as well as the opportunity to train for a prestigious qualification and the potential for a life-long career, it's not hard to see why the top law firms continue to be such a popular choice for new graduates.

Over the last twenty years, a total of eighteen firms have appeared in *The Times Top 100 Graduate Employers,* and three global firms – Clifford Chance, Allen & Overy and Linklaters – have each featured in the rankings every year since 1999.

"Attracting and retaining the best talent to the firm is key. One of the most important aspects of that is providing an exceptional standard of training and development from the outset," says Laura Yeates, Head of Graduate Talent at Clifford Chance.

Like several of the leading firms, Clifford Chance now promotes its training contracts almost as soon as students arrive at university. "We have developed an award-winning scheme for first year undergraduates that helps them understand the landscape of the legal sector and how things are changing", explains Yeates. "The programme includes presentations on our practice areas, case studies, and seminars to develop legal knowledge and commercial awareness. It's an intensive schedule of classroom-based activity, a day shadowing our lawyers and a trip to the Amsterdam office to see the firm's global network in action."

The most successful participants are assessed for a training contact and can be offered a place with the firm a full two years before the end of their degree. Other training contracts are offered through the firm's vacation placements for penultimate and final year students and general applications.

Widening access to the legal

Laura Yeates, Head of Graduate Talent, Clifford Chance

profession is a major priority for Clifford Chance. "We were the first firm to introduce 'blind CVs' during our selection process, in order to reduce unconscious bias about the schools and universities that applicants had studied at," explains Yeates. "And we use contextualised data that takes into consideration a graduate's background when we're assessing their abilities and future potential. Our ethos is that we want to be a broad church of personalities,

experiences and backgrounds."

After graduation, the route to becoming a fully-qualified solicitor includes either one or two years at law school and a further two years of rotational placements, known as 'seats', within a firm.

Yeates believes that to be a successful lawyer, it takes more than academic achievement and a strong CV. "The more you can display an intellectual curiosity and enthusiasm for problem solving, the better. Take interest in what's changing around you, whether it's artificial intelligence, globalisation or another trend, and consider what that could mean for our clients."

As with many other industries and business sectors, technology is transforming how law firms operate. "There is still work to do that is repetitive and time-consuming, but a lot of it is being stripped out by the clever use of AI," says Yeates.

It's no secret that working as a trainee or a newly-qualified solicitor for a top firm can mean very long hours and tough deadlines. "This is a hard career," admits Yeates. "It's demanding – intellectually and personally – but it's also incredibly rewarding."

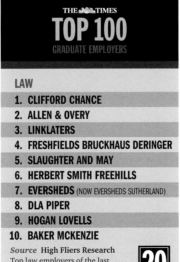

THE TIMES

TOP 100
GRADUATE EMPLOYERS

LAW

1. **CLIFFORD CHANCE**
2. **ALLEN & OVERY**
3. **LINKLATERS**
4. **FRESHFIELDS BRUCKHAUS DERINGER**
5. **SLAUGHTER AND MAY**
6. **HERBERT SMITH FREEHILLS**
7. **EVERSHEDS** (NOW EVERSHEDS SUTHERLAND)
8. **DLA PIPER**
9. **HOGAN LOVELLS**
10. **BAKER MCKENZIE**

Source **High Fliers Research**
Top law employers of the last 20 years, based on their annual rankings in *The Times Top 100 Graduate Employers* 1999-2018.

20 YEARS

We only recruit one type of person

FEMALEBLACKMALEASIAN SCHOOLLEAVERUNIVERSITY GRADUATEDISABLEDGAY BRITISHCITIZEN

You might think there's an MI5 'type'. White. Middle class. Male. Think again.
We need people who can bring a rich mix of skills, experiences and backgrounds
to help us fight the threats we face. Our differences make us stronger.
Together, we help to keep the country safe.

To find out more, please visit www.mi5.gov.uk/careers

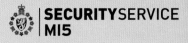

Media

F or seven out of the last twenty years, more final year students have applied for graduate jobs in the media than any other career sector.

One in seven new graduates from the 'Class of 2018' wanted to work in either journalism, broadcasting, publishing, communications, public relations or advertising.

Despite the media's popularity as a career destination for university-leavers, and the increasing number of entry-level vacancies in the sector that are filled by graduates, few media employers offer formal graduate development programmes. Just ten media organisations have been ranked in *The Times Top 100 Graduate Employers* since its launch in 1999.

The sector is led by the BBC which has been rated as one of the UK's top ten graduate employers fourteen times over the last twenty years.

"I think the enduring popularity of the BBC as a graduate employer is a combination of our brand and the public purpose of what we do," says Claire Paul, Head of Leadership Development and New Talent at the BBC. "And if you look at the alumni for the broadcasting industry, it's very hard to find people who are leading the industry who didn't come off a BBC graduate trainee programme."

The BBC offers over a hundred places annually on its graduate training programmes, with entry-level vacancies in several different parts of the organisation.

"Over recent years, we've been building up pathways into the BBC in all disciplines," says Paul. "We now have graduate programmes in areas like software engineering, digital technologies, broadcast engineering and research & development, as well as business and our long-established

Claire Paul, Director of Leadership Development & New Talent, BBC

journalism and production graduate trainee schemes."

For graduates wanting to work in journalism, the BBC's advice is to begin building up experience at university. "You don't need to have studied for a journalism degree in order to be successful. Things like writing for a student newspaper

THE TIMES TOP 100 GRADUATE EMPLOYERS

MEDIA

1. BBC
2. WPP
3. SKY
4. THOMSON REUTERS
5. BLOOMBERG
6. PENGUIN RANDOM HOUSE
7. SAATCHI & SAATCHI
8. VIRGIN MEDIA
9. CHANNEL FOUR
10. J. WALTER THOMPSON

Source **High Fliers Research**
Top media employers of the last 20 years, based on their annual rankings in *The Times Top 100 Graduate Employers* 1999-2018.

or working on student radio can really demonstrate that you're passionate about being a journalist," recommends Paul.

"And in today's age, there are so many other ways that you can communicate, whether that's film-making on your phone, blogging or podcasts," she says. "If you've never written anything or produced anything, then you shouldn't be surprised if you find you're competing with people who have already done a lot."

Across the BBC, there is a strong emphasis on future talent. "The BBC is constantly reinventing itself and the most crucial way we do that is by getting in the best young talent," explains Paul.

"We're always looking for people's underlying potential. So if your degree and your time at university has helped you develop great analytical skills and really honed your ideas and creativity, then that will put you in a strong position when you're applying for one of our schemes."

Oil & Energy

Jonathan Kohn, Vice President Human Resources, Shell

When the first edition of *The Times Top 100 Graduate Employers* was published in 1999, three of the world's best-known oil and gas companies – BP, Shell and ExxonMobil – were named among the UK's top twenty-five graduate recruiters.

All three have continued to be ranked in the *Top 100* every year since then, and have been joined over the last twenty years by a further seven employers from the wider energy sector.

Today's oil & energy sector accounts for less than 2 per cent of the annual vacancies at *The Times Top 100 Graduate Employers*, but boasts some of the country's longest-established graduate programmes.

"Shell's graduate programme can trace its roots right back to the 1960s," says Jonathan Kohn, Vice President of Human Resources for Shell UK, Ireland, Nordics & South Africa. "We've a very long history of recruiting graduates to be the future leadership of the company. Joining as a graduate has always provided a good foundation for a professional career and many people have gone from opportunity to opportunity and have reached the very top of Shell."

This emphasis on leadership remains a key element of Shell's graduate recruitment. "We pick people who'll be leaders when they turn up on day one," Kohn explains. "They may be the most junior members of the team, but they bring leadership in terms of their thoughts and perspectives, and getting their voice heard in the room. If people can't do that on day one, they're probably not going to get through our selection process."

Graduates joining Shell are recruited for a fast-track career path through the company. "We expect our new graduates to be in a significant leadership position in a decade," Kohn explains. "For example, within ten years of joining, you could be the UK finance manager of our retail business, which globally has more branded outlets than either McDonalds or Starbucks."

Three-quarters of Shell's senior managers started as graduates. "You hear so much about the death of 'careers for life', but given the scale and breadth of Shell, it really is possible here. I joined as a graduate and often joke I've just done 25 years by accident," says Kohn.

"At no point did I think I wanted to work for just one employer. But if you do a job and the company is able to offer you exciting, challenging opportunities – one after another – in different roles, in different parts of the business, in different countries, before you know it you're two decades into your career," he says. "For me, it's happened as a result of the quality of the work, the quality of my colleagues and the international dimension of the organisation. I've never needed to go elsewhere to find my next challenge."

At company level, Shell's biggest challenge is moving from being an oil producer to becoming a sustainable energy provider. "You can't turn a big switch and change everything overnight, but there are some incredibly exciting developments," Kohn says. "For example, Prelude is Shell's first floating liquefied natural gas production facility and the largest floating structure on the planet. Graduates have a chance to be part of a company that's playing a leading role in the energy transition that the world is relying on for a sustainable future."

THE TIMES

TOP 100

GRADUATE EMPLOYERS

OIL & ENERGY

1. **BP**
2. **SHELL**
3. **EXXONMOBIL**
4. **CENTRICA**
5. **BNFL** (INCLUDING BRITISH NUCLEAR GROUP)
6. **EDF ENERGY**
7. **E.ON**
8. **NPOWER**
9. **NATIONAL GRID**
10. **SCOTTISH POWER**

Source **High Fliers Research**
Top oil & energy employers of the last 20 years, based on their annual rankings in *The Times Top 100 Graduate Employers* 1999-2018.

Public Sector

At the UK's top universities, one in seven students who graduated in the summer of 2018 applied to work for public sector employers after university, making it a far more popular career choice for graduates than jobs in investment banking, law or accountancy.

This is not a new phenomenon. Twenty-two public sector employers have appeared in *The Times Top 100 Graduate Employers* over the past two decades. The highest-rated employer is the Civil Service, whose Fast Stream programme now recruits on behalf of most major Government departments, including the Foreign & Commonwealth Office, Ministry of Defence, Department for Transport and HM Revenue & Customs. The Fast Stream has been ranked amongst the country's top ten graduate employers every year since 1999, and headed the list in 2003.

Greg Hobbs, Head of the Civil Service Fast Stream, believes its enduring appeal lies in the impact that graduates can have on the programme. "The Civil Service has huge things to deliver for the country, and our Fast Streamers are put straight into challenging and exciting situations from day one," he explains. "We give them significant responsibility and, from the very start of their career, we're asking them to write national policy and contribute to running the country."

The Fast Stream has more than doubled its annual recruitment over the last five years, and there are now fifteen different schemes available. "The Fast Stream is continuing to grow because of the value it brings to Government departments," says Hobbs. "Our biggest intake is for the 'Generalist' scheme which focuses on policy and operations, but we also have schemes offering roles

Greg Hobbs, Deputy Director, Fast Stream & Early Talent, Civil Service

in finance, science & engineering, commercial, communications and digital. The most popular schemes are those for the Diplomatic Service and the Houses of Parliament."

Each scheme typically includes three or four years of placements and rotations in different departments across the Civil Service. By the time they complete the scheme, Fast Streamers can expect to be promoted two grades and achieve a salary of between £45,000 and £55,000.

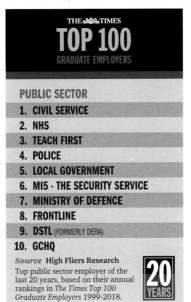

Source High Fliers Research
Top public sector employer of the last 20 years, based on their annual rankings in *The Times Top 100 Graduate Employers* 1999-2018.

"We are training leaders of the future, and recognise that the very best leaders have a range of experiences to draw on, as well as the mentors and learning networks that the Fast Stream provides," says Hobbs.

The multi-stage selection process for the Fast Stream includes online tests, a video interview, plus a half-day assessment centre.

"To be successful, you need to demonstrate qualities like resilience, an openness to change, emotional intelligence and a good awareness of what's happening in society," explains Greg. "It's not about the university you went to or what subject you studied when you were there, it's about what you as an individual can bring to the Fast Stream. More than ever before, we've broadened our reach so we're looking at a diverse range of candidates from a broad range of backgrounds."

Hobbs believes that the Civil Service can only work at its best when it reflects the population that it serves. "We're doing everything we can to make sure that the Fast Stream is as diverse, inclusive and reflective of the whole of society as it possibly can be."

YOU LEAD
THE WAY.

Choose our varied, comprehensive graduate programme and build all-rounder experience and life-changing skills.

BRING YOUR BEST. WE'LL DO THE REST.

lidlgraduatecareers.co.uk

Retail

Sixteen of the country's best-known retailers have appeared in *The Times Top 100 Graduate Employers* over the last two decades, with Marks & Spencer, Tesco and the John Lewis Partnership featuring in the rankings every year since 1999.

"M&S is one of the longest-established names on the high street, but we are continually reshaping, transforming and evolving," says Helen Alkin, Head of Future Talent at M&S. "Graduates have always been an integral part of our talent pipeline because they bring new skills and new thinking which are absolutely critical to us."

Like a number of other leading retailers, M&S recruits graduates into a wide range of entry-level roles within the company, not just retail management.

"We work very hard on campus to explain the breadth and variety of opportunities that M&S can provide," she explains. "People don't necessarily think beyond what they've seen as a consumer and wouldn't associate us with jobs in data analysis and software engineering or the large number of graduate vacancies that we have in logistics and supply chain."

M&S offers a total of fifteen individual graduate programmes in different parts of the organisation, including merchandising, buying, food technology, fashion design and property.

The company is unusual in that it is largely an own-brand retailer. "This means we can offer graduates the chance to be involved in every part of the retail process – from initial product development, right through to selling it to our customers," says Alkin. "And there are few other retailers who have opportunities across food, clothing and home products."

Helen Alkin, Head of Future Talent, M&S

The last two years have been a particularly turbulent time for the retail sector, with well-known brands like New Look, Mothercare, Debenhams, Homebase, Jones the Bootmaker and Carpetright cutting stores, and Toys R Us and Maplins closing down altogether.

"The way that we all shop now is drastically different to how it was ten or fifteen years ago, and more change is on the way," admits Alkin. "But M&S has always been a big innovator on the high street, so for new graduates there's a real opportunity to be part of the transformation and revitalisation that today's retail sector is going through."

Recent new entries in *The Times Top 100 Graduate Employers* include the home-delivery giant Amazon, which joined the list in 2015 and is now ranked just outside the top twenty, and the online fashion and beauty retailer Asos, which is this year's highest newcomer to the *Top 100* list. Together, they expect to hire over 300 graduates in 2019.

"To drive M&S forward, the graduates we're looking for are those with a real digital mindset who can challenge the norm and the status quo," Alkin says. "As a company, we've always valued great communicators and people with real commercial acumen and leadership skills. M&S needs graduates who are prepared to get stuck in from day one and are excited by change."

THE TIMES TOP 100 GRADUATE EMPLOYERS

RETAIL

1. ALDI
2. MARKS & SPENCER
3. TESCO
4. JOHN LEWIS PARTNERSHIP
5. SAINSBURY'S
6. BOOTS
7. MCDONALD'S
8. LIDL
9. ASDA
10. ARCADIA GROUP

Source High Fliers Research
Top retail employers of the last 20 years, based on their annual rankings in *The Times Top 100 Graduate Employers* 1999-2018.

Discover the remarkable.

We're Vodafone. The tech industry's original game changers.

From developing smart cities to enabling the growth of economies in the developing world, we're building the digital infrastructure of the future.

We're looking for curious innovators who embrace technology, who thrive in an environment where their creativity and determination enable us to succeed in the digital world.

Discover our graduate and internship opportunities careers.vodafone.com

The future is exciting.
Ready?

Technology

Candida Mottershead, Human Resources Director, Accenture

The technology sector is fast-changing and, during the last two decades, more than twenty IT firms, software developers, internet companies and telecommunications providers have featured in *The Times Top 100 Graduate Employers*.

Several technology companies that were ranked as leading employers in the early 2000s are no longer operating and just four employers – Accenture, IBM, Microsoft and BT – have appeared in the *Top 100* each year from 1999 onwards.

Accenture was the first employer to be voted number one in *The Times Top 100 Graduate Employers*, and it remained there for four years running until 2002. "We've moved a long way as a business in the last twenty years," says Candida Mottershead, Human Resources Director at Accenture. "Today's graduates have the opportunity to work in an organisation where business meets really cutting-edge technology. We used to find graduates wanted to come into consulting, but now they're really keen on the technology side too."

It isn't a prerequisite for graduates joining Accenture to have studied a computer science or technical degree. "We want people that are really excited by technology, and over the last few years we've been more open about the types of degrees that we're looking for, to recruit a range of backgrounds and experiences," says Mottershead.

"We provide all our new graduates with an intense two-week induction and then a whole cascade of training that they go through for two years which helps them develop their business and commercial acumen, as well as their technical skills," she says. "And they'll be spending time out on client projects to learn from colleagues that they're working alongside."

Accenture recruits around 500 graduates annually for its five businesses – technology, digital, operations, consulting and strategy – and offers industrial placements and summer internships as taster experiences for students. "I think it can help you understand what we do and gives you the confidence that this is what you really want to do when you leave university," Mottershead explains. "We get some fantastic students on our placement schemes and many of them are offered a place on the graduate programme."

The company recruits equal numbers of men and women for its graduate programme. "We have been gender-balanced in our graduate intake for a number of years. It's really working well and it's not the challenge that it used to be to attract women, even for technology roles which have typically been more appealing to men."

Competition for entry-level jobs at Accenture remains tough, but Mottershead is clear about the qualities that graduates need to be successful at the company. "We need our graduates to be passionate about technology and be curious about the world around them," she says. "They are the future of Accenture and we need them to be able to come in and challenge how we do things and challenge the status quo."

Many of Accenture's senior leaders began their careers on the graduate programme. "This is a demanding industry but that means you can learn an awful lot and continue to learn as your career develops," says Mottershead.

THE TIMES TOP 100 GRADUATE EMPLOYERS

TECHNOLOGY

1. **ACCENTURE** (FORMERLY ANDERSEN CONSULTING)
2. **IBM**
3. **MICROSOFT**
4. **BT**
5. **GOOGLE**
6. **VODAFONE**
7. **LOGICA**
8. **NORTEL NETWORKS**
9. **FACEBOOK**
10. **INTEL**

Source **High Fliers Research**
Top technology employers of the last 20 years, based on their annual rankings in *The Times Top 100 Graduate Employers* 1999-2018.

The difference is you

**Demola Aofolaju,
Management Accountant
Finance graduate scheme**

"It's a very exciting time to join Network Rail. By joining us now, you'll get a chance to help shape the future of the rail industry."

We own, operate and develop Britain's railway infrastructure; that's 20,000 miles of track, 30,000 bridges, tunnels and viaducts and the thousands of signals, level crossings and stations. We manage 20 of the UK's largest stations while all the others, over 2,500, are managed by the country's train operating companies.

Every day, more than 4.6 million journeys are made in the UK. People depend on Britain's railway for their daily commute, to visit friends and loved ones and to get them home safe every day. Our role is to deliver a safe and reliable railway, so we carefully manage and deliver thousands of projects every year that form part of the multi-billion pound Railway Upgrade Plan, to grow and expand the nation's railway network to respond to the tremendous growth and demand the railway has experienced – a doubling of passenger journeys over the past 20 years.

We are building a better railway for a better Britain.

Therefore, the railway is crucial to Britain's prosperity. It connects people with jobs, goods with markets, and stimulates new housing and economic growth. The railways are the economic arteries of the nation. We run the safest major railway in Europe. At the same time, Britain's railway is Europe's fastest growing, with the number of rail journeys doubling in the last 20 years and forecast to increase by another 40 % by 2040. It is a growing industry, which offers not only prosperity and connectivity at home, but opens export opportunities for British business overseas.

NetworkRail

Standout graduate and placement opportunities with Network Rail

Through our Railway Upgrade Plan, we are delivering £130m of improvements every week. Working in partnership as one railway, alongside the Government and industry, we are making a £50bn investment, spreading opportunity across the country. This means more trains, and services that are faster, more reliable and more comfortable. This is the biggest and most ambitious upgrade the network has ever seen in over 150 years, and our great people are delivering it.

Network Rail is customer focused. We run the company through devolved route businesses that understand how to meet customer needs. We operate in a matrix structure, which means we work collaboratively across functions. This structure is made up of nine route businesses, group functions and route support services. Eight of the route businesses manage and run the railway network in a defined geographical area and work closely with local train operating companies to deliver the best service possible for their passengers. The ninth route operates nationally serving freight and long-distance operators.

Our nine customer focused route businesses run the railway. They operate, maintain and renew infrastructure to deliver a safe and reliable railway for passengers and freight customers.

Each route is a large, complex business in its own right, employing thousands of people and responsible for billions of pounds of expenditure every year. They are run by a Managing Director and a Senior Leadership Team who are accountable for effectively and efficiently delivering for customers and key stakeholders. These outcomes are made visible through route and customer scorecards.

In Scotland, the route and the train operating company form an alliance, Scotrail. The aim of this partnership is to improve the railway in Scotland for customers by working better together. Both the route and the train operator work to achieve common objectives, they are led by a single managing director, who is a member of the Executive Committee and reports to our Chief Executive.

Find out more at **networkrail.co.uk/graduates**

THE ✦ TIMES
THE SUNDAY TIMES
Know your times

Students pay £26 per year, which is a saving of 90%

Get life ready

Students know more. Students get more. Students save more.

Considered journalism
We provide diverse opinion along with in-depth insight on all the stories that matter.

+

Global news
With 36 correspondents across six continents, read in-depth analysis, anywhere in the world.

+

Exclusive benefits
Enjoy up to 25% off at 2,000 restaurants nationwide and enjoy 2-for-1 cinema tickets every weekend.

THE ⟨crest⟩ TIMES

TOP 100

GRADUATE EMPLOYERS

Index

Graduate Vacancies in 2019 — category columns (left to right): Accountancy, Consulting, Engineering, Finance, General Management, Human Resources, Investment Banking, Law, Logistics, Marketing, Media, Property, Purchasing, Research & Development, Retailing, Sales, Technology, Other

EMPLOYER	TOP 100 RANKING	GRADUATE VACANCIES IN 2019 (areas)	NUMBER OF VACANCIES	PAGE
AECOM	100	Consulting, Engineering, Finance, Media, Sales	350	84
AIRBUS	51	Engineering, Finance, Logistics, Property, Purchasing, Sales	100+	86
ALDI	3	Finance, Retailing	100	88
ALLEN & OVERY	38	Law	80-90	90
AMAZON	23	Consulting, Engineering, Finance, General Management, Human Resources, Marketing, Media, Property, Purchasing, Retailing, Sales, Technology	250+	92
AON	84	Consulting, Finance, Law, Sales	75+	94
APPLE	44	Accountancy, Consulting, Engineering, Finance, General Management, Human Resources, Marketing, Media, Property, Purchasing, Research & Development, Retailing, Sales, Technology	No fixed quota	96
ARMY	28	Engineering, Finance, General Management, Logistics, Marketing, Technology	650+	98
ARUP	27	Accountancy, Consulting, Engineering, Finance	250+	100
ASOS	52	Engineering, General Management, Marketing, Retailing, Technology	No fixed quota	102
ASTRAZENECA	46	Engineering, Finance, Marketing, Property, Purchasing, Sales	80+	104
ATKINS	45	Accountancy, Consulting, Sales	400	106
BAE SYSTEMS	39	Consulting, Engineering, Finance, General Management, Human Resources, Sales	350	108
BAKER MCKENZIE	65	Law	30	110
BANK OF ENGLAND	71	Finance, General Management, Human Resources, Investment Banking, Sales	80+	112
BARCLAYS	18	Finance, General Management, Human Resources, Investment Banking, Marketing, Sales	500+	114
BBC	12	Consulting, Finance, Media, Property, Sales	130	116
BLACKROCK	72	Consulting, Engineering, Finance, Investment Banking, Sales	125+	118
BLOOMBERG	59	Consulting, Finance, Media, Sales, Technology	450	120
BMW GROUP	87	Engineering, Finance, Human Resources, Logistics, Marketing, Sales	20-30	122
BOOTS	54	Finance, General Management, Human Resources, Logistics, Marketing, Sales	30-40	124
BOSTON CONSULTING GROUP	47	Consulting	No fixed quota	126
BP	22	Accountancy, Consulting, Engineering, Finance, Law, Property, Purchasing, Research & Development, Retailing, Sales	100+	128
BRITISH AIRWAYS	82	Accountancy, Finance, General Management, Marketing, Sales	50-100	130
BT	70	Finance, General Management, Human Resources, Logistics, Marketing, Property, Purchasing, Sales, Technology	250+	132
CANCER RESEARCH UK	63	Accountancy, Finance, Marketing, Sales	9	134
CHARITYWORKS	96	Engineering, Finance, General Management, Marketing, Media, Sales, Technology	140	136
CIVIL SERVICE	2	Consulting, Engineering, Finance, General Management, Law, Property, Purchasing	Up to 1,500	138
CLIFFORD CHANCE	36	Law	90+	140
CMS	89	Law	65	142
DANONE	74	Marketing, Purchasing	15-20	144
DELOITTE	6	Accountancy, Consulting, Finance, General Management, Media, Sales	1,000+	146
DLA PIPER	58	Law	70-80	148
DYSON	50	Engineering, Marketing, Sales	75+	150
EXXONMOBIL	61	Consulting, Finance, Marketing	30+	152
FRESHFIELDS BRUCKHAUS DERINGER	62	Law	Up to 80	154
FRONTLINE	26	General Management, Human Resources, Law	452	156
GOLDMAN SACHS	17	Investment Banking, Sales	450	158
GOOGLE	5	Consulting, Engineering, Finance, Marketing, Media, Retailing, Sales	No fixed quota	160
GRANT THORNTON	86	Accountancy	400-450	162
GSK	10	Accountancy, Consulting, Engineering, Finance, Logistics, Marketing, Property, Purchasing, Sales	60+	164
HERBERT SMITH FREEHILLS	48	Law	Up to 60	166
HOGAN LOVELLS	76	Law	50	168

EMPLOYER	TOP 100 RANKING	ACCOUNTANCY	CONSULTING	ENGINEERING	FINANCE	GENERAL MANAGEMENT	HUMAN RESOURCES	INVESTMENT BANKING	LAW	LOGISTICS	MARKETING	MEDIA	PROPERTY	PURCHASING	RESEARCH & DEVELOPMENT	RETAILING	SALES	TECHNOLOGY	OTHER	NUMBER OF VACANCIES	PAGE
HSBC	14	●				●		●									●	●		600+	170
IBM	25		●															●		150+	172
IRWIN MITCHELL	95								●											50	174
JAGUAR LAND ROVER	19	●		●	●		●			●	●		●	●	●		●	●		250-300	176
JOHNSON & JOHNSON	77			●	●						●				●					25-30	178
J.P. MORGAN	13			●	●	●		●							●			●		400+	180
KPMG	8	●	●		●	●	●	●										●		Around 1,200	182
L'ORÉAL	85				●					●	●						●			28	184
LIDL	15				●					●							●			60	186
LINKLATERS	40								●											100	188
LLOYD'S	97				●															10	190
LLOYDS BANKING GROUP	24	●	●	●	●	●		●			●						●	●		250+	192
MARKS & SPENCER	35			●	●	●				●	●		●	●	●	●				200	194
MARS	41	●		●	●	●				●	●			●	●		●	●		25-30	196
MCDONALD'S	68				●															30	198
MI5 - THE SECURITY SERVICE	79				●															200+	200
MORGAN STANLEY	43			●	●		●	●										●		200+	202
NETWORK RAIL	81		●	●	●	●							●							Around 170	204
NEWTON	34		●																	100	206
NGDP FOR LOCAL GOVERNMENT	73	●		●	●	●		●		●	●	●	●	●			●			140	208
NHS	7	●		●	●	●									●		●			500	210
PENGUIN RANDOM HOUSE	53									●	●					●				20+	212
PINSENT MASONS	99								●											68	214
POLICE NOW	90																		●	350	216
PWC	1	●	●		●				●									●		1,350	218
ROLLS-ROYCE	16			●		●	●							●			●	●		300+	220
ROYAL AIR FORCE	83			●		●		●	●									●		500-600	222
ROYAL NAVY	78			●	●	●	●		●	●		●			●			●		No fixed quota	224
SANTANDER	56		●		●		●	●									●			100	226
SAVILLS	92												●							100	228
SHELL	29			●	●	●			●	●				●			●	●		38+	230
SIEMENS	91			●	●	●								●	●		●	●		70-80	232
SKY	30				●						●						●			90+	234
SLAUGHTER AND MAY	60								●											80-85	236
TEACH FIRST	4																		●	1,750	238
TESCO	37				●					●	●			●		●	●			80+	240
THINK AHEAD	42																		●	100-112	242
TPP	75									●					●	●	●			50+	244
UNILEVER	11			●	●	●		●			●				●		●	●		40-50	246
VIRGIN MEDIA	57			●	●	●									●			●		60+	248
WELLCOME	67	●			●	●	●	●	●			●	●			●		●		12	250
WHITE & CASE	80								●											50	252
WPP	64										●	●								To be confirmed	254

MAKE AMAZING HAPPEN
Start your career in infrastructure and environment here:
aecom.com/amazing

AECOM Graduates make a real difference to the built and natural environment in which we live. The company is a leader in all of the key markets that it serves, including transportation, facilities, environmental, energy, oil and gas, water, high-rise buildings and government.

AECOM is a global network of experts working with clients, communities and colleagues to develop and implement innovative solutions to the world's most complex challenges.

Delivering clean water and energy. Building iconic skyscrapers. Planning new cities. Restoring damaged environments. Connecting people and economies with roads, bridges, tunnels and transit systems. Designing parks where children play. Helping governments maintain stability and security. AECOM connects expertise across services, markets, and geographies to deliver transformative outcomes. Worldwide, AECOM designs, builds, finances, operates and manages projects and programs that unlock opportunities, protect the environment and improve people's lives.

The AECOM Graduate Development Programme lasts for two years, and will provide graduates with full financial and development support towards their relevant professional qualification, including an assigned mentor, regular residential training modules, an opportunity to work on live client projects, external training courses where required, and multi-disciplinary exposure.

AECOM is seeking applicants from around 35 disciplines, including civil, structural, mechanical, electrical, building services, industrial, fire and sustainable buildings engineering, as well as quantity & building surveying, project management, planning & design, ecology, acoustics, environmental, water and energy related disciplines.

GRADUATE VACANCIES IN 2019

CONSULTING
ENGINEERING
FINANCE
PROPERTY
TECHNOLOGY

NUMBER OF VACANCIES
350 graduate jobs

LOCATIONS OF VACANCIES

STARTING SALARY FOR 2019
£24,000-£27,000

UNIVERSITY VISITS IN 2018-19
BATH, BELFAST, BIRMINGHAM, BRISTOL, CARDIFF, TRINITY COLLEGE DUBLIN, UNIVERSITY COLLEGE DUBLIN, DURHAM, EDINBURGH, EXETER, GLASGOW, HERIOT-WATT, IMPERIAL COLLEGE LONDON, LEEDS, LOUGHBOROUGH, MANCHESTER, NEWCASTLE, NOTTINGHAM, PLYMOUTH, READING, SHEFFIELD, SOUTHAMPTON, STRATHCLYDE, SURREY, UNIVERSITY COLLEGE LONDON, WARWICK, YORK
Please check with your university careers service for full details of local events.

MINIMUM ENTRY REQUIREMENTS
2.2 Degree

APPLICATION DEADLINE
Year-round recruitment
Early application advised.

FURTHER INFORMATION
www.Top100GraduateEmployers.com
Register now for the latest news, campus events, work experience and graduate vacancies at AECOM.

" AMAZING IS BEING RECOGNISED AS A LEADING BIRD AND BOTANY SURVEYOR AFTER JUST ONE YEAR IN THE JOB. "

CAMERON
GRADUATE ECOLOGIST,
BIRMINGHAM

MAKE AMAZING HAPPEN
Start your career in infrastructure
and environment here:
aecom.com/amazing

AIRBUS

Airbus is a global leader in aerospace, offering the most comprehensive range of passenger airliners, and civil and military rotorcraft. As well as having strong capabilities in military aircraft and cybersecurity, Airbus is also Europe's number one space enterprise.

Graduates at Airbus can take their first steps towards building a big career. Over the course of their programme, they can explore the breadth of the business through a series of rotational placements – allowing them to build the knowledge, experience and understanding needed to progress within the organisation.

Airbus' UK graduate programme is both structured and flexible. Why? Because Airbus is a strong believer in career mobility, as it allows the organisation and its people to move forward. So placements are tailored to suit each graduate's needs, as well as those of the business, encouraging individuals to take control of their own career. Add to that outstanding training and development, a comprehensive induction, various technical and business modules, and graduates have everything they need to succeed in either commercial aircraft or defence and space. While the majority of roles are engineering-based, Airbus also recruits people with degrees in everything from Materials Sciences and IT to Business and Finance.

Airbus' placements last between two and three years and are designed to accelerate learning development – helping graduates to discover new career paths and open their mind to the company's possibilities.

What's more, working alongside passionate and determined people, graduates will help to accomplish the extraordinary – on the ground, in the sky, and in space.

GRADUATE VACANCIES IN 2019

ENGINEERING
FINANCE
LOGISTICS
PURCHASING
RESEARCH & DEVELOPMENT
TECHNOLOGY

NUMBER OF VACANCIES
100+ graduate jobs

LOCATIONS OF VACANCIES

STARTING SALARY FOR 2019
£27,000
Plus a £2,000 welcome bonus.

UNIVERSITY VISITS IN 2018-19
ASTON, BRISTOL, CARDIFF, IMPERIAL COLLEGE LONDON, LIVERPOOL, LOUGHBOROUGH, MANCHESTER, READING.
Please check with your university careers service for full details of local events.

MINIMUM ENTRY REQUIREMENTS
2.2 Degree

APPLICATION DEADLINE
November 2018

FURTHER INFORMATION
www.Top100GraduateEmployers.com
Register now for the latest news, campus events, work experience and graduate vacancies at Airbus.

With roots dating back to 1913, Aldi (short for Albrecht Discount) came to the UK in 1990 and customers were amazed to see a fantastic example of 'no frills' shopping. Aldi are now one of the UK's fastest-growing supermarkets and one of the world's most successful retailers.

All graduates enter the business on the Area Manager Training Programme. It's gained a reputation for offering an enormous amount of responsibility, and rightly so. Over 12 months, graduates get everything they need to take control of a multi-million pound area of up to four stores. Graduates also receive incredible support throughout their training, with a dedicated mentor and regular one-to-one sessions with talented colleagues.

It's the perfect introduction to Aldi and a superb foundation for future success. It gives graduates a wider lens to make critical business decisions later on in their journey. Three to four years into the role, graduates may get the chance to take on a project role within one of Aldi's Regions, Corporate departments, Logistics, or even an International Secondment in countries such as the US or Australia. Further in the future, high-performing Area Managers could even move into a Director role within (for example) Buying, Finance or Operations.

Aldi is built on an attitude. It's about never giving up; always striving for smarter, simpler ways of doing things. They're a business with integrity: they're fair to their partners and suppliers, and everything they do is for the benefit of their customers and their people. They look for graduates who are incredibly hardworking with a positive, 'roll their sleeves up' attitude. Those who join Aldi will blend intellect with a practical, business-focused mindset as they achieve impressive results with a world-class team.

GRADUATE VACANCIES IN 2019

GENERAL MANAGEMENT
RETAILING

NUMBER OF VACANCIES
100 graduate jobs

LOCATIONS OF VACANCIES

STARTING SALARY FOR 2019
£44,000

UNIVERSITY VISITS IN 2018-19
ASTON, BIRMINGHAM, BRISTOL, CARDIFF, DURHAM, EAST ANGLIA, EDINBURGH, EXETER, KEELE, LEEDS, LEICESTER, LIVERPOOL, LOUGHBOROUGH, MANCHESTER, NEWCASTLE, NORTHUMBRIA, NOTTINGHAM, READING, ST ANDREWS, STRATHCLYDE, WARWICK, YORK
Please check with your university careers service for full details of local events.

MINIMUM ENTRY REQUIREMENTS
2.1 Degree
96 UCAS points
240 UCAS points for those who passed exams before 2017.

APPLICATION DEADLINE
Year-round recruitment
Early application advised.

FURTHER INFORMATION
www.Top100GraduateEmployers.com
Register now for the latest news, campus events, work experience and graduate vacancies at Aldi.

It's tougher than you think.

Turns out I'm tougher than I thought.

Graduate Area Manager Programme

- **£44,000 starting salary (rising to £75,360 after four years)**
- **Pension • Healthcare • Audi A4 • All-year round recruitment but places fill quickly**

The Area Manager role is tough. Not many employers would ask you to run a £multi-million business after 14 weeks. But that's the beauty of Aldi. You'll need to be driven, determined and ready to work outside your comfort zone. In return you'll get world-class training and support from your very first day. In fact, my mentor helped me make the most of my skills, determination and strength of character. And that's why I wouldn't want to be anywhere else right now.

aldirecruitment.co.uk/graduates

ALLEN & OVERY

aograduate.com

twitter.com/AllenOveryGrads
@AllenOveryGrads
facebook.com/AllenOveryGrads
linkedin.com/company/Allen-&-Overy

Allen & Overy is a leading global law firm operating in over 30 countries. It covers 99% of the world's economy, working with companies, organisations and governments on issues of incredible scope and complexity, applying new ways of thinking to the ever-changing world around us.

Allen & Overy are pioneers in the industry: the only firm to have topped the Financial Times Innovative Law Firm ranking five times, as well as being TARGETjobs most popular graduate recruiter in law for the last thirteen years. They look for trainees who want to push the limits of law, and in return who can expect a rewarding experience that will prepare them for a career at the very pinnacle of the profession. In each of their seats they'll support a senior associate or partner on work that crosses departments and borders – in fact, 73% of the firm's work involves two or more jurisdictions. Around 80% of trainees have the chance to spend six months in one of the firm's 44 overseas offices, or on secondment to one of its corporate clients – who include 87% of Forbes' top 100 public companies.

As the world changes, the legal industry needs to evolve with it. A&O is investing in its people to ensure they have the skills and knowledge they will need to operate in the legal landscape of the future. For trainees, this means an in-house training programme characterised by flexibility, choice and opportunity – like having the chance to take a litigation course alongside their rotations.

A&O is dedicated to challenging the status quo and leading the way in commercial law. So whatever they've studied – and around half have a degree in a subject other than law – A&O helps its trainees develop into exceptional lawyers and learn to do work of the highest possible standard. All they look for in return is for graduates to bring confidence, creativity and the desire to learn.

GRADUATE VACANCIES IN 2019

LAW

NUMBER OF VACANCIES
80-90 graduate jobs
For training contracts starting in 2021.

LOCATIONS OF VACANCIES

STARTING SALARY FOR 2019
£45,000
Plus a £10,000 maintenance grant for the A&O LPC, and also a £9,000 grant for the GDL in London.

UNIVERSITY VISITS IN 2018-19
BATH, BELFAST, BIRMINGHAM, BRISTOL, CAMBRIDGE, CARDIFF, TRINITY COLLEGE DUBLIN, UNIVERSITY COLLEGE DUBLIN, DURHAM, EDINBURGH, EXETER, KING'S COLLEGE LONDON, LEEDS, LEICESTER, LONDON SCHOOL OF ECONOMICS, MANCHESTER, NOTTINGHAM, OXFORD, SHEFFIELD, SOUTHAMPTON, ST ANDREWS, WARWICK, YORK
Please check with your university careers service for full details of local events.

MINIMUM ENTRY REQUIREMENTS
2.1 Degree
135 UCAS points
340 UCAS points for those who passed exams before 2017.

APPLICATION DEADLINE
31st December 2018

FURTHER INFORMATION
www.Top100GraduateEmployers.com
Register now for the latest news, campus events, work experience and graduate vacancies at Allen & Overy.

ALLEN & OVERY

MADE
FOR
MORE

IT'S TIME

The world around us is changing. New ways of working create new opportunities, and we're looking for people who are ready to make an impact. With our world-class development programme and industry leading experts behind you, you can become a lawyer of the future. If you're made for more, we want to hear from you. Visit our website to find out more.

A career in Law
aograduate.com

@AllenOveryGrads   /allenoverygrads   AllenOveryGrads

amazon

Amazon is driven by the excitement of building technologies, inventing products, and providing services that change lives. They embrace new ways of doing things, make decisions quickly, and are not afraid to fail. They have the scope and capabilities of a large company, and the spirit of a small one.

Earth's most customer-centric company is looking for the world's most talented individuals to be a part of new technologies that improve the lives of customers, shoppers, sellers, content creators, and developers around the world. Amazon gives graduates responsibility and hands-on training to help them succeed.

Amazon has opportunities available in many different areas; for example, Area Managers are in charge of a department within warehouses, also known as Fulfillment Centres. They manage the day-to-day operations to deliver on the targeted key performance indicators. They are also responsible for leading a team whilst driving process improvement within their area.

For graduates with previous work experience, Amazon offers the Pathways Leadership Development Programme, which leads them through a number of positions that help them acquire leadership skills and prepare them to be the next VP or GM within Amazon Operations. Besides that, the operations network offers roles within Engineering, Finance, HR, IT, and Logistics.

Amazon also offers opportunities in Retail, Finance, Design, and Amazon Media Group. There are software development engineering roles at Amazon's Development Centres, supporting businesses like Amazon Instant Video and Amazon Data Services. They strive to hire the brightest minds from universities around the globe, and have various opportunities for graduates who believe in their mission and want to be part of the team.

GRADUATE VACANCIES IN 2019

ENGINEERING
FINANCE
GENERAL MANAGEMENT
HUMAN RESOURCES
LOGISTICS
MARKETING
PURCHASING
RESEARCH & DEVELOPMENT
RETAILING
SALES
TECHNOLOGY

NUMBER OF VACANCIES
250+ graduate jobs

LOCATIONS OF VACANCIES

Vacancies also available in Europe and elsewhere in the world.

STARTING SALARY FOR 2019
£Competitive
Plus a sign-on bonus and RSUs.

UNIVERSITY VISITS IN 2018-19
BIRMINGHAM, BRISTOL, CAMBRIDGE, DURHAM, EDINBURGH, EXETER, GLASGOW, IMPERIAL COLLEGE LONDON, LONDON SCHOOL OF ECONOMICS, MANCHESTER, NEWCASTLE, OXFORD, ST ANDREWS, UNIVERSITY COLLEGE LONDON, WARWICK
Please check with your university careers service for full details of local events.

MINIMUM ENTRY REQUIREMENTS
2.1 Degree

APPLICATION DEADLINE
Year-round recruitment
Early application advised.

FURTHER INFORMATION
www.Top100GraduateEmployers.com
Register now for the latest news, campus events, work experience and graduate vacancies at Amazon.

...the impossible, possible.

...oblem solver? Curious to learn and innovate daily?
...to learn to lead by example? If so, the Amazon Area
... in one of our many Fulfillment Centers could be the
... for you. We will help you develop outstanding leadership
...u will get to make history at one of the world's fastest
...panies.

...MORE AT AMAZON JOBS

AON

Aon is a leading global professional services firm providing a broad range of risk, retirement and health solutions. Its 50,000 colleagues in 120 countries empower results for clients by using proprietary data and analytics to deliver insights that reduce volatility and improve performance.

Few things are certain in life. Economic upheaval, political crises, natural disasters – and plenty more besides – all mean the world can be full of surprises. Aon draw on the expertise of its colleagues to help the biggest names in business plan for every eventuality. Its size, global network and emphasis on innovation mean that, where they lead, the industry follows.

Depending on the area graduates join, they will be using their analytical mindset and strong communication skills to help clients address key questions that affect their businesses. What will be the impact of rising life expectancy? How would the collapse of the Eurozone affect the world economy? Aon's business is to provide the answers.

Graduates join a range of consulting and broking roles across business areas including Insurance & Reinsurance, Actuarial, Investment, Reward & Remuneration, Talent & Employee Engagement, Employee Benefits or Cyber Security.

Aon's graduate development programme complements the technical training it provides, helping graduates to build their business knowledge, develop professional skills and learn how to grow effective relationships with clients and colleagues. In addition to the technical training, colleagues are fully supported to study for relevant professional qualifications to enable them to have a greater impact on Aon's clients and progress professionally within their chosen career path.

GRADUATE VACANCIES IN 2019

CONSULTING
FINANCE
INVESTMENT BANKING
TECHNOLOGY

NUMBER OF VACANCIES
75+ graduate jobs

LOCATIONS OF VACANCIES

Vacancies also available in Europe, the USA, Asia, and elsewhere in the world.

STARTING SALARY FOR 2019
£Competitive
Plus a discretionary bonus scheme.

UNIVERSITY VISITS IN 2018-19
BATH, BIRMINGHAM, BRISTOL, CAMBRIDGE, CITY, DURHAM, EDINBURGH, EXETER, HERIOT-WATT, IMPERIAL COLLEGE LONDON, LEEDS, LEICESTER, MANCHESTER, NOTTINGHAM, OXFORD, SOUTHAMPTON, ST ANDREWS, SURREY, UNIVERSITY COLLEGE LONDON, WARWICK
Please check with your university careers service for full details of local events.

MINIMUM ENTRY REQUIREMENTS
2.1 Degree

APPLICATION DEADLINE
Varies by function

FURTHER INFORMATION
www.Top100GraduateEmployers.com
Register now for the latest news, campus events, work experience and graduate vacancies at Aon.

Find what's possible

At Aon, we draw on the expertise of over 50,000 people to help the biggest names in business plan for every eventuality. Our size, global network and emphasis on innovation mean where we lead, the industry follows.

We have consulting & broking opportunities for graduates, interns and apprentices available in Actuarial, Investment, Insurance & Reinsurance, Employee Benefits, Insurance Strategy, Reward & Remuneration, Talent and Employee Engagement, Cybersecurity.

Find out more on
aonearlycareers.co.uk

Ruohan,
Aon Graduate

GRADUATE VACANCIES IN 2019
ACCOUNTANCY
ENGINEERING
FINANCE
GENERAL MANAGEMENT
HUMAN RESOURCES
LAW
LOGISTICS
MARKETING
MEDIA
PROPERTY
PURCHASING
RESEARCH & DEVELOPMENT
RETAILING
SALES
TECHNOLOGY

NUMBER OF VACANCIES
No fixed quota

LOCATIONS OF VACANCIES

STARTING SALARY FOR 2019
£Competitive

UNIVERSITY VISITS IN 2018-19
Please check with your university careers service for full details of local events.

APPLICATION DEADLINE
Year-round recruitment

FURTHER INFORMATION
www.Top100GraduateEmployers.com
Register now for the latest news, campus events, work experience and graduate vacancies at Apple.

Apple revolutionised personal technology with the introduction of the Macintosh in 1984. Today, Apple leads the world in innovation with iPhone, iPad, Mac and Apple Watch. Apple's software platforms provide seamless experiences across all Apple devices and empower people with breakthrough services.

Apple does things differently, and the results have revolutionised entire industries. Every year, new graduates become a part of that as they start their career with Apple. This is a company that values curiosity and individuality, and provides opportunities to develop professional skills, get hands-on experience, and work with some of the best minds in the business.

Because Apple is at the intersection of technology and the liberal arts, the company hires great minds from every field of study. With so many ways to contribute, chances are good that employees will find a way to do what they love, whether they work in the UK or at one of Apple's locations around the world.

Apple seeks a wide variety of talent because it manages virtually every aspect of the business, from research and development, through manufacturing, to sales and support and even the customers' retail experience in the Apple Store. Beyond the roles that are focused directly on Apple technology, the company counts on talented people who can meet the challenges of running a unique global business. At Apple, this also means using its leadership position as a socially responsible corporate citizen to influence change in the world.

Everything Apple creates is the result of people working together to make each other's ideas stronger. That happens because everyone at Apple strives towards a common goal — creating the best customer experiences. And because Apple believes its most important resource is its people, it offers various benefits to help further the well-being of employees and their families in meaningful ways.

Where your impact will have the most impact.

www.apple.com/jobs/uk

GRADUATE VACANCIES IN 2019

ENGINEERING

GENERAL MANAGEMENT

HUMAN RESOURCES

LAW

LOGISTICS

TECHNOLOGY

NUMBER OF VACANCIES
650+ graduate jobs

LOCATIONS OF VACANCIES

Lead from the front, do something that really matters and put other people first. Officers in the British Army have the responsibility of leading their soldiers to help make the world a safer, better place. The rewards are exceptional, the challenge is incredible and there's no bigger adventure in life.

STARTING SALARY FOR 2019
Over £31,000
After training.

The journey to becoming a British Army Officer begins at the Royal Military Academy Sandhurst, where Officer Cadets learn all the skills they need – from weapons handling to outdoor survival – as well as what it takes to lead their team to tackle any challenge. Then, once they commission, they take command of a platoon of up to 30 soldiers and start the specialist training they need to be experts in their role – whether that's engineering, intelligence gathering or piloting an Apache helicopter.

UNIVERSITY VISITS IN 2018-19
BIRMINGHAM, BRISTOL, DURHAM, EXETER, LEEDS, LOUGHBOROUGH, NEWCASTLE, NORTHUMBRIA, NOTTINGHAM, SOUTHAMPTON
Please check with your university careers service for full details of local events.

From skiing in the Alps to white water rafting in Colorado, Army Officers take part in adventurous training around the world, all whilst earning a starting salary of over £31,000 (after training) and enjoying all the benefits that come with Army life, from sports and state-of-the-art training facilities, to gaining professional qualifications and continually progressing their career. The Army also provides financial support for its future leaders, offering Army Undergraduate Bursaries to those who are interested in a career as an Army Officer after university.

MINIMUM ENTRY REQUIREMENTS
72 UCAS points
180 UCAS points for those who passed exams before 2017.

The Army looks for leadership potential, a sense of purpose and the drive to achieve great things. With these qualities in place, they can provide the world-class leadership training required to become a successful Officer, as well as a clear path for future career progression.

APPLICATION DEADLINE
Year-round recruitment

Becoming an Army Officer offers people with potential a focus for their ambition, a life full of challenge and adventure, and somewhere they can truly belong.

FURTHER INFORMATION
www.Top100GraduateEmployers.com
*Register now for the latest news, campus events, work experience and graduate vacancies at the **British Army**.*

THIS IS BELONGING

FIND WHERE YOU BELONG

ARMY
BE THE BEST

ARUP

An independent firm offering a broad range of professional services, Arup believes that by bringing great people together, there are infinite possibilities. With experts in design, engineering, planning, business consultancy, project management and much more, Arup people work together to shape a better world.

Arup has offices in more than 30 countries across the world, making international team-working part of everyday life and bringing together professionals from diverse disciplines and with complementary skills on a uniquely global scale.

The firm is owned in trust for Arup's employees and this independence translates through the thoughts and actions of its people. Commitment to sustainability is paramount and Arup strives not only to embrace this in projects, but also to embed it into everyday thinking and working.

Graduate opportunities span a wide range of disciplines and offer exceptional experience for individuals who are ambitious, friendly and approach work with fresh eyes and enthusiasm. Arup's diversity helps to foster the creativity that is its hallmark; and the support and freedom for innovation that is encouraged has made Arup the driving force behind some of the most iconic and sustainable designs in the world.

Arup offers competitive benefits and continuous professional development built around employees and their ambitions. Graduates can undertake a professional training programme, accredited by leading organisations such as the Institution of Civil Engineers and the Association for Project Management. As a firm, Arup seeks exceptional people with innovative ideas and curious minds who want to make a real difference to the environment; passion, drive and creativity are a must.

GRADUATE VACANCIES IN 2019
ACCOUNTANCY
CONSULTING
ENGINEERING
FINANCE

NUMBER OF VACANCIES
250+ graduate jobs

LOCATIONS OF VACANCIES

Vacancies also available in Europe, Asia, the USA and elsewhere in the world.

STARTING SALARY FOR 2019
£22,000-£26,500
Plus a welcome bonus of up to £4,000, and a bi-annual profit share scheme.

UNIVERSITY VISITS IN 2018-19
ABERDEEN, ASTON, BATH, BELFAST, BIRMINGHAM, BRISTOL, CAMBRIDGE, CARDIFF, DURHAM, EXETER, GLASGOW, HERIOT-WATT, IMPERIAL COLLEGE LONDON, LEEDS, LIVERPOOL, LOUGHBOROUGH, MANCHESTER, NEWCASTLE, NOTTINGHAM, OXFORD, SHEFFIELD, SOUTHAMPTON, STRATHCLYDE, SWANSEA, UNIVERSITY COLLEGE LONDON, WARWICK, YORK
Please check with your university careers service for full details of local events.

MINIMUM ENTRY REQUIREMENTS
2.1 Degree
Relevant degree required for some roles.

APPLICATION DEADLINE
Varies by function

FURTHER INFORMATION
www.Top100GraduateEmployers.com
Register now for the latest news, campus events, work experience and graduate vacancies at Arup.

Infinite possibilities.

At Arup our people are always on the lookout for new and innovative ways to transform the world's infrastructure and built environment. We help to turn the challenges and obstacles of the past into the achievements of the future. We approach our work with fresh eyes and enthusiasm – working to take our industry in exciting directions. This philosophy has helped us design and deliver groundbreaking and iconic work across the world. Involving everyone from design teams and engineers, through consultants, project managers and a myriad of other professions and disciplines.

Early exposure and responsibility is a given. Work life balance is a reality, not an aspiration. And we share our success with everyone – we deliver results collaboratively and we all benefit from those results. It's about making the impossible happen, making a real difference to the world around us. It's about infinite possibilities.

Explore an opportunity where the possibilities are endless...

www.arup.com/ukmeagrads

We are committed to equal opportunities.

ARUP
We shape a better world

asos

Authentic, brave and creative to their core. ASOS focus on fashion as a force for good, inspiring young people to express their best selves and achieve amazing things. They believe fashion thrives on individuality and should be fun for everyone.

ASOS is a global fashion destination for 20-somethings, selling cutting-edge clothes and offering a wide variety of fashion-related content, making ASOS.com the hub of a thriving community.

The online retailer sells over 85,000 branded and own-label products through localised mobile and web experiences, delivering from their fulfilment centres in the UK, US and Europe to almost every country in the world. Tailoring the mix of their own-label, global and local brands, they sell through eight local language websites: UK, US, France, Germany, Spain, Italy, Australia and Russia.

ASOS are thrilled to have been selected as a company where graduates aspire to work. They drive innovation through technology and continue to push the boundaries of online retail. In addition to a competitive salary, 40% discount and a benefits package, every graduate is offered support and guidance throughout their time at ASOS.

Passionate about their people, ASOS acknowledge that they are the future of the business, helping their ASOSers to develop both personally and professionally throughout their career, by offering a range of bespoke and tailored learning solutions. Career coaching, mentors from within the business, team development days, career planning and sponsored qualification support are all part of what ASOS offers.

ASOS is the place to be for any graduates who like the idea of working in a fast-paced, innovative environment where everyone is passionate about what they do.

GRADUATE VACANCIES IN 2019

FINANCE

HUMAN RESOURCES

LOGISTICS

MARKETING

RETAILING

TECHNOLOGY

NUMBER OF VACANCIES
No fixed quota

LOCATIONS OF VACANCIES

STARTING SALARY FOR 2019
£Competitive

UNIVERSITY VISITS IN 2018-19
Please check with your university careers service for full details of local events.

APPLICATION DEADLINE
Varies by function

FURTHER INFORMATION
www.Top100GraduateEmployers.com
Register now for the latest news, campus events, work experience and graduate vacancies at ASOS.

WE'RE AUTHENTIC
WE'RE BRAVE
WE'RE CREATIVE

We're always on the lookout for great people with the passion and commitment to push ASOS into bold and innovative new places. If you love what we do at ASOS, become a part of it. Join us!

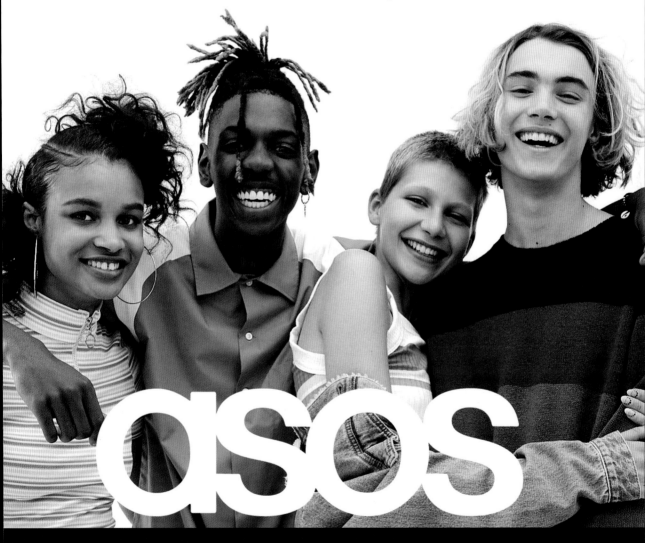

Subsidised Cafe	ASOS Academy	Summer Friday 3pm Finishes
Generous Salary	Flexible Benefits	Regular Sample Sales
Industry Leading Projects	Amazing Offices & Culture	40% Staff Discount On Clothing
Subsidised Beauty Treatments	Free Gym & Fitness Classes	20% Staff Discount On Beauty

GRADUATE VACANCIES IN 2019

ENGINEERING

GENERAL MANAGEMENT

LOGISTICS

PURCHASING

RESEARCH & DEVELOPMENT

TECHNOLOGY

NUMBER OF VACANCIES
80+ graduate jobs

LOCATIONS OF VACANCIES

Vacancies also available in Europe, the USA, Asia, and elsewhere in the world.

STARTING SALARY FOR 2019
£29,000+
Plus a sign-on bonus / relocation allowance (where appropriate).

UNIVERSITY VISITS IN 2018-19
CAMBRIDGE, IMPERIAL COLLEGE LONDON, KING'S COLLEGE LONDON, LEEDS, LIVERPOOL, LONDON SCHOOL OF ECONOMICS, MANCHESTER, OXFORD, SHEFFIELD, UNIVERSITY COLLEGE LONDON, WARWICK, YORK
Please check with your university careers service for full details of local events.

MINIMUM ENTRY REQUIREMENTS
2.1 Degree

APPLICATION DEADLINE
Varies by function

FURTHER INFORMATION
www.Top100GraduateEmployers.com
Register now for the latest news, campus events, work experience and graduate vacancies at AstraZeneca.

AstraZeneca is a global biopharmaceutical business that pushes the boundaries of science to deliver life-changing medicines. It is an agile company that invests over $5bn in R&D each year to pursue discoveries beyond imagination. They thrive on a unique spirit of innovation and collaboration.

Graduates from any discipline who are inspired by what science can do thrive in AstraZeneca's diverse and international culture. They will take real responsibility from day one, and throughout the various programmes will have the opportunity to contribute to ground-breaking projects and gain an extensive understanding of the global biopharmaceutical industry, from discovery to patients.

There are many paths that graduates at AstraZeneca can follow to achieve their career objectives. Outstanding personal development plans are devised with managers. Passionate leaders can be found at all levels. And there is a strong support network which includes mentors and 'buddies' for all graduates, to help set them up for success – and all within an energising and entrepreneurial environment.

Some programmes provide graduates with opportunities to work abroad. And as they explore their potential in a new location, they'll find that AstraZeneca is a company that offers a rich array of different experiences, perspectives and challenges.

Graduates at AstraZeneca work with bold thinkers whose ideas are as diverse as the cultures that have helped shape them. The company is proud to have gained a host of awards for its progressive working practices. It also recognises that diverse teams are innovative teams which strengthen the connections between employees, patients, stakeholders and the communities in which they work.

To find out more about each of their programmes, visit their careers site.

ATKINS

Atkins is one of the world's most respected design, engineering and project management consultancies. Together with fully-integrated, global SNC-Lavalin, Atkins works to defy today's most challenging issues – helping clients plan, design and enable major capital projects, while transforming people's lives.

Atkins wants bright, agile minds who share their drive to make the world a better place. The business is creating a tomorrow where lives are enriched through innovations, from developing driverless cars to solving pressing energy problems of the future. Graduates will find opportunities in aerospace, defence, energy, infrastructure, management consultancy, transportation, security & technology, quantity surveying and building surveying.

The programme puts graduates in a diverse environment where wellbeing and work-life balance is valued. Graduates are offered competitive packages with flexible holidays, chartership bonuses, volunteer days and a settling-in payment. Graduates are empowered and supported to 'hit the ground running' on exciting, complex projects for major global clients – from Boeing KC-46, to the International Thermonuclear Experimental Reactor, Thames Tideway Tunnel, Smart Motorways, and the Freedom Tower & World Trade Center site.

Entering the three-year Graduate Development Programme, graduates develop the skills and knowledge to progress thriving, early careers. While encouraged to drive their own development, they are well-supported by line managers, graduate representatives, and the Learning & Development team, not to mention a thriving graduate community. World-class training also includes professional specific schemes that lead to chartered status.

SNC-Lavalin's Atkins business invites graduates to join them for the best possible start to an exceptional career in engineering.

GRADUATE VACANCIES IN 2019

CONSULTING
ENGINEERING
TECHNOLOGY

NUMBER OF VACANCIES
400 graduate jobs

LOCATIONS OF VACANCIES

STARTING SALARY FOR 2019
£26,500
Plus a £2,000 settling-in bonus.

UNIVERSITY VISITS IN 2018-19
BATH, BIRMINGHAM, BRISTOL, CARDIFF, IMPERIAL COLLEGE LONDON, LIVERPOOL, MANCHESTER, NOTTINGHAM, SHEFFIELD, STRATHCLYDE, SURREY, SWANSEA
Please check with your university careers service for full details of local events.

MINIMUM ENTRY REQUIREMENTS
Relevant degree required for some roles.

APPLICATION DEADLINE
Varies by job function

FURTHER INFORMATION
www.Top100GraduateEmployers.com
Register now for the latest news, campus events, work experience and graduate vacancies at Atkins.

All images © Crossrail

Shaping a better future, together.

It's never been a more exciting time to work in SNC-Lavalin's Atkins business. We're already meeting fast growing demands for innovation and technology, from breakthroughs in transport to making Virtual Reality part of the delivery process.

Find out how this enhances your career opportunities, visit careers.atkinsglobal.com

 snclavalin.com | atkinsglobal.com

BAE SYSTEMS

BAE Systems help their customers to stay a step ahead when protecting people and national security, critical infrastructure and vital information. This is a long-term commitment involving significant investments in skills. They also work closely with local partners to support economic development through the transfer of knowledge, skills and technology.

By demonstrating passion and enthusiasm to improve, graduates will receive the support needed to be creative and pioneering throughout their development, to set the stage for an amazing future with BAE Systems.

The Graduate Development Framework (GDF) is a two-year scheme which develops people who are passionate about their chosen field. As this is their largest scheme, BAE Systems have a range of business and engineering opportunities available, covering everything from Naval Architecture and Electrical & Software Engineering to Human Resources, Procurement and Commercial, to name just a few.

For those with an interest in finance, there's the five-year Finance Leader Development Programme (FLDP) which is a fast-track finance graduate scheme, preparing individuals to become Finance Directors of the future. The programme includes a structured and fully supported route to the highly respected Chartered Institute of Management Accountants (CIMA) qualification.

Alongside this, BAE Systems Applied Intelligence offer a range of early career positions in Consulting, Engineering and Project Management. Graduates will be involved in supporting the delivery of solutions which help clients to protect against cyber threats and enhance their critical assets in the connected world.

BAE Systems also have a number of summer internship and industrial placements available in a range of business, consulting, finance and engineering roles.

GRADUATE VACANCIES IN 2019
CONSULTING
ENGINEERING
FINANCE
GENERAL MANAGEMENT
HUMAN RESOURCES
TECHNOLOGY

NUMBER OF VACANCIES
350 graduate jobs

LOCATIONS OF VACANCIES

STARTING SALARY FOR 2019
£28,000-£30,000
Plus a £2,000 welcome payment.

UNIVERSITY VISITS IN 2018-19
ASTON, BATH, BIRMINGHAM, BRISTOL, CAMBRIDGE, CARDIFF, DURHAM, GLASGOW, IMPERIAL COLLEGE LONDON, LANCASTER, LEEDS, LIVERPOOL, LOUGHBOROUGH, MANCHESTER, NEWCASTLE, OXFORD, SHEFFIELD, SOUTHAMPTON, STRATHCLYDE, SURREY, UNIVERSITY COLLEGE LONDON, WARWICK, YORK
Please check with your university careers service for full details of local events.

MINIMUM ENTRY REQUIREMENTS
Requirements vary by function – please see website for details.

APPLICATION DEADLINE
Varies by function

FURTHER INFORMATION
www.Top100GraduateEmployers.com
Register now for the latest news, campus events, work experience and graduate vacancies at BAE Systems.

Baker McKenzie prides itself on being the global law firm that offers a personal and professional approach to its graduates and clients alike. It's this approach that ensures the firm is ideally placed to offer graduates the best possible start to their legal career.

With 77 offices in 47 countries, and a presence in all leading financial centres, Baker McKenzie is the world's premier global law firm. London is home to the firm's largest office, where Baker McKenzie has been well established since its opening in 1961. With more than 400 lawyers, they deliver high-quality local solutions across a broad range of practices and offer global advice in conjunction with their international offices. With a strong international client base, Baker McKenzie have considerable expertise in acting on, and coordinating, complex cross border transactions and disputes.

The firm offers 1st Year Insight Schemes and Vacation Schemes, and these provide the ideal opportunity to experience what it's like to work for a City-based, global law firm. Training is provided to familiarise individuals with some of their typical transactions and to help them develop key skills. Baker McKenzie place great emphasis on involving candidates in 'live' work with both Associates and Partners.

The two-year training contract comprises four six-month seats, which include a transactional and a contentious seat along with the possibility of a secondment abroad or with a client. The training contract commences with a highly interactive and practical induction which focuses on key skills including practical problem solving, presenting and the application of information technology. Formal and informal reviews are undertaken to support Trainees' ongoing development.

GRADUATE VACANCIES IN 2019
LAW

NUMBER OF VACANCIES
30 graduate jobs
For training contracts starting in 2021.

LOCATIONS OF VACANCIES

STARTING SALARY FOR 2019
£45,000
Plus an annual bonus and a maintenance grant for GDL / LPC.

UNIVERSITY VISITS IN 2018-19
BELFAST, BRISTOL, CAMBRIDGE, DURHAM, EDINBURGH, EXETER, GLASGOW, KING'S COLLEGE LONDON, LEEDS, LEICESTER, LONDON SCHOOL OF ECONOMICS, MANCHESTER, NOTTINGHAM, OXFORD, QUEEN MARY LONDON, SOUTHAMPTON, ST ANDREWS, WARWICK, YORK
Please check with your university careers service for full details of local events.

MINIMUM ENTRY REQUIREMENTS
2.1 Degree

APPLICATION DEADLINE
Varies by function
Please see website for full details.

FURTHER INFORMATION
www.Top100GraduateEmployers.com
Register now for the latest news, campus events, work experience and graduate vacancies at Baker McKenzie.

Baker McKenzie.

Working side by side with partners.

GRADUATE LAW CAREERS

Whether it's a recent Trainee or one of our partners, everyone at Baker McKenzie is ready and willing to support you. That's what makes working here so special. We pride ourselves on fostering a non-hierarchical work culture. One in which people are friendly and approachable, and where whatever level you're at, your ideas will always be listened to.

Learn more at **bakermckenzie.com/londongraduates**

Law-struck

BANK OF ENGLAND

The impact of the Bank of England's work is uniquely far-reaching. As the country's central bank, they promote the good of the people of the UK by maintaining monetary and financial stability. The work they do, and the decisions they make, influences the daily lives of millions of people.

The Bank's primary role hasn't changed for over 300 years. But the range of work they do, and the ways in which they deliver it, is changing all the time. Today it's changing quicker than ever before. And their graduates are a key part of this progress.

Despite the nature of the Bank's work, economics is not the only way in. They welcome graduates from all degree disciplines, because quality of thinking is what counts here. Their culture is open and collaborative, where ideas are shared freely and people at every level are empowered to speak up. It is refreshingly diverse too. The Bank looks for people from all backgrounds, and individual perspectives are embraced. Successful applicants will find a wide range of societies, clubs and employee networks open to them.

Wherever graduates work – from Regulation, Technology and Policy Analysis to Economics and Communications – they'll take on complex work that they can be proud of. They'll tackle projects that support, shape and challenge the biggest ideas in the economy. And the work they do will benefit every single person in the UK.

As training is at the heart of the Bank's programme, graduates will be able to grow into real experts in their field. Equally, the support is there to explore other parts of the Bank if they wish. There are many and varied pathways available. Graduates who are keen to broaden their horizons will have every opportunity to define their own future as the Bank itself moves forward.

GRADUATE VACANCIES IN 2019

FINANCE
GENERAL MANAGEMENT
HUMAN RESOURCES
INVESTMENT BANKING
TECHNOLOGY

NUMBER OF VACANCIES
80+ graduate jobs

LOCATIONS OF VACANCIES

STARTING SALARY FOR 2019
£30,000

UNIVERSITY VISITS IN 2018-19
BATH, BIRMINGHAM, BRISTOL, BRUNEL, CARDIFF, DURHAM, EDINBURGH, EXETER, GLASGOW, LANCASTER, LEEDS, LIVERPOOL, LOUGHBOROUGH, NEWCASTLE, READING, SURREY, YORK
Please check with your university careers service for full details of local events.

MINIMUM ENTRY REQUIREMENTS
2.1 Degree

APPLICATION DEADLINE
12th November 2018

FURTHER INFORMATION
www.Top100GraduateEmployers.com
Register now for the latest news, campus events, work experience and graduate vacancies at the Bank of England.

BANK OF ENGLAND

PICTURE WHAT TOMORROW'S ECONOMY COULD BE THEN GUIDE IT

We have one clear aim — to ensure stability at the heart of the UK's economy. But there are countless ways in which you could help us achieve this. From HR and Technology to Economics and Risk, you'll be encouraged and supported to follow the path that inspires you the most. And you'll enjoy real influence — not just over the projects you're involved in, but also over where your future with us goes next.

The Bank of England is changing today. **You define tomorrow.**

bankofenglandearlycareers.co.uk

BARCLAYS

GRADUATE VACANCIES IN 2019

FINANCE
GENERAL MANAGEMENT
HUMAN RESOURCES
INVESTMENT BANKING
MARKETING
SALES
TECHNOLOGY

NUMBER OF VACANCIES
500+ graduate jobs

LOCATIONS OF VACANCIES

Vacancies also available in Europe, the USA and Asia.

STARTING SALARY FOR 2019
£Competitive

UNIVERSITY VISITS IN 2018-19
BATH, BIRMINGHAM, BRISTOL, CAMBRIDGE, CITY, DURHAM, EDINBURGH, EXETER, GLASGOW, IMPERIAL COLLEGE LONDON, KING'S COLLEGE LONDON, LANCASTER, LEEDS, LIVERPOOL, LONDON SCHOOL OF ECONOMICS, LOUGHBOROUGH, MANCHESTER, NEWCASTLE, NOTTINGHAM, OXFORD, QUEEN MARY LONDON, SOUTHAMPTON, ST ANDREWS, STRATHCLYDE, UNIVERSITY COLLEGE LONDON, WARWICK
Please check with your university careers service for full details of local events.

APPLICATION DEADLINE
Rolling recruitment
Early application advised.

FURTHER INFORMATION
www.Top100GraduateEmployers.com
*Register now for the latest news, campus events, work experience and graduate vacancies at **Barclays**.*

Healthy economies need innovative banks to help transform and drive social progress. Barclays' ambition for bigger thinking is simple. By encouraging fresh ideas they can make a bigger difference. Interns and graduates at Barclays have many opportunities to get involved. To share big ideas. To show a better way. And to challenge what's already been done.

Barclays is a transatlantic consumer, corporate and investment bank offering products and services across personal, corporate and investment banking, credit cards and wealth management, with a strong presence in its two home markets of the UK and the US.

With over 325 years of history and expertise in banking, Barclays operates in over 40 countries and employs approximately 85,000 people. Barclays moves, lends, invests and protects money for customers and clients worldwide.

Barclays was the first bank to appoint a female bank manager, introduce ATMs, and launch credit cards and contactless payment. From the products and services they develop to the partnerships they build, they seek to improve lives and drive growth that benefits everyone.

Those joining can expect immediate responsibility. Collective challenges and inspiring collaborations will expand their minds, while ongoing training will turn fledgling ideas into groundbreaking concepts, providing the expertise that drives the bank and profession as a whole.

Barclays offers a wealth of opportunities for students from all degree disciplines. All graduates need is a commercial outlook, curious nature, and the ambition to help Barclays become the best bank it can be. In a positive, supportive environment, graduates will have the freedom to create smarter solutions every day.

The latest thinking?
Time to out-think it.

At Barclays, we believe opportunities are created by those who like to challenge convention, explore new possibilities and run with bold ideas.

Whether the result is a product that makes our customers' and clients' lives easier, a deal that helps to ensure a company's future success, or a wider initiative that benefits the communities we serve, that's what makes this an inspiring place to build a career.

But that's just our thoughts. It's yours we're interested in.

So tell us, what do you think?

joinus.barclays

BARCLAYS

BBC

In 1922, a Scottish engineer called John Reith was the first Director General of the BBC. He famously said he "hadn't the remotest idea as to what broadcasting was". The BBC has come a long way since then, with over 21,000 staff spread out across the world.

The BBC has nine national TV services, ten national radio stations, regional TV and Radio, online services across News, Sport, Weather, CBBC and iPlayer, international services such as the BBC World Service and World News, and its commercial arm, BBC Worldwide.

Structured entry-level trainee schemes for graduates (and also non-graduates) are available across most of the BBC's business areas; in Production, Journalism, Broadcast Engineering, Software Engineering, Research and Development, UX Design, Legal, Information Security and Communications.

The BBC's training arm, the BBC Academy, has specialists who work alongside the BBC's subject-matter experts to design industry-leading training programmes; alumni from these programmes have consistently gone on to become leaders across the broadcasting sector. Competition for places is tough, with several thousand applicants routinely applying for Production and Journalism trainee programmes.

Opportunities are available across the UK, in London, Birmingham, Salford, Bristol, Cardiff, Glasgow and Belfast. Whilst academic achievement is an important entry requirement for some of the BBC's programmes, attitude, curiosity and passion are likely to impress BBC recruiters, as is a good dose of life experience and the ability to communicate and work in a team.

Recruitment takes place at various times throughout the year; the BBC's Careers website has a comprehensive list of every trainee programme and when it is open for applications. Most trainee programmes start in September.

GRADUATE VACANCIES IN 2019

ENGINEERING
GENERAL MANAGEMENT
MEDIA
RESEARCH & DEVELOPMENT
TECHNOLOGY

NUMBER OF VACANCIES
130 graduate jobs

LOCATIONS OF VACANCIES

STARTING SALARY FOR 2019
£20,800
£25,000 in London.

UNIVERSITY VISITS IN 2018-19
ABERYSTWYTH, CARDIFF, LEEDS,
LIVERPOOL, OXFORD, YORK
*Please check with your university careers
service for full details of local events.*

APPLICATION DEADLINE
Varies by function

FURTHER INFORMATION
www.Top100GraduateEmployers.com
*Register now for the latest news, campus
events, work experience and graduate
vacancies at the BBC.*

Be part of something special. Join the BBC.

Graduate Opportunities | UK Wide | £20,800+ pa

The BBC is the world's leading public service broadcaster, known and loved internationally for its radio, television and online content.

Our aim is simple – to enrich people's lives with programmes and services that inform, educate and entertain by being the most creative organisation in the world.

Creativity is the lifeblood of our organisation. We're brave. We innovate and demonstrate creative ambition, trying new things and embracing new technology.

We're looking for the next generation of talent to keep the BBC at its very best with fresh ideas and different perspectives. The more diverse our workforce, the better able we are to respond to and reflect our audiences in all their diversity.

As a BBC graduate you will be making a difference, working on products and services that are enjoyed every day by millions of people. Our graduate schemes include journalism, software engineering, broadcast engineering, research & development, legal and production to name a few.

Be part of something special and join the BBC.

To find out more visit **www.bbc.co.uk/careers/trainee-schemes-and-apprenticeships**

The world's watching

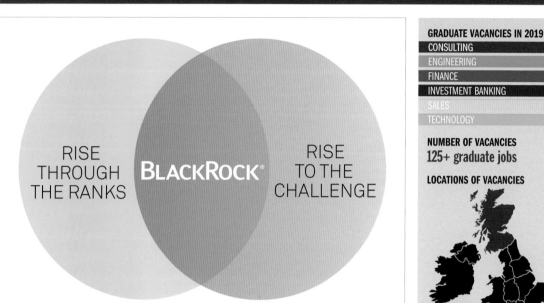

RISE THROUGH THE RANKS — BLACKROCK® — RISE TO THE CHALLENGE

GRADUATE VACANCIES IN 2019
- CONSULTING
- ENGINEERING
- FINANCE
- INVESTMENT BANKING
- SALES
- TECHNOLOGY

NUMBER OF VACANCIES
125+ graduate jobs

LOCATIONS OF VACANCIES

Vacancies also available in Europe.

STARTING SALARY FOR 2019
£Competitive

UNIVERSITY VISITS IN 2018-19
ASTON, BATH, BIRMINGHAM, BRADFORD, BRISTOL, BRUNEL, CAMBRIDGE, CITY, TRINITY COLLEGE DUBLIN, UNIVERSITY COLLEGE DUBLIN, DUNDEE, DURHAM, EAST ANGLIA, EDINBURGH, ESSEX, EXETER, GLASGOW, HERIOT-WATT, HULL, IMPERIAL COLLEGE LONDON, KEELE, KING'S COLLEGE LONDON, KENT, LANCASTER, LEEDS, LEICESTER, LIVERPOOL, LONDON SCHOOL OF ECONOMICS, LOUGHBOROUGH, MANCHESTER, NEWCASTLE, NORTHUMBRIA, NOTTINGHAM, NOTTINGHAM TRENT, OXFORD, OXFORD BROOKES, PLYMOUTH, QUEEN MARY LONDON, READING, ROYAL HOLLOWAY, SHEFFIELD, SOUTHAMPTON, STIRLING, STRATHCLYDE, UNIVERSITY COLLEGE LONDON, WARWICK, YORK
Please check with your university careers service for full details of local events.

MINIMUM ENTRY REQUIREMENTS
2.1 Degree

APPLICATION DEADLINE
11th November 2018

FURTHER INFORMATION
www.Top100GraduateEmployers.com
Register now for the latest news, campus events, work experience and graduate vacancies at BlackRock.

BlackRock was founded 30 years ago by eight entrepreneurs who wanted to start a very different company. One that focused on a singular purpose: making a difference in the lives of the parents and grandparents, the doctors and teachers who entrust them with their money – and their futures – every day.

Today, as the world's largest asset manager, with more than $6.3 trillion under management, BlackRock brings together financial leadership, worldwide reach and state-of-the-art technology to provide answers to the millions of investors who entrust their financial futures to the company.

The story of BlackRock's success rests not just with its founders, but with the thousands of talented people who have brought their ideas and energy to the firm every day since. That's why BlackRock always looks for fresh perspectives and new ideas, and views its differences as strengths. It knows that its success depends on its ability to use collective experiences and ideas to achieve more for its clients and the business. BlackRock strongly believes that diverse skill sets and perspectives lead to more innovative solutions and better results.

BlackRock's programmes are an ideal opportunity for natural-born problem solvers, innovators and future leaders to work for a firm that has been called in by some of the world's largest companies and governments to find solutions for their most pressing financial challenges.

BlackRock is committed to harnessing every graduate's potential. The programme begins with an orientation in New York, followed by a structured curriculum of ongoing training designed to maximise business knowledge and individual effectiveness. BlackRock offers opportunities across Advisory & Client Services, Analytics & Risk, Corporate Functions & Business Operations, Investments, Relationship Management & Sales and Technology.

Our work is diverse and your opportunities are limitless. Explore the possibilities at BlackRock.

BlackRock was founded in 1988 by eight entrepreneurs who wanted to start a very different company. One that combined the best of a financial leader and a technology pioneer. Our mission is to create a better financial future for our clients and we are looking for the future leaders to help us do that. We recognize that talent comes in many forms and we value diverse perspectives. So, whatever your background, whatever you're studying, there's a place for you here.

If you're at the beginning of your university career, we offer early insight programmes, which give you a glimpse of life at BlackRock. If you're in the penultimate year of study, our summer internships offer an immersive experience which give you a realistic insight into life at the world's largest asset manager. Our global Analyst Programme is for students who are in their final year of university and is designed to prepare you for a career at BlackRock.

We offer opportunities across Advisory & Client Services, Analytics & Risk, Corporate Functions & Business Operations, Investments, Relationship Management & Sales and Technology.

To learn more:
careers.blackrock.com/campusrecruitment

BLACKROCK®

Bloomberg

bloomberg.com/careers

twitter.com/BloombergCareer 🐦 facebook.com/BloombergCareers f
instagram.com/Bloomberg 📷 linkedin.com/company/Bloomberg-LP in

GRADUATE VACANCIES IN 2019

ENGINEERING
FINANCE
MEDIA
SALES
TECHNOLOGY

NUMBER OF VACANCIES
450 graduate jobs

LOCATIONS OF VACANCIES

Vacancies also available in the USA and Asia.

STARTING SALARY FOR 2019
£Competitive
Plus a competitive bonus.

UNIVERSITY VISITS IN 2018-19
BATH, BRISTOL, CAMBRIDGE, TRINITY
COLLEGE DUBLIN, EDINBURGH, GLASGOW,
LEEDS, IMPERIAL COLLEGE LONDON,
KING'S COLLEGE LONDON, LONDON
SCHOOL OF ECONOMICS, MANCHESTER,
OXFORD, QUEEN MARY LONDON,
SOUTHAMPTON, ST ANDREWS, UNIVERSITY
COLLEGE LONDON, WARWICK, YORK
*Please check with your university careers
service for full details of local events.*

APPLICATION DEADLINE
Year-round recruitment
Early application advised.

FURTHER INFORMATION
www.Top100GraduateEmployers.com
*Register now for the latest news, campus
events, work experience and graduate
vacancies at Bloomberg.*

As a global information and technology company, Bloomberg use its dynamic network of data, ideas and analysis to solve difficult problems every day. Its customers around the world rely on them to deliver accurate, real-time business and market information that helps them make important financial decision.

Bloomberg is guided by four core values: innovation, collaboration, customer service, and doing the right thing. The new European Headquarters in London is a testament to that innovation, as it's the world's most sustainable office building.

Bloomberg offers internships and full-time entry-level roles at their London office across a range of business areas including Analytics & Sales, Engineering, Global Data, Operations, and more. Candidates who join Bloomberg can build and define their own unique career, rather than a pre-defined path. Bloomberg is proud to have a truly global dynamic organization, so all employees are empowered to have an impact and are measured by their contributions. All graduate starters will participate in team-specific training that continues throughout their career via robust career development resources.

Bloomberg also offers internships to provide an unparalleled combination of learning, networking, and project responsibilities. The internship programme aims to provide first-hand exposure to its business and unique culture, and is filled with training, seminars, senior leader speaker series, philanthropic events, and more.

Candidates apply online on Bloomberg's career website. The interview process will depend on the business area they have applied to, but typically involves a video and/or telephone interview followed by in-person interviews and assessment days. Bloomberg hire on a rolling basis, so early application is advised.

How does a tsunami affect microchip prices?

At Bloomberg,
we ask hard questions
and then build tools
to answer them.
It's our purpose.

**Come find yours.
bloomberg.com/careers**

Make connections **on purpose.**

Bloomberg

Rolls-Royce
Motor Cars Limited

GRADUATE VACANCIES IN 2019

ENGINEERING
FINANCE
HUMAN RESOURCES
LOGISTICS
MARKETING
SALES
TECHNOLOGY

NUMBER OF VACANCIES
20-30 graduate jobs

LOCATIONS OF VACANCIES

STARTING SALARY FOR 2019
£31,000

With its three brands BMW, MINI and Rolls-Royce Motor Cars, the BMW Group is the world's leading manufacturer of premium automobiles and motorcycles, and provider of premium financial and mobility services. It operates 30 production and assembly facilities in 14 countries and has a global sales network.

As a global leader in their field, BMW Group are always looking for passionate graduates who are interested in developing their business experience to join their 24-month UK Graduate Programme or their 18-month Global Leader Development Programme (GLDP).

Offered across a variety of disciplines, the UK Graduate Programme is a unique chance for graduates to strengthen their business profile through involvement in a range of projects and rotational placements, as well as individually-tailored development opportunities. Supervised by mentors and surrounded by fellow graduates, they'll gain invaluable insights into business processes and strategy, as well as the opportunity to get to know BMW Group's culture and brands from the inside.

The GLDP is a unique talent development opportunity that will equip successful applicants, step-by-step, with the skills they need to succeed. Supported by an experienced mentor, they'll be able to benefit from this structured scheme in several ways: they'll have the chance to work abroad, share know-how across borders, join teams to tackle exciting and varied projects and build their own global network of contacts.

With the UK Graduate Programme and the GLDP, graduates who share BMW Group's passion for future mobility solutions, who are willing to strengthen their strategic and operational competencies, and who welcome the opportunity to take on new responsibilities are in good company.

UNIVERSITY VISITS IN 2018-19
ASTON, BATH, BIRMINGHAM, EXETER, LOUGHBOROUGH, NOTTINGHAM TRENT, OXFORD BROOKES, PLYMOUTH, READING, SHEFFIELD, SOUTHAMPTON, SURREY, SUSSEX
Please check with your university careers service for full details of local events.

MINIMUM ENTRY REQUIREMENTS
2.1 Degree

APPLICATION DEADLINE
Varies by function

FURTHER INFORMATION
www.Top100GraduateEmployers.com
Register now for the latest news, campus events, work experience and graduate vacancies at BMW Group.

GET THE SKILLS TO LEAD AND SUCCEED.

THE BMW GROUP UK GRADUATE PROGRAMME AND THE GLOBAL LEADER DEVELOPMENT PROGRAMME.

Those who want to
lead can learn it here, step
by step, with a global leader driven
by passion for innovative mobility solutions.

If you share our passion, enjoy taking on responsibilities
and want to lay the foundation for a rewarding and successful
career, join us on our 24-month Graduate Programme or our
Global Leader Development Programme.

Apply now at www.bmwgroup.jobs/uk

BMW
GROUP

THE NEXT
100 YEARS

BMW · MINI · Rolls-Royce Motor Cars Limited

www.boots.jobs/graduate-schemes

graduates@boots.co.uk

twitter.com/Boots_Talent   facebook.com/TalentProgrammes

Boots is the UK's leading pharmacy-led health and beauty
retailer and its purpose is to champion everyone's right to feel
good. With 2,486 stores in the UK and a heritage spanning
over 165 years, Boots has a unique place in the heart of the
communities it serves.

Boots is also part of a global enterprise, Walgreens Boots Alliance, which has a
presence in over 25 countries. They are looking for talented, passionate graduates,
who want to make a real difference, who are innovative and proactive go-getters
and who can help the business grow. In return, Boots have a whole lot to offer.

The Support Office graduate programmes are based in Nottingham, with
opportunities in the commercial teams, HR, Global Brands and many more.
All of Boots' graduates will have the chance to spend time in stores,
understanding the customers, seeing how the organisation operates and
working alongside fantastic store and healthcare colleagues to learn how to
deliver legendary customer care.

Helping graduates to identify their strengths and preferences is very
important, so Boots also offers access to a unique learning and development
programme which helps them to develop skills and knowledge that can help
accelerate their career with the organisation.

Boots offers a pre-registration programme for MPharm students who can
gain a true breadth and depth of experience within a community pharmacy.
The programme provides the opportunity to experience delivering individual
patient care as well as a range of innovative clinical services, supported by
experienced tutors and pharmacist trainers.

For undergraduates, Boots also offers Year in Industry placements and
Summer Internships, which will provide invaluable on-the-job experience.

the bigger picture
whichever way you look at it
#boots360

Boots

let's feel good

GRADUATE VACANCIES IN 2019

ACCOUNTANCY
ENGINEERING
FINANCE
HUMAN RESOURCES
LOGISTICS
PURCHASING
RESEARCH & DEVELOPMENT
RETAILING
SALES
TECHNOLOGY

NUMBER OF VACANCIES
100+ graduate jobs

LOCATIONS OF VACANCIES

STARTING SALARY FOR 2019
£35,000+
Plus a £3,000 settling-in allowance.

UNIVERSITY VISITS IN 2018-19
ABERDEEN, BATH, BIRMINGHAM,
CAMBRIDGE, DURHAM, HERIOT-WATT,
IMPERIAL COLLEGE LONDON,
LONDON SCHOOL OF ECONOMICS,
MANCHESTER, NOTTINGHAM, OXFORD,
SHEFFIELD, STRATHCLYDE,
UNIVERSITY COLLEGE LONDON
*Please check with your university careers
service for full details of local events.*

MINIMUM ENTRY REQUIREMENTS
2.1 Degree

APPLICATION DEADLINE
Varies by function

FURTHER INFORMATION
www.Top100GraduateEmployers.com
*Register now for the latest news, campus
events, work experience and graduate
vacancies at BP.*

BP delivers energy products and services around the world. From finding, developing and producing oil and gas resources, to refining, manufacturing and selling related products directly to customers and on the world's markets, it keeps the world moving.

BP's challenge for the future is to balance environmental and climate change concerns with the fact that oil and gas will still play a big role. So it continually looks to develop innovative ways of lowering emissions, while meeting the world's growing energy needs. It takes a diverse group of talented people to help BP create the real change the world needs. From engineers, automotive experts, geoscientists and chemists to accountants, analysts, technologists and traders.

Its graduate programmes and internships offer opportunities to make a real contribution, with all the support interns and graduates need to achieve their full potential. BP's programmes give them a platform to become business leaders, leading scientists or ground-breaking engineers. It offers the scope to contribute at any stage of the energy lifecycle from day one, and to build a challenging and varied career. Graduates on their two- or three-year programmes gain a full range of skills and experience. Their paid 11-week and year-long internships offer hands-on business experience to undergraduates or postgraduates who are about to start the final year of their degree or PhD.

BP's diverse and inclusive environment focuses on teamwork, respect and ambition as much as academic achievements. And safety is a priority, as they develop the energy of tomorrow. To find out what life as a BP intern or graduate is really like, go to BP's website and hear from the people who live it. Or, to find the right role, take a look at BP's degree matcher tool at *www.bp.com/degreematcher.*

www.britishairwaysgraduates.co.uk

youtube.com/FlyBritishAirways ▶ linkedin.com/company/British-Airways in

British Airways matters. They matter to the 40 million people who fly with them every year to and from their many bases around the world. They matter to its brilliant people. And, as the national flag carrier, they matter because they represent the very best in British hospitality.

British Airways can trace its origins back to the birth of civil aviation, and they're proud of their history. But it's the future that counts, and British Airways wants its graduates to be the new generation of visionary pioneers that will help it continue to innovate and define its future success. Consistently offering the service British Airways customers expect. However they choose to fly, wherever they fly to.

They represent all that is great about being British: innovation, expertise and exceptional service. But none of it would be possible without its people. These are people with determination, teamwork and passion. People with insight, commerciality and intelligence. People with drive. British Airways graduates can expect to shape the future of the nation's flag carrier, and fuel change in an ever-expanding industry. Always challenging the status quo, and never settling for second best.

Whether they join the Commercial, Finance, Logistics, Future Leaders, Analysts, Operational Research or Head Office Business Placement Programme, they can expect an immersive induction, followed by a structured development plan, plus plenty of support. Whatever the role, they'll discover BA's ambitious way of life and how their creativity, commercial awareness and agile thinking can help take a British icon even further. Then there are all the attractive travel benefits to look forward to. So for those who feel ready to shape the future of the airline industry, British Airways is the place to do it.

GRADUATE VACANCIES IN 2019

ACCOUNTING
FINANCE
GENERAL MANAGEMENT
LOGISTICS
MARKETING
RESEARCH & DEVELOPMENT
SALES

NUMBER OF VACANCIES
50-100 graduate jobs

LOCATIONS OF VACANCIES

STARTING SALARY FOR 2019
£27,500-£32,000
Plus an attractive benefits package, including staff travel.

UNIVERSITY VISITS IN 2018-19
EDINBURGH, LEEDS, LIVERPOOL, LOUGHBOROUGH, SOUTHAMPTON, WARWICK
Please check with your university careers service for full details of local events.

MINIMUM ENTRY REQUIREMENTS
2.1 Degree

APPLICATION DEADLINE
Varies by function
Please see website for full details.

FURTHER INFORMATION
www.Top100GraduateEmployers.com
*Register now for the latest news, campus events, work experience and graduate vacancies at **British Airways**.*

BRITISH AIRWAYS

AMBITION, VISION AND A PIONEERING SPIRIT. THAT'S WHAT IT TAKES.

From data and technology to customer expectations, our world is changing fast. That's why we need the brightest minds to ensure we stay ahead of the curve. Fresh ideas and different perspectives. People who can shape the future of the airline industry and take it to exciting new places. Collaborators, challengers and visionaries. The only question is: do you have what it takes?

careers.ba.com/emerging-talent

BE PART OF
PROGRESS

Every day, BT's people are able to touch the lives of millions, providing the key services everyone needs to get the most out of life. BT knows that with great power, comes great responsibility. That's why they are committed to a much higher purpose – to use the power of communication to create a better world.

The company's reach spans far and wide across the globe, operating in over 180 countries – making them one of the world's leading and most diverse communication providers. It's little wonder then that BT is one of the top picks when it comes to their graduate opportunities and schemes.

As graduates know all too well, the world today brings many challenges for those starting out in the ever-changing and highly competitive world of work. In response to this, BT is on a mission to help eager grads to kick-start their careers, encouraging them to adapt and reinvent themselves, as their roles, values and skillsets shift and grow around them. In this respect, the company is offering the young talent of today something completely unique – the promise of a diverse career in a company that doesn't stand still.

Diversity is at the very heart of BT. In order to provide the very best products and services to a varied customer base, they need a diverse workforce to imagine, create and deliver solutions, required both now and in the future. This means creating and maintaining a working environment that includes and values graduates.

BT's commitment to creating a diverse and people-led business is the driving force behind their core purpose. So any graduate who is ready to embrace the dynamic world of work, and who is seeking an environment that provides them with the space to discover their strengths, will be right at home. This could be the perfect time to join their cause and Be Part of Progress.

Let's create the future

Connectivity and collaboration – here at BT we believe that's what makes the world go round.

 btplc.com/Careercentre

We're global innovators, thriving on the power of communication to make a better world and truly bring people together.

We always want more out of life. Always moving forward, always pushing for progress. Our development teams have created exciting new tech for everyone, from festival goers to car manufactures.

We're proud to be the UK's number one tech sector investor – but we're not stopping there.

If you share our passions for innovation, collaboration and amazing customer service, it's time to put your career future in our hands.

CANCER RESEARCH UK

graduates.cancerresearchuk.org

graduate@cancer.org.uk

twitter.com/CR_UK   facebook.com/CancerResearchUK

youtube.com/CancerResearchUK   linkedin.com/company/Cancer-Research-UK

Cancer. Be afraid. CRUK is a world-leading organisation funding science through exceptional fundraising efforts, raising £634m last year. Its ambition is to see ¾ of people surviving within the next 20 years – focusing on prevention, early diagnosis, and developing and personalising treatments to be more effective.

Graduates who join CRUK do something different, something extraordinary. They're changing lives. CRUK are looking for smart, sharp minded graduates to help achieve their goals. Their graduates are passionate in their work, determined, standout communicators and effective relationship builders.

What does a graduate scheme at an organisation like this offer? All graduates are put through their paces from the very beginning. Whether joining Fundraising & Marketing; Scientific Strategy and Funding; Project Management & Digital; Finance, HR or Policy, Information and Communications streams, they will have the exciting opportunity to rotate across four diverse business areas over the course of two years.

Graduates receive support and challenges from senior mentors, peers and placement managers along their journey with formal training whilst transitioning between placements. Placements are varied, stretching and business critical. From day one, graduates will be working on high profile projects with leaders across the organisation; drawing on and developing their individual strengths, talents and experience. CRUK invests in their talent, therefore all of their graduate placements are permanent roles.

As well as graduate opportunities, Cancer Research UK offers a vast array of entry-level jobs for recent graduates, sandwich placements and volunteering opportunities including award winning twelve week internships.

CRUK wants like minds, and the best minds, to help beat cancer sooner.

GRADUATE VACANCIES IN 2019
ACCOUNTANCY
FINANCE
MARKETING
RESEARCH & DEVELOPMENT
TECHNOLOGY

NUMBER OF VACANCIES
9 graduate jobs

LOCATIONS OF VACANCIES

STARTING SALARY FOR 2019
£25,000

UNIVERSITY VISITS IN 2018-19
BIRMINGHAM, CITY, QUEEN MARY LONDON
Please check with your university careers service for full details of local events.

MINIMUM ENTRY REQUIREMENTS
2.1 Degree

APPLICATION DEADLINE
November 2018

FURTHER INFORMATION
www.Top100GraduateEmployers.com
Register now for the latest news, campus events, work experience and graduate vacancies at Cancer Research UK.

AMBITIOUS

SMART FAST-PACED INSPIRING

DRIVING CHANGE SHARP

UNITED

PIONEERING

VERSATILE CHALLENGING PERCEPTIONS

LIFE-SAVING

THIS IS HOW IT FEELS HELPING TO BEAT CANCER.

For your chance to experience it, go to cruk.org/graduates

CANCER
RESEARCH
UK

Charityworks is the UK non-profit sector's graduate scheme, recruiting around 140 graduates each year. It's a 12-month, paid full-time job in a partner charity or housing association and an acclaimed leadership programme, introducing graduates to what they need to work and lead in the non-profit sector.

In a placement, graduates could be providing vital business support and evaluation at a national charity like NSPCC, leading on the improvement of infrastructure projects with a major housing charity, driving international business with the RNLI, or serving a community in a local project. Wherever they're based, they'll have a chance to make a real impact through their work.

Alongside the placement, graduates will take part in a leadership development programme. They'll be matched with an external mentor in the sector to help them make the most of the year. Twice a month they'll come together with their fellow trainees and leaders across the sector to explore and debate the key issues affecting their work and society as a whole and grow in their leadership ability. Graduates will also produce their own research, helping to raise their profile and develop their understanding of their environment.

At the end of the 12-month scheme they will have the experience and skills to kick-start a professional career in the UK non-profit sector and beyond. Charityworks graduates are highly desired, with 98% securing employment within three months if they were looking for it. Typically, over 66% of graduates stay in their host organisations at the end of the year, and 96% of graduates since 2009 have remained within the non-profit or public sector – some have even gone on to start their own organisations.

Whatever graduates want to do in the long-term, Charityworks is a fantastic way to launch their career and change the world for a living.

GRADUATE VACANCIES IN 2019
FINANCE
GENERAL MANAGEMENT
HUMAN RESOURCES
MARKETING
MEDIA
RESEARCH & DEVELOPMENT
SALES
TECHNOLOGY

NUMBER OF VACANCIES
140 graduate jobs

LOCATIONS OF VACANCIES

STARTING SALARY FOR 2019
£18,000-£20,000

UNIVERSITY VISITS IN 2018-19
BIRMINGHAM, BRADFORD, BRISTOL, BRUNEL, CAMBRIDGE, CARDIFF, DURHAM, EAST ANGLIA, EDINBURGH, EXETER, GLASGOW, KING'S COLLEGE LONDON, KENT, LANCASTER, LEEDS, LEICESTER, LIVERPOOL, LONDON SCHOOL OF ECONOMICS, MANCHESTER, NEWCASTLE, NORTHUMBRIA, NOTTINGHAM, NOTTINGHAM TRENT, OXFORD, QUEEN MARY LONDON, READING, ROYAL HOLLOWAY, SCHOOL OF AFRICAN STUDIES, SHEFFIELD, SUSSEX, UNIVERSITY COLLEGE LONDON, WARWICK, YORK
Please check with your university careers service for full details of local events.

MINIMUM ENTRY REQUIREMENTS
2.1 Degree

APPLICATION DEADLINE
28th February 2019

FURTHER INFORMATION
www.Top100GraduateEmployers.com
Register now for the latest news, campus events, work experience and graduate vacancies at Charityworks.

POVERTY.
AFFORDABLE HOUSING.
DOMESTIC VIOLENCE.
CLIMATE CHANGE.
SOCIAL CARE.

WHAT ROLE WILL YOU PLAY?

Charityworks.
Change the world
for a living.

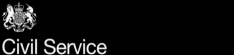

Be Yourself.

Be a Future Leader.

Be a Fast Streamer.

The Civil Service Fast Stream is a unique development opportunity for high potential graduates to become the future senior leaders of the Civil Service. The Fast Stream offers stretching and challenging work, contributing to addressing some of the most pressing issues facing the UK today.

Joining an organisation that impacts every aspect of society, graduates pursue a career path within their chosen government profession. They take up roles working across the Civil Service and contribute to shaping the future for generations to come. They benefit from a structured learning programme and, on many schemes, also have the opportunity to study for a professional qualification. Fast Streamers also benefit from a career path beyond the programme with infinite possibilities. Fast Stream alumni have progressed their careers to some of the most influential senior leadership roles.

In the Civil Service, graduates will be immersed in a culture where people genuinely matter and can confidently be themselves at work each day. People from all backgrounds influence decision-making, form life-long friendships and support one another on their development journeys. In addition, flexible working arrangements offer the space to achieve work-life balance, while a range of Fast Stream networks create a vibrant social life around work.

The Fast Stream has no upper age limit and, regardless of the degree subject studied, there's a scheme that's right for everyone. When graduates apply to the Fast Stream, they have a choice of 15 different schemes, each designed to accelerate their progression to the most senior Civil Service roles.

There is no typical Fast Streamer. The Fast Stream community includes people of all ages, cultures and backgrounds. And with postings available with multiple government departments, there is no typical role.

GRADUATE VACANCIES IN 2019
ENGINEERING
FINANCE
GENERAL MANAGEMENT
HUMAN RESOURCES
MARKETING
PURCHASING
RESEARCH & DEVELOPMENT
TECHNOLOGY

NUMBER OF VACANCIES
Up to 1,500 graduate jobs

LOCATIONS OF VACANCIES

STARTING SALARY FOR 2019
£25,000-£28,000

UNIVERSITY VISITS IN 2018-19
ABERYSTWYTH, ASTON, BELFAST, BIRMINGHAM, BRADFORD, BRISTOL, BRUNEL, CARDIFF, CITY, DURHAM, EAST ANGLIA, EDINBURGH, ESSEX, EXETER, GLASGOW, HULL, IMPERIAL COLLEGE LONDON, KING'S COLLEGE LONDON, KENT, LANCASTER, LEEDS, LEICESTER, LIVERPOOL, LONDON SCHOOL OF ECONOMICS, MANCHESTER, NEWCASTLE, NORTHUMBRIA, NOTTINGHAM, NOTTINGHAM TRENT, PLYMOUTH, QUEEN MARY LONDON, READING, ROYAL HOLLOWAY, SCHOOL OF AFRICAN STUDIES, SHEFFIELD, SOUTHAMPTON, SUSSEX, UNIVERSITY COLLEGE LONDON, WARWICK, YORK
Please check with your university careers service for full details of local events.

MINIMUM ENTRY REQUIREMENTS
2.2 Degree

APPLICATION DEADLINE
Late October 2018

FURTHER INFORMATION
www.Top100GraduateEmployers.com
Register now for the latest news, campus events, work experience and graduate vacancies at the Civil Service Fast Stream.

Civil Service
Fast Stream

Goal Defender.
Media Planner.
Fast Streamer.

There's no such thing as a typical Civil Service Fast Streamer, because all that matters to us is your potential to progress. Join us in this unique leadership development opportunity and, whichever degree subject you studied, you'll find a career path that's right for you. Take netball fan, Phoebe. She studied Anthropology, and now she's thriving on our Government Communication Service scheme. Whatever you achieve on the Fast Stream, you'll still find time for your life outside work. So there's nothing to stop you from becoming a future leader, or from being yourself.

faststream.gov.uk

graduate.recruitment@cliffordchance.com ✉
twitter.com/CCGradsUK 🐦 facebook.com/CliffordChanceGrads f
youtube.com/CliffordChanceGrads ▶ linkedin.com/company/Clifford-Chance-llp in
@CCcareers 👻 instagram.com/CliffordChanceCareers 📷

CLIFFORD CHANCE

GRADUATE VACANCIES IN 2019
LAW

NUMBER OF VACANCIES
90+ graduate jobs
For training contracts starting in 2021.

LOCATIONS OF VACANCIES

Clifford Chance is a leading global law firm with thousands of lawyers based across offices in five continents. They offer expert advice in all areas of commercial law. And with more top-ranked global practices than any other firm, it's clear why renowned organisations trust them with their biggest deals.

It's a firm where bright minds meet and collaborate across borders, languages and legal systems. Their six practice areas include: Corporate; Finance; Capital Markets; Real Estate; Litigation & Dispute Resolution; and Tax, Pensions & Employment. And they're looking for talented, committed graduates who can rise to the challenges of commercial law.

The opportunities at Clifford Chance range from their award-winning first-year initiative, SPARK, to Open Days and technology-focused training contracts. Their Open Days welcome graduates who want to experience their working culture. Attendees meet their brightest people and get tips on how to submit an outstanding Training Contract application.

For graduates ready to dive in, there's the Clifford Chance Training Contract. Over two years, trainees rotate across their core areas, learn from established experts and work on high-profile deals. Responsibility starts from day one – it's how they transform talented beginners into confident professional lawyers.

And now there's IGNITE, a brand-new Training Contract with an emphasis on technology. Trainees still rotate across the firm, but with a focus on shaping the future. They'll have the time and space to develop new skills. To reconsider what tech can do for law. To redefine how the firm delivers the best results for clients.

Across all of their graduate opportunities, Clifford Chance provide in-depth training, mentoring and support for their trainees' aspirations. Which explains why so many of their trainees stay and build long-term careers with them.

STARTING SALARY FOR 2019
£46,600

UNIVERSITY VISITS IN 2018-19
BIRMINGHAM, BRISTOL, CAMBRIDGE, DURHAM, EAST ANGLIA, EDINBURGH, EXETER, GLASGOW, KING'S COLLEGE LONDON, KENT, LANCASTER, LEEDS, LEICESTER, LONDON SCHOOL OF ECONOMICS, MANCHESTER, NOTTINGHAM, OXFORD, QUEEN MARY LONDON, SHEFFIELD, SOUTHAMPTON, ST ANDREWS, UNIVERSITY COLLEGE LONDON, WARWICK, YORK
Please check with your university careers service for full details of local events.

APPLICATION DEADLINE
16th December 2018

FURTHER INFORMATION
www.Top100GraduateEmployers.com
Register now for the latest news, campus events, work experience and graduate vacancies at Clifford Chance.

CMS is a future-facing law firm combining top quality sector expertise with international scale and a strategy to become a progressive technology-driven firm. The firm focuses on delivering rewarding futures for its clients, its communities and its people.

The culture at CMS is open, honest and approachable, and it values innovation, collaboration and inclusivity. And there is great momentum; employing more than 4,500 fee earners worldwide and with a total staff of 7,500, it creates exceptional relationships with clients and staff. This means it is looking for lawyers who possess excellent personal skills alongside a deep understanding of the business of law. In return, CMS offers world-class training and development opportunities, genuine recognition and inspiring work.

Across its six core sectors of Energy, Financial Services, Infrastructure & Project Finance, Life Sciences & Healthcare, Real Estate & Technology and Media & Communications, CMS has some of the most creative legal minds. Its lawyers are immersed in the clients' worlds, are genuine experts in their fields and are knowledgeable about the business issues organisations face day-to-day.

The CMS Academy is CMS's next-generation vacation scheme. It starts with a one-week 'business of law' training programme in London. This includes panel discussions with clients, case studies, work simulation exercises and client visits, amongst other things. It is an intense but fully rewarding week where students will experience first-hand the commitment from the firm to make them the best lawyer for the future. The second part of the programme includes a two-week internship within one of their UK offices, and participants gain real experience in a commercial environment and develop skills needed to succeed as a trainee solicitor.

GRADUATE VACANCIES IN 2019
LAW

NUMBER OF VACANCIES
65 graduate jobs
For training contracts starting in 2021.

LOCATIONS OF VACANCIES

STARTING SALARY FOR 2019
£25,000-£43,000

UNIVERSITY VISITS IN 2018-19
ABERDEEN, BRISTOL, CAMBRIDGE, CARDIFF, DUNDEE, DURHAM, EDINBURGH, EXETER, GLASGOW, KING'S COLLEGE LONDON, LEEDS, LONDON SCHOOL OF ECONOMICS, MANCHESTER, NOTTINGHAM, OXFORD, QUEEN MARY LONDON, SHEFFIELD, STRATHCLYDE, UNIVERSITY COLLEGE LONDON, WARWICK, YORK
Please check with your university careers service for full details of local events.

MINIMUM ENTRY REQUIREMENTS
2.1 Degree
128 UCAS points
320 UCAS points for those who passed exams before 2017.

APPLICATION DEADLINE
4th January 2019

FURTHER INFORMATION
www.Top100GraduateEmployers.com
Register now for the latest news, campus events, work experience and graduate vacancies at CMS.

Law.Tax

It's not just what you do, it's how you do it

At CMS, we anticipate and create sustainable and rewarding futures for our clients, our people and our communities. We are committed to giving all our talent inspiring work, genuine recognition and exceptional learning opportunities. You will experience a dynamic, empowering and inclusive culture, underpinned by trust and respect.

We offer the very best start to your career with our First Steps programme or CMS Academy, our next generation vacation scheme.

Advance with CMS

CMS ACADEMY
THE NEXT GENERATION VACATION SCHEME

Your World First

graduates.cms-cmno.com

DANONE
ONE PLANET. ONE HEALTH

PRODUCTS AND SERVICES
FOR EVERY STAGE OF LIFE.

For over 100 years, a unique purpose to 'bring health through food and beverages to as many people as possible', has inspired world leading brands such as Evian, Activia, Cow&Gate and Nutricia. Today, this purpose unites 100,000 Danone employees behind products that reach nine million consumers worldwide.

The UK Danone graduate scheme is designed for motivated individuals who are passionate about Danone's mission and values. In return, Danone provides them with the essential skills and behaviours needed to grow into committed and inspirational leaders.

Although a global business, Danone has a non-hierarchical structure that ensures every employee is equally valued, respected and empowered to make a difference. For graduates, that means they are placed in influential roles, with independence and autonomy, gaining extensive experience to support their personal progression. Graduates will be at the cutting edge of the business, playing a key role from the start.

Individual growth and development are an integral part of the company's DNA. A graduate's learning journey is completely personalised, based on their career aspirations and developmental targets. Along the way, they are fully supported by an internal coach and a network of key individuals who are committed to helping them achieve their goals.

Danone was built on the pioneering spirit of its founders. It's their spirit that underpins the core values of the entire organisation and their legacy is the development of a business that began and remains at the forefront of innovation. In its graduates, Danone is looking for new and exciting visionaries to continue this legacy and to contribute to a healthier world.

GRADUATE VACANCIES IN 2019
MARKETING
RESEARCH & DEVELOPMENT
SALES

NUMBER OF VACANCIES
15-20 graduate jobs

LOCATIONS OF VACANCIES

STARTING SALARY FOR 2019
£30,500
Plus a 3% bonus.

UNIVERSITY VISITS IN 2018-19
ASTON, BATH, BIRMINGHAM,
BRISTOL, DURHAM, EXETER,
KING'S COLLEGE LONDON, LANCASTER,
NOTTINGHAM, WARWICK
Please check with your university careers service for full details of local events.

MINIMUM ENTRY REQUIREMENTS
2.1 Degree

APPLICATION DEADLINE
11th November 2018

FURTHER INFORMATION
www.Top100GraduateEmployers.com
Register now for the latest news, campus events, work experience and graduate vacancies at Danone.

OUR SALES OF WATER GENERATES €4.7 BILLION...

Join Danone and help us to continue our mission to bring health through food.

Applications now open.

evian

EAU MINERALE NATURELLE
NATURAL MINERAL WATER

®

50 cL

...BUT WE NEVER TAKE MORE THAN NATURE OFFERS*

*Danone ensures reasoned use of every water source, under the control of hydro-geologists, so that the sources continue to replenish themselves at a natural rate. The amount drawn respects the resource, which is replenished by nature year after year.

danone.co.uk/graduates

DANONE
ONE PLANET. ONE HEALTH

Deloitte is a business that doesn't just recognise the need to remain curious, but fully embraces it. At Deloitte, graduates follow a career path that enables them to be true to themselves. To dream bigger, think creatively and deliver real impact. Deloitte is reshaping both the business and technology landscape.

In this ever more complex world, it's the smartest and most curious people that make the difference, because they're driven by imagination and the desire to add value. Deloitte is a business that doesn't just recognise the need to remain curious, but fully embraces it. Here, graduates will follow a career path that enables them to be true to themselves. To dream bigger, think creatively and deliver real impact. This is a place for go-getters, problem solvers, those who want to make a difference.

Deloitte is reshaping both the business and technology landscape. From Human Capital and Tax Consulting to Technology and Cyber they're delivering end-to-end improvement programmes, turning disruption into opportunity, and redesigning the art of Audit through automation.

It's not the background or experience of graduates that matters most, it's their mind, and how they'll use it to make an impact for clients, as well as their own career. Deloitte has opportunities across their entire business, so whatever their passion, graduates will find something that's right for them.

Deloitte have 29 offices across the UK and Northern Ireland, including Aberdeen, Belfast, Cardiff, Channel Islands, Gatwick, London, Manchester, Reading, St Albans and many more. Whichever location is chosen, graduates can be sure of joining a business that is both local and global, with networks, connections and values that reach right across the world.

This is the home of the imaginative – be part of it.

GRADUATE VACANCIES IN 2019

ACCOUNTANCY

CONSULTING

FINANCE

HUMAN RESOURCES

PROPERTY

TECHNOLOGY

NUMBER OF VACANCIES
1,000+ graduate jobs

LOCATIONS OF VACANCIES

STARTING SALARY FOR 2019
£Competitive

UNIVERSITY VISITS IN 2018-19
ABERDEEN, ASTON, BATH, BELFAST, BIRMINGHAM, BRISTOL, BRUNEL, CAMBRIDGE, CARDIFF, CITY, DURHAM, EAST ANGLIA, EDINBURGH, ESSEX, EXETER, GLASGOW, IMPERIAL COLLEGE LONDON, KING'S COLLEGE LONDON, KENT, LANCASTER, LEEDS, LEICESTER, LIVERPOOL, LONDON SCHOOL OF ECONOMICS, LOUGHBOROUGH, MANCHESTER, NEWCASTLE, NOTTINGHAM, NOTTINGHAM TRENT, OXFORD, PLYMOUTH, QUEEN MARY LONDON, READING, ROYAL HOLLOWAY, SHEFFIELD, SOUTHAMPTON, ST ANDREWS, STRATHCLYDE, SURREY, SUSSEX, SWANSEA, ULSTER, UNIVERSITY COLLEGE LONDON, WARWICK, YORK
Please check with your university careers service for full details of local events.

MINIMUM ENTRY REQUIREMENTS
2.1 Degree
104 UCAS points
260 UCAS points for those who passed exams before 2017.

APPLICATION DEADLINE
Early November
Early application advised.

FURTHER INFORMATION
www.Top100GraduateEmployers.com
Register now for the latest news, campus events, work experience and graduate vacancies at Deloitte.

Deloitte.

Where are solutions before they're found?

Welcome to the home of the curious.
A place for those who know that imagination,
ingenuity and solution finding are what
humans are made of. We offer life-changing
careers and professional qualifications,
across all industries, to those who are true
to themselves. Those who set no limits to
their dreams and ambitions.

deloitte.co.uk/careers
What impact will you make?

DLA PIPER

DLA Piper is one of the world's leading business law firms. As a trusted advisor to clients, it delivers quality, consistency and value, helping them achieve their goals. With over 90 offices across more than 40 countries, the firm provides seamless local and cross-border advice.

DLA Piper's ten sector groups cover the full range of business law services, and provide insight on industry trends, opportunities and challenges. Clients include multinationals, emerging companies, public sector bodies and governments. Across the two leading legal directories, the firm has over 2,400 lawyer rankings, and over 1,200 practice group/sector rankings.

DLA Piper is progressive, innovative and responsible. Through its global non-profit initiative, the firm contributed over 200,000 pro bono hours in 2017 alone, supporting under-served regions on access to justice, social and economic development, and women's advancement. The firm has also pledged US$6.5 million to UNICEF to improve child justice.

People are the heart of DLA Piper. By making diversity and inclusion core principles, the firm fosters a culture of mutual respect, where everyone is valued as an individual.

DLA Piper is looking for ambitious, capable and forward-thinking graduates from any degree discipline to join its journey. Graduates will be based in one of the firm's seven UK offices: Birmingham, Edinburgh, Leeds, Liverpool, London, Manchester or Sheffield.

During their two-year training contract, graduates will complete four six-month rotations, and the majority will undertake an international or client secondment. As part of DLA Piper's future, all graduates are given the resources and opportunities to build an exciting, fulfilling career.

GRADUATE VACANCIES IN 2019
LAW

NUMBER OF VACANCIES
70-80 graduate jobs
For training contracts starting in 2021.

LOCATIONS OF VACANCIES

STARTING SALARY FOR 2019
£45,000
London salary. £28,000 in other offices.

UNIVERSITY VISITS IN 2018-19
ABERDEEN, BIRMINGHAM, BRISTOL, CAMBRIDGE, DURHAM, EDINBURGH, GLASGOW, IMPERIAL COLLEGE LONDON, KING'S COLLEGE LONDON, LANCASTER, LEICESTER, LIVERPOOL, LONDON SCHOOL OF ECONOMICS, MANCHESTER, NEWCASTLE, NOTTINGHAM, OXFORD, QUEEN MARY LONDON, SHEFFIELD, ST ANDREWS, STRATHCLYDE, UNIVERSITY COLLEGE LONDON, WARWICK, YORK
Please check with your university careers service for full details of local events.

MINIMUM ENTRY REQUIREMENTS
2.1 Degree
128 UCAS points
320 UCAS points for those who passed exams before 2017.

APPLICATION DEADLINE
November-December 2018
November for Training Contracts, December for Summer Internships.

FURTHER INFORMATION
www.Top100GraduateEmployers.com
Register now for the latest news, campus events, work experience and graduate vacancies at DLA Piper.

DLA PIPER

SHARE OUR VISION
SHAPE YOUR FUTURE

Our goal is simple. We want to create the future leaders
of the firm. That means giving you the skills you need to
become a successful lawyer, but also the experiences
to discover where your true interests lie.

Find out more at
DLAPIPERGRADUATES.COM

Dyson is a global technology enterprise. They transform every category they enter with iconic re-inventions that simply work better. Dyson people apply 'wrong thinking', experiment without fear, and create machines that defy convention. The future is bright and the next few years will be their busiest yet.

Dyson is transforming globally. In 2012 they were just 3,120 people – today they're approaching 12,000. With ever-expanding interests, from personal care to electric vehicles, they are on the lookout for people who have a passion for solving problems that can contribute to the future of cutting-edge technology.

Since its early success Dyson has always gone against the grain and carved out its own path, from bagless vacuums to bladeless fans, revolutionary hairdryers to building its own degree. Whether someone is an intern, graduate or industry leader at Dyson, they all share the same values. It's helped them to stick to their roots, build the technologies they have today and bolster the ones they're creating for tomorrow.

At Dyson, graduates learn their trade from true experts in-house, not by shadowing, but by being in the spotlight. It's an approach that brings out the best in their new talent – turning them from first-timers into major achievers. They gain invaluable exposure to the inner workings at Dyson through tough projects with real responsibility. Past graduates across the business have found themselves presenting ideas to James Dyson within a matter of weeks into their new role.

A lot goes on at Dyson – in and outside the engineering labs. They're on the lookout for people to join teams across marketing, engineering and more: people who share Dyson's core values and a passion for technology, those who won't settle for 'good enough' and can push the boundaries without fear.

GRADUATE VACANCIES IN 2019

ENGINEERING

MARKETING

TECHNOLOGY

NUMBER OF VACANCIES
75+ graduate jobs

LOCATIONS OF VACANCIES

STARTING SALARY FOR 2019
£26,500
Plus a £2,000 sign-on bonus.

UNIVERSITY VISITS IN 2018-19
BATH, BRISTOL, CAMBRIDGE,
IMPERIAL COLLEGE LONDON, LEEDS,
LOUGHBOROUGH, SHEFFIELD,
SOUTHAMPTON, WARWICK
Please check with your university careers service for full details of local events.

MINIMUM ENTRY REQUIREMENTS
2.1 Degree

APPLICATION DEADLINE
Varies by function

FURTHER INFORMATION
www.Top100GraduateEmployers.com
*Register now for the latest news, campus events, work experience and graduate vacancies at **Dyson**.*

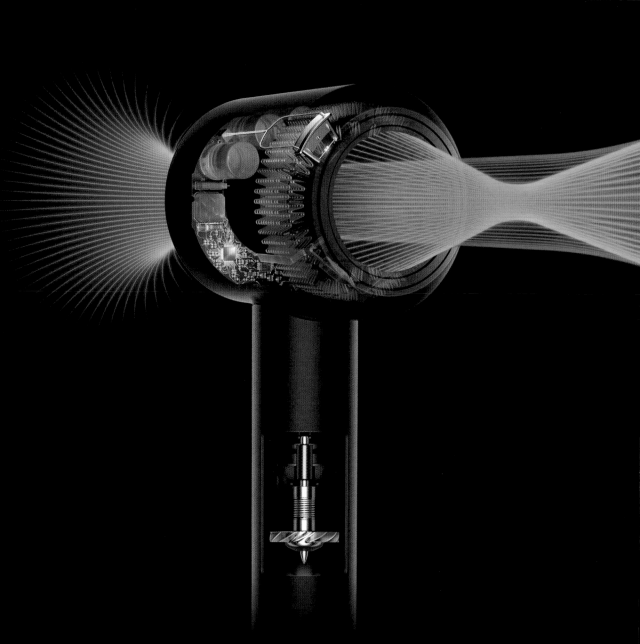

Re-think the rules.

We're looking for the best and brightest graduates to shape
our future. There's nothing conventional about a Dyson career,
so only the most ambitious need apply. At the forefront of our
global business, you won't just learn how things are done –
you'll find ways to make them better.

careers.dyson.com/early-careers

ExxonMobil

Global fundamentals

Consider how modern energy enriches your life. Now consider the 7 billion other people on earth who also use energy each day to make their own lives richer, more productive, safer and healthier. Then you will recognize what is perhaps the biggest driver of energy demand: the human desire to sustain and improve the well-being of ourselves, our families and our communities. Through 2040, population and economic growth will drive demand higher, but the world will use energy more efficiently and shift toward lower-carbon fuels.

25%

The world's population will rise by more than 25 percent from 2010 to 2040, reaching nearly 9 billion people. Population and economic growth are key factors behind increasing demand for energy.

Imagine working for the world's largest publicly traded oil and gas company, on tasks that affect nearly everyone in the world today and for future generations to come. ExxonMobil in the UK is better known for its Esso and Mobil brands due to the success of its service stations and high performance lubricants.

ExxonMobil offers challenging long-term careers to high performing graduates, as well as summer and year placements with real responsibility!

There's no such thing as an average day at ExxonMobil and there are many different career paths available from a technical career to a leadership position to a commercial role. For graduates who are looking for a long-term career that will be challenging, rewarding and certainly varied, then a career with ExxonMobil might just be for them.

What are ExxonMobil looking for? For the technical schemes, applications are welcomed from Chemical, Electrical and Mechanical (and related) Engineers with a 2:1 minimum. For the commercial schemes, applications from a number of disciplines including Science/Engineering/IT/Business degrees with a 2:1 minimum are accepted.

In addition to the competitive base salary and relocation allowance, employees are also offered a matched 2-for-1 share scheme, final salary pension plan, private health care scheme, 33 days holiday per annum (including public holidays), interest-free loan, tailored graduate training and continuous development, support towards studying for professional qualifications such as IChemE, free sports facilities and subsidised dining facilities at most locations, voluntary community activities, international opportunities and regular job rotations (typically every one to three years) with opportunities to develop and hone skills.

GRADUATE VACANCIES IN 2019
ENGINEERING
HUMAN RESOURCES
MARKETING

NUMBER OF VACANCIES
30+ graduate jobs

LOCATIONS OF VACANCIES

STARTING SALARY FOR 2019
£38,500+

UNIVERSITY VISITS IN 2018-19
BATH, BIRMINGHAM, BRISTOL, CAMBRIDGE, EDINBURGH, IMPERIAL COLLEGE LONDON, LOUGHBOROUGH, MANCHESTER, NEWCASTLE, NOTTINGHAM, SHEFFIELD, SOUTHAMPTON, STRATHCLYDE
Please check with your university careers service for full details of local events.

MINIMUM ENTRY REQUIREMENTS
2.1 Degree

APPLICATION DEADLINE
Year-round recruitment
Early application advised.

FURTHER INFORMATION
www.Top100GraduateEmployers.com
Register now for the latest news, campus events, work experience and graduate vacancies at ExxonMobil.

careers.exxonmobil.com

Freshfields Bruckhaus Deringer advises some of the world's biggest companies on how to grow, strengthen and defend their businesses. For aspiring lawyers keen to pursue a career in commercial law, Freshfields can offer some of the best and most interesting work there is.

Freshfields advise on every type of regulatory issue, from financial services regulation to tax, combating bribery and corruption to buying and selling property; and risk management and disputes work to help defend their clients' businesses and reputations – this involves not only litigation to arbitration but also handling major global investigations by regulatory authorities.

Freshfields divides its business into five practice groups, which divide further into specialist teams. Trainees must experience at least one seat in corporate, dispute resolution and finance; other seats are available in antitrust, competition and trade; people and reward; real estate; and tax.

Prior to starting a training contract, successful applicants will be supported through their LPC or GDL course. The LPC is available to law students and the GDL is for non-law students. When trainees first arrive there's a two-week induction which includes practical skills workshops and advice to help new trainees hit the ground running. After that, Freshfields offer legal training on a departmental basis and business skills training in how to work productively, delegate and handle pressure.

Throughout a training contract, trainees are offered plenty of guidance. Much of this is on-the-job work with partners and associates – operating on an open-door policy, so there's always a supportive team around and the opportunity to learn from their fantastic network of lawyers.

GRADUATE VACANCIES IN 2019

LAW

NUMBER OF VACANCIES
Up to 80 graduate jobs
For training contracts starting in 2021.

LOCATIONS OF VACANCIES

STARTING SALARY FOR 2019
£45,000

UNIVERSITY VISITS IN 2018-19
BELFAST, BIRMINGHAM, BRISTOL, CAMBRIDGE, CARDIFF, TRINITY COLLEGE DUBLIN, UNIVERSITY COLLEGE DUBLIN, DURHAM, EDINBURGH, EXETER, GLASGOW, KING'S COLLEGE LONDON, LEEDS, LEICESTER, LONDON SCHOOL OF ECONOMICS, MANCHESTER, NEWCASTLE, NOTTINGHAM, OXFORD, QUEEN MARY LONDON, READING, SCHOOL OF ORIENTAL AND AFRICAN STUDIES, SHEFFIELD, SOUTHAMPTON, ST ANDREWS, UNIVERSITY COLLEGE LONDON, WARWICK, YORK
Please check with your university careers service for full details of local events.

MINIMUM ENTRY REQUIREMENTS
2.1 Degree

APPLICATION DEADLINE
Varies by eligibility
See website for details.

FURTHER INFORMATION
www.Top100GraduateEmployers.com
Register now for the latest news, campus events, work experience and graduate vacancies at Freshfields.

Expect great things.

We do.
And as a trainee at Freshfields, so will you.

Ask about our culture and the same words come up: supportive, collaborative, inclusive. That might not be what you'd expect of a 275-year-old Magic Circle firm. But our long history is based on being adaptable and innovative.

Join us and you'll be learning from the best, with unique training and benefits, and access to opportunities across our global network. You'll also be making a difference: we're committed to responsibility, sustainability and diversity.

 To find out more, visit
freshfields.com/ukgraduates

We recruit fantastic trainees. We want them all to qualify with us and go on to become great lawyers.

Never get tired of the views from our London office.

Freshfields Bruckhaus Deringer

FRONTLINE

CHANGING LIVES

thefrontline.org.uk

facebook.com/FrontlineChangingLives **f**   recruitment@thefrontline.org.uk ✉

linkedin.com/company/Frontline-org **in**   twitter.com/FrontlineSW **y**

instagram.com/Frontline_SW **◉**   youtube.com/FrontlineSW **▶**

At least half a million children in England don't have a safe or stable home. These children and their families face some of the worst life chances, but great social work has the power to change this. That's why Frontline recruits and develops outstanding individuals to be social workers and transform the lives of the most vulnerable children and families.

Frontline's two-year Leadership Development programme offers graduates an exciting new route into one of Britain's toughest and most rewarding professions. Frontline prioritise hands-on experience through practice-based learning, and participants will benefit from tailored intensive practical and academic training, as they join a new generation of children's social workers.

Following a five-week residential training programme, participants spend two years working in a local authority children's services department. The first year qualifies participants as social workers through direct work with children and families. In the second year they work as a newly qualified social worker responsible for their own caseload, and will complete a fully funded master's qualification.

Frontline participants work directly with children, families, schools, courts and the police, to empower families to achieve positive change. They will develop a whole range of invaluable and transferable skills including leadership, relationship-building and conflict resolution. Participants will inspire, persuade and be part of a leadership profession which brings out the best in diverse groups of people. Additionally, participants will benefit from ongoing leadership development coaching.

Joining Frontline provides the opportunity to make a real difference to the lives of vulnerable children and their families. Frontline welcomes applications from students from a range of degree disciplines.

GRADUATE VACANCIES IN 2019

GENERAL MANAGEMENT

HUMAN RESOURCES

LAW

NUMBER OF VACANCIES
452 graduate jobs

LOCATIONS OF VACANCIES

STARTING SALARY FOR 2019
£Competitive

UNIVERSITY VISITS IN 2018-19
ASTON, BATH, BIRMINGHAM, BRISTOL, CAMBRIDGE, CARDIFF, CITY, DURHAM, EAST ANGLIA, EDINBURGH, ESSEX, EXETER, KING'S COLLEGE LONDON, KENT, LANCASTER, LEEDS, LEICESTER, LIVERPOOL, LONDON SCHOOL OF ECONOMICS, MANCHESTER, NEWCASTLE, NORTHUMBRIA, NOTTINGHAM, NOTTINGHAM TRENT, OXFORD, QUEEN MARY LONDON, READING, SHEFFIELD, SOUTHAMPTON, ST ANDREWS, UNIVERSITY COLLEGE LONDON, WARWICK, YORK
Please check with your university careers service for full details of local events.

MINIMUM ENTRY REQUIREMENTS
2.1 Degree

APPLICATION DEADLINE
19th November 2018

FURTHER INFORMATION
www.Top100GraduateEmployers.com
Register now for the latest news, campus events, work experience and graduate vacancies at **Frontline.**

CHANGE YOUR LIFE
TRANSFORM THEIRS

Join a movement of leaders working to address social disadvantage through children's social work

FRONTLINE

Goldman Sachs

Goldman Sachs turns ideas into reality for its clients and communities around the world. In every area of Goldman Sachs, from the trading floor to their tech stacks, wealth management to risk management, each one of its teams contributes to innovations that drive progress around the world.

At Goldman Sachs, graduates' skills and experiences create a world of possibilities for their clients. New joiners will work alongside industry experts and strategic thinkers at all levels, gaining hands-on experience unlike anywhere else. All at a place where ideas matter, and personal and professional growth are front of mind.

Goldman Sachs is structured in a series of divisions: Engineering, Executive Office, Finance, Global Compliance, Global Investment Research, Consumer and Commercial Banking, Human Capital Management, Internal Audit, Investment Banking, Investment Management, Legal, Merchant Banking, Operations, Realty Management, Risk, Securities and Services.

From a graduate's first day, they will be immersed in a collaborative environment with people of all levels who share the firm's values. Nearly everyone – from junior analysts to the most senior leaders – is actively involved in recruiting talented people from a variety of backgrounds, because Goldman Sachs recognises that a diverse workforce enables them to serve their clients most effectively and in the most innovative ways.

The diversity of talents and educational backgrounds at the firm is crucial to its performance and business success. To that end, Goldman Sachs is committed to an environment that values diversity, promotes inclusion and encourages teamwork. Whatever an individual's background or area of academic study, Goldman Sachs values their intellect, personality and integrity.

GRADUATE VACANCIES IN 2019

INVESTMENT BANKING

TECHNOLOGY

NUMBER OF VACANCIES
450 graduate jobs

LOCATIONS OF VACANCIES

Vacancies also available in Europe, the USA, Asia, and elsewhere in the world.

STARTING SALARY FOR 2019
£Competitive
Plus a competitive bonus.

UNIVERSITY VISITS IN 2018-19
BATH, BIRMINGHAM, BRISTOL, CAMBRIDGE, CITY, TRINITY COLLEGE DUBLIN, UNIVERSITY COLLEGE DUBLIN, DURHAM, EDINBURGH, GLASGOW, IMPERIAL COLLEGE LONDON, KING'S COLLEGE LONDON, LONDON SCHOOL OF ECONOMICS, LOUGHBOROUGH, MANCHESTER, NOTTINGHAM, OXFORD, QUEEN MARY LONDON, READING, SHEFFIELD, SOUTHAMPTON, ST ANDREWS, STRATHCLYDE, SURREY, UNIVERSITY COLLEGE LONDON, WARWICK
Please check with your university careers service for full details of local events.

APPLICATION DEADLINE
2nd December 2018
Deadline for all Engineering programmes is 6th January 2019. Warsaw and Off-Cycle internships accepted on a rolling basis.

FURTHER INFORMATION
www.Top100GraduateEmployers.com
Register now for the latest news, campus events, work experience and graduate vacancies at Goldman Sachs.

Make **things** possible.

At Goldman Sachs, your skills and experiences will create a world of possibilities for our clients. From the latest IPO and market insights to investments in clean energy and infrastructure, each one of our teams contributes to innovations that drive progress around the world.

You'll work alongside industry experts and strategic thinkers at all levels, gaining hands-on experience unlike anywhere else. All at a place where your ideas matter and your personal and professional growth are front of mind.

Come embrace the opportunity to move industries, make markets and empower communities.

Make things possible at goldmansachs.com/careers.

APPLICATION DEADLINES

2 December, 2018

All applications for the following programmes (excluding Engineering, Off-Cycle and Warsaw*):

- Spring Programme
- Summer Analyst
- Work Placement
- New Analyst

6 January, 2019

Engineering Programme

- Spring Programme
- Summer Analyst
- New Analyst

*Off-Cycle and Warsaw will be a rolling-deadline.

goldmansachs.com/careers

Google

GRADUATE VACANCIES IN 2019

CONSULTING
ENGINEERING
HUMAN RESOURCES
MARKETING
MEDIA
SALES
TECHNOLOGY

NUMBER OF VACANCIES
No fixed quota

LOCATIONS OF VACANCIES

Vacancies also available in the USA, Asia, and elsewhere in the world.

Larry Page and Sergey Brin founded Google in September 1998 with a mission to organise the world's information and make it universally accessible and useful. Since then, the company has grown to more than 80,000 employees worldwide, with a wide range of popular products and platforms like Search, Maps, Cloud, Ads, Gmail, Android, the Assistant and YouTube.

A problem isn't truly solved until it's solved for all. Googlers build products that help create opportunities for everyone, whether down the street or across the globe. They bring insight, imagination, and a healthy disregard for the impossible. They bring everything that makes them unique. It's really the people that make Google the kind of company it is. Google hires people who are smart and determined, and favour ability over experience.

Google hires graduates from all disciplines, from humanities and business related courses to engineering and computer science. The ideal candidate is someone who can demonstrate a passion for the online industry and someone who has made the most of their time at university through involvement in clubs, societies or relevant internships. Google hires graduates who have a variety of strengths and passions, not just isolated skill sets. For technical roles within engineering teams, specific skills will be required. The diversity of perspectives, ideas, and cultures, both within Google and in the tech industry overall, leads to the creation of better products and services.

Whether it's providing online marketing consultancy, selling an advertising solution to clients, hiring the next generation of Googlers, or building products, Google has full-time roles and internships available across teams like Global Customer Experience, Sales, People Operations, Legal, Finance, Operations, Cloud and Engineering.

STARTING SALARY FOR 2019
£Competitive
Plus world-renowned perks and benefits.

UNIVERSITY VISITS IN 2018-19
Please check with your university careers service for full details of local events.

MINIMUM ENTRY REQUIREMENTS
Relevant degree required for some roles.

APPLICATION DEADLINE
Year-round recruitment

FURTHER INFORMATION
www.Top100GraduateEmployers.com
Register now for the latest news, campus events, work experience and graduate vacancies at Google.

BRING QUESTIONS

BUILD ANSWERS

Google

www.google.com/careers/students

Grant Thornton

HARK

"You don't need to know much about accounting and finance. If you're willing to learn and have got the right attitude, we'll teach you everything you need to know."

**Public Sector Trainee
Birmingham**

Grant Thornton is one of the world's leading independent assurance, tax and advisory firms. They are driven by independent thinkers that provide high quality business and financial advice to a wide range of clients in countries all over the world. Shape more than just your career at Grant Thornton.

In Grant Thornton's Graduate Programme, graduates get the training and support to help them grow in confidence and to develop the skills they need to become a future leader. But they'll also do so much more than that. They will work with people who are driven by their purpose of shaping a vibrant economy in the UK and beyond.

Graduates join a three-year programme to become professionally qualified advisers, specialising in either advisory, audit or tax. In this training programme, they'll get hands-on experience working with clients, from multinationals to start-ups, across public and private sectors.

Grant Thornton's graduate programme is just the beginning. Once graduates get their qualification, all kinds of career routes will open up to them, from audit, tax and advisory to people management and business development. What happens next and how fast they progress is up to them.

Grant Thornton has a flexible approach to academic entry requirements. The firm will consider applicants' academic achievements, but their strengths, motivations and connection with the business and its values are more important. They are looking for people with a broad range of interests and experiences.

Grant Thornton does things differently. They give their people the freedom to drive change and shape their own destinies. Their people are inspired to make a difference. Their collaborative culture means they share ideas as well as the responsibility for making them happen.

GRADUATE VACANCIES IN 2019
ACCOUNTANCY

NUMBER OF VACANCIES
400-450 graduate jobs

LOCATIONS OF VACANCIES

STARTING SALARY FOR 2019
£Competitive

UNIVERSITY VISITS IN 2018-19
ASTON, BATH, BIRMINGHAM, BRISTOL, CAMBRIDGE, CARDIFF, CITY, DURHAM, EDINBURGH, EXETER, GLASGOW, HERIOT-WATT, KING'S COLLEGE LONDON, KENT, LEEDS, LEICESTER, LIVERPOOL, LOUGHBOROUGH, MANCHESTER, NEWCASTLE, NOTTINGHAM, NOTTINGHAM TRENT, OXFORD BROOKES, QUEEN MARY LONDON, READING, SHEFFIELD, SOUTHAMPTON, STIRLING, STRATHCLYDE, SURREY, UNIVERSITY COLLEGE LONDON, WARWICK, YORK
Please check with your university careers service for full details of local events.

APPLICATION DEADLINE
Year-round recruitment
Early application advised.

FURTHER INFORMATION
www.Top100GraduateEmployers.com
Register now for the latest news, campus events, work experience and graduate vacancies at Grant Thornton.

SHAPE MORE THAN JUST YOUR CAREER

At Grant Thornton we have a unique culture where thinking differently is encouraged, your opinions are heard and your contributions are valued. If you are looking to make a difference, come and share in our bold purpose of shaping a vibrant economy in the UK and beyond. So bring your passion, ambitions and inspiration, and together let's make it happen.

trainees.grant-thornton.co.uk

 Grant Thornton

An instinct for growth™

gsk
do more
feel better
live longer

GSK is a science-led global healthcare company of over 100,000 individuals united by their mission and four values of patient focus, integrity, respect for people and transparency. GSK put these values at the heart of everything they do to better help meet the needs of their patients and consumers.

Based in the UK with employees in over 150 countries, GSK research and develop a broad range of healthcare products from lifesaving prescription medicines and vaccines to popular consumer products such as Beechams, Sensodyne, Savlon and Panadol. Every year GSK screens millions of compounds and make billions of packs of medicines and consumer healthcare products, with a commitment to widening access to their products, so more people can benefit, no matter where they live in the world or what they can afford to pay.

Dedicated to helping millions of people around the world to do more, feel better and live longer, GSK is revolutionising its business to meet changing global healthcare needs. GSK invested £3.9 billion in R&D in 2017 and has consistently topped the Access to Medicine Index, reinforcing the company's commitment to tackle some of the world's worst diseases by embracing new, open and innovative ways of working.

GSK is deeply committed to developing people through a range of ongoing opportunities that includes tailored 2-3 year rotational graduate Future Leaders programmes, industrial or summer placements. Successful graduates will be stretched to forge new relationships, seek out new experiences and be responsible for driving their own development. GSK will be there every step of the way, helping to build the skills that will allow them to reach their potential.

Most of all, GSK graduates enjoy the sense of purpose that comes from leading change in an industry that touches millions every day.

facebook.com/HSFgraduatesUK **f**   graduatesUK@hsf.com ✉

linkedin.com/company/Herbert-Smith-Freehills **in**   twitter.com/HSFgraduatesUK **y**

instagram.com/HSFgraduatesUK 🅞   youtube.com/HSFlegal ▶

Herbert Smith Freehills work on some of the world's biggest cases. With award-winning expertise in multiple fields, their progressive approach sets them apart. They advise more FTSE 100 clients than any other US or UK-headquartered firm – and their inclusive ethos means trainees can be a part of it all.

By combining perspectives and potential from diverse backgrounds, Herbert Smith Freehills views and practices law differently. This allows them to break new ground, whether it's a complex international dispute or a billion-pound, cross-border deal. And trainees can add their expertise to the mix.

Herbert Smith Freehills operates at the forefront of a range of global legal practice areas. For example, their dispute resolution team is recognised as number one in the UK, Asia and Australia. That also includes their leading international arbitration practice and award-winning in-house advocacy unit, allowing them to offer a complete litigation service, and a realistic alternative to the Bar.

At the same time, Herbert Smith Freehills has worldwide reach, with over 3,000 lawyers in 27 different offices, and 18 international trainee secondments. The firm gives those who are looking to stay at the cutting-edge of law the scope to work in a truly international way.

Herbert Smith Freehills' trainees can be a part of it all. The training contract balances contentious and non-contentious work with pro bono opportunities and real responsibility. All trainees will sit in dispute resolution and corporate, as well as having the opportunity to experience specialist areas such as finance, competition, regulation and trade, intellectual property, and tax. This firm's truly global and progressive approach allows them to offer trainees a unique and comprehensive learning experience.

GRADUATE VACANCIES IN 2019
LAW

NUMBER OF VACANCIES
Up to 60 graduate jobs
For training contracts starting in 2021.

LOCATIONS OF VACANCIES

STARTING SALARY FOR 2019
£44,000

UNIVERSITY VISITS IN 2018-19
BATH, BELFAST, BIRMINGHAM, BRISTOL, CAMBRIDGE, CARDIFF, CITY, TRINITY COLLEGE DUBLIN, UNIVERSITY COLLEGE DUBLIN, DUNDEE, DURHAM, EAST ANGLIA, EDINBURGH, ESSEX, EXETER, GLASGOW, IMPERIAL COLLEGE LONDON, KING'S COLLEGE LONDON, KENT, LANCASTER, LEEDS, LEICESTER, LONDON SCHOOL OF ECONOMICS, MANCHESTER, NEWCASTLE, NOTTINGHAM, OXFORD, QUEEN MARY LONDON, SCHOOL OF AFRICAN STUDIES, SHEFFIELD, SOUTHAMPTON, UNIVERSITY COLLEGE LONDON, WARWICK, YORK
Please check with your university careers service for full details of local events.

MINIMUM ENTRY REQUIREMENTS
2.1 Degree

APPLICATION DEADLINE
Year-round recruitment
Early application advised.

FURTHER INFORMATION
www.Top100GraduateEmployers.com
Register now for the latest news, campus events, work experience and graduate vacancies at Herbert Smith Freehills.

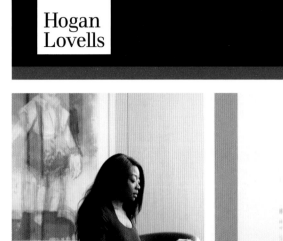

hoganlovells.com/graduates

graduate.recruitment@hoganlovells.com ✉

twitter.com/HLGraduatesUK 🐦 facebook.com/HoganLovellsGradsUK **f**

instagram.com/HoganLovellsGradsUK 📷 linkedin.com/company/HoganLovells **in**

Hogan Lovells

When graduates choose Hogan Lovells, they're not just choosing a career in law. They're choosing a more progressive international outlook, a clearer focus on innovation and a sharper commercial edge. They're choosing to challenge accepted wisdom. They're choosing to be a global game-changer.

It's why many prestigious, forward-thinking clients choose to work with them. The firm has a reputation not just for the consistently high quality of its 2,600 lawyers, but also for its sense of community. The network of over 48 global offices collaborates closely. Together, their teams of corporate, finance, dispute resolution, government regulatory and intellectual property lawyers tackle some of the most intricate legal and commercial issues that businesses face.

Their trainee solicitors don't just master law. They develop industry expertise and explore the principles of business, entrepreneurship and social enterprise. Each year, the firm takes on up to 50 trainee solicitors – both law and non-law graduates. The two-year training contract is split into four six-month 'seats'. During this time, trainee solicitors move around four different practice areas, including corporate, finance, and dispute resolution. Graduates will gain exposure to and develop a rounded understanding of international law, and they will have an opportunity to apply for an international or client secondment.

Hogan Lovells also runs highly-regarded summer and winter vacation schemes. Up to 55 places are available in total. Each lasts up to three weeks, and gives participants the chance to work alongside partners, associates and trainees in major practice areas. Students are exposed to two or three practice areas and learn to draft documents, carry out legal research, attend meetings and in some cases attend court. This hands-on learning is complemented by tailored workshops, case studies and social events.

GRADUATE VACANCIES IN 2019
LAW

NUMBER OF VACANCIES
50 graduate jobs
For training contracts starting in 2021.

LOCATIONS OF VACANCIES

STARTING SALARY FOR 2019
£45,000

UNIVERSITY VISITS IN 2018-19
BELFAST, BIRMINGHAM, BRISTOL, CAMBRIDGE, CARDIFF, DURHAM, EAST ANGLIA, EDINBURGH, EXETER, HULL, KING'S COLLEGE LONDON, LANCASTER, LEEDS, LEICESTER, LONDON SCHOOL OF ECONOMICS, MANCHESTER, NEWCASTLE, NOTTINGHAM, OXFORD, QUEEN MARY LONDON, SCHOOL OF AFRICAN STUDIES, SHEFFIELD, ST ANDREWS, UNIVERSITY COLLEGE LONDON, WARWICK, YORK
Please check with your university careers service for full details of local events.

MINIMUM ENTRY REQUIREMENTS
2.1 Degree

APPLICATION DEADLINE
31st January 2019

FURTHER INFORMATION
www.Top100GraduateEmployers.com
Register now for the latest news, campus events, work experience and graduate vacancies at Hogan Lovells.

HSBC

With a network of some 3,900 offices in 67 countries and territories, serving around 38 million customers, HSBC is one of the largest global banks. HSBC's purpose is connecting customers to opportunities, enabling businesses and economies to prosper. Their international network covers 90 per cent of world trade.

HSBC is looking for students and graduates who are collaborative and curious thinkers, with the courage to challenge the status quo and the motivation to make a positive impact for customers worldwide.

HSBC embeds sustainability in the way they do business and is committed to balancing social, environmental and economic considerations in the decisions it makes. They want a connected international workforce of unique thinkers that reflects the communities and markets in which they serve. They recognise the importance of having a diverse workforce to meet the needs of their customers. That's why they hire, develop, and promote employees based on merit, and provide an open, supportive, and inclusive working environment. They also provide tailored training and support to help employees flourish in their chosen career path. HSBC is an organisation where everyone can be themselves.

Students and graduates can apply to join internship and graduate programmes in one of four global businesses: Commercial Banking, Global Banking & Markets, Global Private Banking or Retail Banking & Wealth Management, including Global Asset Management. The journey begins with an induction followed by a number of rotations across the chosen business area. Successful applicants will work with talented colleagues and be supported by mentors and a buddy as they progress. The technical and personal development training ensures they're well equipped to achieve their full potential and flourish in their chosen career path regardless of the degree subject they have studied.

GRADUATE VACANCIES IN 2019

ACCOUNTANCY
GENERAL MANAGEMENT
INVESTMENT BANKING
RETAILING
SALES

NUMBER OF VACANCIES
600+ graduate jobs

LOCATIONS OF VACANCIES

Vacancies also available in Europe, the USA, Asia, and elsewhere in the world.

STARTING SALARY FOR 2019
£Competitive
Plus a competitive bonus.

UNIVERSITY VISITS IN 2018-19
ASTON, BATH, BIRMINGHAM, BRISTOL, CAMBRIDGE, DURHAM, EAST ANGLIA, EDINBURGH, EXETER, IMPERIAL COLLEGE LONDON, KING'S COLLEGE LONDON, LANCASTER, LEEDS, LEICESTER, LIVERPOOL, LONDON SCHOOL OF ECONOMICS, LOUGHBOROUGH, MANCHESTER, NEWCASTLE, NOTTINGHAM, OXFORD, QUEEN MARY LONDON, SHEFFIELD, SOUTHAMPTON, SURREY, UNIVERSITY COLLEGE LONDON, WARWICK, YORK
Please check with your university careers service for full details of local events.

MINIMUM ENTRY REQUIREMENTS
2.1 Degree
120 UCAS points
300 UCAS points for those who passed exams before 2017.

APPLICATION DEADLINE
Varies by function

FURTHER INFORMATION
www.Top100GraduateEmployers.com
Register now for the latest news, campus events, work experience and graduate vacancies at HSBC.

We value your courage.
Because we're just as courageous.

At HSBC we encourage all our employees to have the courage to challenge the status quo. Because it's often the people who are bold enough to share and voice their opinions who can change the world for the better.

That's why we're looking for people who think, see and do things differently and who can represent and relate to our diverse global customer base. Regardless of your degree discipline, we have a variety of internship and graduate opportunities across our four global business areas:

- Commercial Banking
- Global Banking and Markets
- Retail Banking and Wealth Management
- Global Private Banking

So, if you're a courageous mind wanting a career in banking visit hsbc.com/earlycareers

IBM

ibm.biz/uk-graduates

facebook.com/IBMcareersUKI **f**

linkedin.com/company/IBM **in**   twitter.com/IBMcareersUKI **y**

instagram.com/IBM **O**   youtube.com/IBM **►**

GRADUATE VACANCIES IN 2019

CONSULTING

TECHNOLOGY

NUMBER OF VACANCIES
150+ graduate jobs

LOCATIONS OF VACANCIES

IBM are experts in nearly every technical, scientific and business field. IBM are citizens of, and apply their expertise in, more than 170 countries, with over 380,000 employees worldwide. Since it was founded in 1911, IBM have moved from producing hardware to being at the forefront of artificial intelligence.

STARTING SALARY FOR 2019
£30,000-32,000

IBM's Graduate Scheme will give successful applicants everything they need to build the kind of career they want. With graduate salaries starting at £30k, a flexible benefits package and opportunities in Business, Consulting, Technology & Design, they will work on challenging projects, have real responsibility and have access to world-class opportunities. They'll be able to collaborate with people who are open-minded and excited about the same things as they are.

IBM are looking for enthusiastic, driven and innovative individuals from any degree background. IBM's most successful graduates share a distinct set of characteristics. These begin with energy and creativity, along with a clear focus on delivering exceptional customer service. IBM look for eight specific competencies during the application process: Adaptability, Communication, Client Focus, Creative Problem Solving, Teamwork, Passion for IBM and Taking Ownership.

Skills development is key to an IBMer's success. To help successful applicants on their journey of discovery, IBM's cognitive cloud-based learning platform learns about them and creates a personalised learning plan. To further enhance their Professional Development, there are opportunities for coaching and mentoring, and these graduates will even get a dedicated manager. They will then have the opportunity to apply their knowledge in a commercial environment, via 'on-the-job training', adding value to IBM and its clients.

UNIVERSITY VISITS IN 2018-19
BIRMINGHAM, LEEDS, LOUGHBOROUGH, MANCHESTER, NEWCASTLE, SOUTHAMPTON, SURREY, WARWICK
Please check with your university careers service for full details of local events.

MINIMUM ENTRY REQUIREMENTS
2.1 Degree

APPLICATION DEADLINE
Varies by function

FURTHER INFORMATION
www.Top100GraduateEmployers.com
Register now for the latest news, campus events, work experience and graduate vacancies at IBM.

DO YOUR BEST WORK EVER.

What can you do at IBM?

Our Graduate scheme will give you everything you need to build the kind of career you want. You will work on challenging projects, have real responsibility and have access to world class opportunities. With the support of 380,000 colleagues worldwide, you'll gain the experience, skills and contacts you need to help us solve some of our client's toughest challenges.

ibm.biz/uk-graduates

Ellie
Joined IBM 2014

IBMCareersUKI

IBMCareersUKI

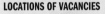
(IM) irwinmitchell
solicitors

Irwin Mitchell is the UK's largest full service law firm. Founded in 1912, they have a strong national presence, covering corporate law, personal injury and private wealth. The 'expert hand, human touch' philosophy resonates throughout the firm, with over one million clients helped through their history.

As a national firm, there are 10 different locations where Irwin Mitchell offer training contracts. There is a choice of either the Business Legal Services (BLS) or Personal Legal Services (PLS) stream. Within business legal services, expect seat rotations in areas such as banking & finance, insolvency and employment. Personal legal services contains both the personal injury seats, such as serious injury and medical negligence, but also private wealth seats, in areas such as will, trust and estate disputes, court of protection and family law.

Trainees will complete four training seats over their two years, each with a high level of partner and senior associate interaction, giving them the chance to gain a diverse set of experiences whilst learning and working with some of the most highly regarded solicitors and legal minds in the UK. At Irwin Mitchell, the trainees are passionate, creatively minded, have high emotional intelligence and possess strong analytical and problem-solving skills.

A large number of training contracts are offered to those who have completed a legal work placement, which is a great way to get a real insight into what life is actually like at the firm. They also offer a first year programme, which gives candidates an earlier opportunity to gain an insight into both the PLS and BLS streams at the firm.

Irwin Mitchell seek to provide opportunities to those who have a passion for the law and who want to make a positive difference to both society and their future careers.

GRADUATE VACANCIES IN 2019
LAW

NUMBER OF VACANCIES
50 graduate jobs
For training contracts starting in 2021.

LOCATIONS OF VACANCIES

STARTING SALARY FOR 2019
£25,000-£36,000

UNIVERSITY VISITS IN 2018-19
BIRMINGHAM, BRISTOL, CAMBRIDGE, CARDIFF, DURHAM, EXETER, LEEDS, LIVERPOOL, MANCHESTER, NEWCASTLE, NOTTINGHAM, SHEFFIELD, SOUTHAMPTON, SUSSEX, WARWICK, YORK
Please check with your university careers service for full details of local events.

APPLICATION DEADLINE
13th January 2019

FURTHER INFORMATION
www.Top100GraduateEmployers.com
Register now for the latest news, campus events, work experience and graduate vacancies at Irwin Mitchell.

A tech-driven revolution is transforming the industry, and Jaguar Land Rover are on a journey to lead that transformation: a journey that requires people who can see the opportunity in a challenge. So, finding the next generation of innovators – bright and passionate people – is crucial.

Jaguar Land Rover is a British technology company with a global reach, and, as the UK's largest car manufacturer, it is now producing and selling more cars than at any time in its history. But there are still ambitious plans for more profitable, sustainable growth. So to keep that momentum going, any new recruits need a creative and commercially focused approach to their work. Bring that, and Jaguar Land Rover has all the opportunities and rewards that graduates want and need.

But the opportunities do not stop there. The graduate scheme has been designed to be as inspiring as the vehicles that successful applicants will help to design, engineer and sell. As the UK's largest investor in research and innovation, education is a critical part of Jaguar Land Rover's business strategy and ambition. It aims to hire the best talent and, then, through a lifelong education and training programmes, to help those people fulfil their potential. These opportunities lie right across the business, from engineering, manufacturing and software design to commercial and business areas.

As would be expected from two of the world's most revered brands, a range of rewards and benefits await those who have the initiative, vision and drive to contribute to the organisation's global success – including a competitive salary, joining bonus, pension scheme and discount car purchase scheme. There is also the opportunity to study for a chartered qualification as part of the programme.

All this, and more, makes Jaguar Land Rover an enviable place for graduates to start their journey.

IMAGINE WHAT'S POSSIBLE.
SEE B≡YOND

Embrace a future of brand new possibilities. Now's the time to be part of a truly transformational journey – both for our business and your career.

As we surge forwards with our plans for autonomous and connected vehicles, electrification and game-changing technology, we've opened up a world of new challenges, ideas and opportunities. If you want to have the chance to think beyond what's gone before and make a difference, this is it.

jaguarlandrovercareers.com

Johnson&Johnson

www.jnjuniversityrecruitment.com

studentcareers@its.jnj.com

GRADUATE VACANCIES IN 2019
ENGINEERING
FINANCE
MARKETING
RESEARCH & DEVELOPMENT
SALES

NUMBER OF VACANCIES
25-30 graduate jobs

LOCATIONS OF VACANCIES

STARTING SALARY FOR 2019
£Competitive

UNIVERSITY VISITS IN 2018-19
ASTON, BATH, EXETER, LANCASTER,
LEEDS, LOUGHBOROUGH, NEWCASTLE,
READING, SHEFFIELD
*Please check with your university careers
service for full details of local events.*

MINIMUM ENTRY REQUIREMENTS
2.1 Degree

APPLICATION DEADLINE
Varies by function

FURTHER INFORMATION
www.Top100GraduateEmployers.com
*Register now for the latest news, campus
events, work experience and graduate
vacancies at Johnson & Johnson.*

'Caring for the world, one person at a time' is a principle that unites the people of J&J. J&J embraces research and science – bringing innovative ideas, products and services to advance the health and wellbeing of people. With a team of 134,000 people in 60 countries, J&J can offer unparalleled opportunities.

Johnson & Johnson's graduate opportunities span many areas of the business – from sales and marketing to engineering and finance – and they are looking for talented individuals to take on full-time roles after graduation. The company offers structured on-the-job learning and leadership development opportunities, working alongside managers who are committed to developing the next generation of leaders within their global organisation.

The Consumer Health Care group work with leading products in a broad range of categories, including skin care, baby care, beauty, over-the-counter medicines, oral care and VisionCare. Their products connect clinically proven consumer insights – bringing science to the art of healthy living.

The Medical Devices group markets products for women's health, surgical oncology, orthopaedics, traditional and minimally invasive surgeries, and wound management. This comprehensive care group also includes diagnostic procedures and interventional vascular technologies.

The Pharmaceutical group (Janssen) produce and market over 100 medicines in areas of unmet medical need in such areas as cardiovascular & metabolic diseases, immunology, infectious diseases & vaccines, neuroscience and oncology.

J&J know that every invention and every breakthrough they've brought to human health and wellbeing has been powered by their people. By joining a company that has been involved in defining the future of healthcare for the past 132 years, graduates will be offered career opportunities as limitless as the lives they will touch.

Discover opportunities to create a lasting impact.

Johnson&Johnson

FAMILY OF COMPANIES

It's more than a job. It's a calling. To those who are driven to do something remarkable. Rare. These are the people we want on our team. People that bring creativity, expertise, and passion to their work. And these are the ones we empower every day to drive their dynamic careers forward across more than 250 leading businesses in consumer products, pharmaceuticals and medical technology.

The world needs you. Let's get started.

LEARN MORE AT
CAREERS.JNJ.COM

J.P.Morgan

facebook.com/JPMorganChase f
linkedin.com/company/J-P-Morgan in   twitter.com/JPMorgan y
instagram.com/JPMorgan ⊙   youtube.com/JPMorgan ▶

GRADUATE VACANCIES IN 2019

FINANCE
GENERAL MANAGEMENT
HUMAN RESOURCES
INVESTMENT BANKING
RESEARCH & DEVELOPMENT
SALES
TECHNOLOGY

NUMBER OF VACANCIES
400+ graduate jobs

LOCATIONS OF VACANCIES

Vacancies also available in Europe, the USA, Asia, and elsewhere in the world.

J.P. Morgan are committed to helping businesses and markets grow and develop in more than 100 countries. Over the last 200 years, they have evolved to meet the complex financial needs of some of the world's largest companies, as well as many of the smaller businesses driving industry change.

J.P. Morgan work hard to do the right thing for their clients, shareholders and the firm every day. Joining the firm means learning from experts in a supportive and collaborative team environment where successful applicants will be supported to make an immediate impact from the start.

They want to see applicants' creativity, communications skills and drive. Whilst academic achievements are important, they're also looking for individuality and passion, as demonstrated by extra curricular activities. J.P. Morgan invest in helping graduates fulfil their potential as they build their career at the firm.

Internship and graduate positions are available firmwide, so applicants are encouraged to learn as much as possible about the different business areas and roles. J.P. Morgan also offer pre-internship programs, such as Spring Week, which provide insight into the finance industry and their programs. They often hire directly from these opportunities – giving successful applicants early exposure to the firm and how they do business.

The different lines of business they hire into are: Asset Management, Global Finance & Business Management, Global Risk Management, Global Treasury Management, Human Resources, Investment Banking, Markets, Quantitative Research, Technology, and Wealth Management.

Working with a team committed to doing their best, earning the trust of their clients, and encouraging employees to fulfil their potential. That's what it means to be part of J.P. Morgan.

STARTING SALARY FOR 2019
£Competitive

UNIVERSITY VISITS IN 2018-19
BATH, CAMBRIDGE, EDINBURGH, EXETER, GLASGOW, IMPERIAL COLLEGE LONDON, LONDON SCHOOL OF ECONOMICS, OXFORD, SOUTHAMPTON, ST ANDREWS, STRATHCLYDE, UNIVERSITY COLLEGE LONDON, WARWICK
Please check with your university careers service for full details of local events.

MINIMUM ENTRY REQUIREMENTS
2.1 Degree

APPLICATION DEADLINE
25th November 2018

FURTHER INFORMATION
www.Top100GraduateEmployers.com
Register now for the latest news, campus events, work experience and graduate vacancies at J.P. Morgan.

J.P.Morgan

All minds wanted. Especially yours.

Our programs open on 1 September

We're looking for students from all majors and backgrounds to join our diverse, global team.

As a top employer in financial services, J.P. Morgan does much more than manage money. We create unexpected solutions to help individuals, companies, institutions and governments tackle financial and business challenges. That's why we need diverse minds like yours.

Here, you'll have more chances to continuously innovate, learn and make a positive impact for our clients, customers and communities. We offer internships in over 20 different business areas with more than 10 Early Insight Programs to introduce you to the industry and our company.

To see how you can join our collaborative team, visit jpmorgan.com/careers to learn more about our programs and upcoming on-campus and virtual events.

We look forward to meeting you.

KPMG in the UK is part of a global network of firms offering Audit, Tax & Pensions, Consulting, Deal Advisory and Technology services. KPMG works shoulder-to-shoulder with clients to help them solve some of the most complex business challenges, applying insight, expertise and new technologies.

Graduate and undergraduate trainees at KPMG have the opportunity to join a people-led organisation, be part an inspiring team and work with some of the brightest minds in business – all while embracing technologies of the future. The firm works across the broadest range of clients and sectors, from the biggest multinationals through to the most innovative start-ups. Focused on delivering the highest quality, the firm has a simple vision: to be the clear choice for its clients, its people, and the communities it works in.

KPMG colleagues come from all sorts of degree disciplines and universities, bringing their own unique perspectives and backgrounds, but sharing a natural curiosity, and a desire to work together to explore new ideas, inspire change and deliver real results for clients.

The firm's innovative Launch Pad assessment, at the final stage of the process, ensures successful candidates receive a job offer in just two working days. Right from the start, graduate and undergraduate trainees will gain exposure to a variety of interesting projects and clients, whilst receiving the support they need to succeed. Equally, through exceptional training, mentoring, professional qualifications and initiatives that give back to communities, trainees will be encouraged to develop a rewarding career within the firm.

Life at KPMG means being part of a fast-moving, intellectually challenging and supportive community, where graduates and undergraduates are empowered to learn, grow and thrive.

GRADUATE VACANCIES IN 2019

ACCOUNTANCY

CONSULTING

FINANCE

GENERAL MANAGEMENT

HUMAN RESOURCES

TECHNOLOGY

NUMBER OF VACANCIES
Around 1,200 graduate jobs

LOCATIONS OF VACANCIES

STARTING SALARY FOR 2019
£Competitive
Plus a great range of benefits – see website for details.

UNIVERSITY VISITS IN 2018-19
ABERDEEN, ASTON, BIRMINGHAM, BRISTOL, CAMBRIDGE, CARDIFF, CITY, EXETER, GLASGOW, HERIOT-WATT, IMPERIAL COLLEGE LONDON, KING'S COLLEGE LONDON, LANCASTER, LEEDS, LEICESTER, LIVERPOOL, LONDON SCHOOL OF ECONOMICS, MANCHESTER, NEWCASTLE, NOTTINGHAM TRENT, PLYMOUTH, QUEEN MARY LONDON, READING, ROYAL HOLLOWAY, SHEFFIELD, SOUTHAMPTON, STRATHCLYDE, SURREY, UNIVERSITY COLLEGE LONDON, WARWICK
Please check with your university careers service for full details of local events.

MINIMUM ENTRY REQUIREMENTS
2.1 Degree
120 UCAS points
300 UCAS points for those who passed exams before 2017.
KPMG takes a range of factors into account, and offers places based on a rounded view – see website for details.

APPLICATION DEADLINE
Year-round recruitment
Early application advised.

FURTHER INFORMATION
www.Top100GraduateEmployers.com
Register now for the latest news, campus events, work experience and graduate vacancies at KPMG.

The big picture is all about small detail.

Graduate and undergraduate opportunities

At KPMG in the UK, you can work side-by-side with some of the brightest minds in business, helping us to solve our clients' most complex challenges. Guided by a natural curiosity, you'll focus on the details to deliver quality results for our people, clients and communities.

Whichever programme you choose, across Audit, Consultancy, Technology, Tax, Deal Advisory or Business Services, you'll gain exposure to a variety of clients and projects – and be a part of our vibrant community. At the same time, we'll support you to learn every day, inspire you to grow and, ultimately, develop an incredibly rewarding career.

kpmgcareers.co.uk

Anticipate tomorrow. Deliver today.

L'ORÉAL

Think 34 iconic international brands, selling in 130 countries. Think Ralph Lauren. Think Diesel. Think Garnier. Think Urban Decay. And now, think about the change graduates can bring, when they work for the world's number one cosmetics group. It's time to lead the change at L'Oréal.

At the forefront of a booming £10 billion industry in the UK, L'Oréal continues to invent and revolutionise. In 2017, the group registered a stunning 498 patents for newly invented products and formulae. That constant creativity and determined exploration is what makes L'Oréal a global success symbol.

So when it comes to their Management Trainee Programme, L'Oréal need more than just graduates. They need inventors, explorers, leaders, and entrepreneurs. Graduates who know that when it comes to success, inspirational talent and hard work go hand in hand. Graduates who know that they should never stop exploring.

L'Oréal believe in developing their talent from the ground up, providing their employees with the opportunity to grow within the company and build a career with them. This is why 100% of their Management Trainee roles are filled with individuals from their Apprenticeships, Internships and Spring Insight Programmes, creating a well-rounded junior talent journey at L'Oréal.

On the Management Trainee Programme, graduates work in functions across the business, gaining a sense of life at L'Oréal. With three different rotations in their chosen stream, they're free to develop their talent and discover new possibilities. With on-the-job training and their own HR sponsor, graduates will progress into operational roles within as little as 18 months. They'll take on real responsibility, and make a palpable contribution to an international success story. From the start, they'll shape their own career; leading the change with L'Oréal.

GRADUATE VACANCIES IN 2019
FINANCE
LOGISTICS
MARKETING
SALES

NUMBER OF VACANCIES
28 graduate jobs

LOCATIONS OF VACANCIES

STARTING SALARY FOR 2019
£30,000

UNIVERSITY VISITS IN 2018-19
ASTON, BATH, BIRMINGHAM, CARDIFF, DURHAM, EXETER, LANCASTER, LIVERPOOL, MANCHESTER, NEWCASTLE, NOTTINGHAM, NOTTINGHAM TRENT, READING, SHEFFIELD, SOUTHAMPTON, SWANSEA, WARWICK, YORK
Please check with your university careers service for full details of local events.

APPLICATION DEADLINE
Year-round recruitment

FURTHER INFORMATION
www.Top100GraduateEmployers.com
Register now for the latest news, campus events, work experience and graduate vacancies at L'Oréal.

L'ORÉAL

#wearelоreal
#leadthechange

CAREERS.LOREAL.COM

Lidl are proud pioneers in the world of retail. With over 700 stores, 12 warehouses and 20,000 employees in the UK alone, they're undoubtedly an established retailer. But it doesn't stop there. With their recent expansion into the US and ambitious plans for UK growth, they don't like to stand still.

Continually challenging and changing the world of grocery retail, Lidl want to make their stores, products and shopping experience better than ever. Lidl is committed to driving various responsibility programmes, including charity partnership, food redistribution and recycling schemes.

Lidl is a brave and dynamic business, and that's exactly what they're looking for in their graduates. They're not looking for one type of person, or polished abilities and substantial experience. They're looking for ambitious, committed people with personality and potential. Potential to become one of Lidl's future leaders.

Lidl's structured graduate programmes, across all areas of the business, are designed to develop students and graduates quickly by challenging them to reach their potential. Experiences span Lidl's stores, warehouses and regional offices, giving graduates the best possible exposure to the key areas of the business along with a range of opportunities to develop their skills and leadership expertise.

Throughout each individual role, graduates will receive soft skills and operational development through a carefully structured training plan, giving them a clear development path to follow. These graduates learn from the best managers and develop their operational and management abilities from day one – and progression from there is down to the individual.

Lidl is an award-winning employer: graduates benefit from competitive salaries, fast-tracked development and stimulating work with world-class teams. Join Lidl now.

GRADUATE VACANCIES IN 2019
GENERAL MANAGEMENT
LOGISTICS
SALES

NUMBER OF VACANCIES
60 graduate jobs

LOCATIONS OF VACANCIES

STARTING SALARY FOR 2019
£36,540

UNIVERSITY VISITS IN 2018-19
ASTON, BATH, BIRMINGHAM, BRADFORD, BRISTOL, CARDIFF, DURHAM, EDINBURGH, EXETER, GLASGOW, IMPERIAL COLLEGE LONDON, KING'S COLLEGE LONDON, LANCASTER, LEEDS, LEICESTER, LIVERPOOL, LOUGHBOROUGH, NEWCASTLE, NOTTINGHAM, NOTTINGHAM TRENT, OXFORD, READING, SOUTHAMPTON, STIRLING, STRATHCLYDE, SURREY, SUSSEX, SWANSEA, UNIVERSITY COLLEGE LONDON, WARWICK
Please check with your university careers service for full details of local events.

MINIMUM ENTRY REQUIREMENTS
2.2 Degree

APPLICATION DEADLINE
Late December 2018

FURTHER INFORMATION
www.Top100GraduateEmployers.com
Register now for the latest news, campus events, work experience and graduate vacancies at Lidl.

CHOOSE YOUR FUTURE.

Our rotational graduate programmes give huge variety, all-rounder experience and the skills to grow a career that's going places.

BRING YOUR BEST. WE'LL DO THE REST.

lidlgraduatecareers.co.uk

Linklaters

From a shifting geopolitical landscape to the exponential growth in FinTech, this is a time of unprecedented change. Linklaters is ready. They go further to support clients, with market-leading legal insight and innovation. And they go further for each other, too.

When people join Linklaters, they find colleagues they want to work with. Inspiring, personable professionals who are generous with their time and always happy to help. Because, to be best in class, Linklaters looks for open minded, team-spirited individuals who will collaborate – and innovate – to deliver the smartest solutions for clients. Linklaters recruits candidates from a range of different backgrounds and disciplines, not just law. Why? Because those candidates bring with them a set of unique skills and perspectives that can help to challenge conventional thinking and inspire different approaches to client problems.

All Linklaters trainees benefit from pioneering learning and development opportunities, and an inclusive working culture that encourages them to fulfil their potential. Non-law graduates can take a one-year conversion course, the Graduate Diploma in Law. And all graduates complete the bespoke, accelerated Legal Practice Course before starting training contracts.

Then, over two years, trainees take four six-month seats (placements) in different practice areas and sometimes abroad. They work on high-profile deals across a global network of 30 offices, and gain the knowledge they need to qualify. And throughout their career, they enjoy the advantage of world-class training, courtesy of the Linklaters Law & Business School.

With their uniquely future-focused culture and high-profile, global opportunities, Linklaters provides the ideal preparation for a rewarding career, no matter what the future holds. Great change is here. Get ready.

GRADUATE VACANCIES IN 2019

LAW

NUMBER OF VACANCIES

100 graduate jobs

For training contracts starting in 2021.

LOCATIONS OF VACANCIES

STARTING SALARY FOR 2019

£44,000

UNIVERSITY VISITS IN 2018-19

BELFAST, BIRMINGHAM, BRISTOL, CAMBRIDGE, TRINITY COLLEGE DUBLIN, UNIVERSITY COLLEGE DUBLIN, DURHAM, EDINBURGH, EXETER, GLASGOW, KING'S COLLEGE LONDON, LEEDS, LEICESTER, LONDON SCHOOL OF ECONOMICS, MANCHESTER, NOTTINGHAM, OXFORD, QUEEN MARY LONDON, SHEFFIELD, SOUTHAMPTON, ST ANDREWS, UNIVERSITY COLLEGE LONDON, WARWICK, YORK

Please check with your university careers service for full details of local events.

MINIMUM ENTRY REQUIREMENTS

2.1 Degree

Relevant degree required for some roles.

APPLICATION DEADLINE

8th January 2019

FURTHER INFORMATION

www.Top100GraduateEmployers.com

Register now for the latest news, campus events, work experience and graduate vacancies at Linklaters.

Great change is here.

Linklaters

Are you ready?

From a shifting geopolitical landscape
to the exponential growth in FinTech,
this is a time of unprecedented change.

At Linklaters, we're ready. Our people
go further to support our clients,
with market-leading legal insight and
innovation. And we go further for each
other, too. We're people you want to work
with, generous with our time and ready
to help. So no matter what the future
holds, with us you'll be one step ahead.
Great change is here. Get ready.

Find out more at careers.linklaters.com

LLOYD'S

NUMBER OF VACANCIES
10 graduate jobs

LOCATIONS OF VACANCIES

Lloyd's is the foundation of the insurance industry and the future of it. Led by expert underwriters and brokers who cover more than 200 territories across the world, the Lloyd's market develops the complex insurance needed to empower human progress.

At Lloyd's, graduates help to make new endeavours possible, from space tourism to huge, groundbreaking events. They safeguard the world against risks from cyber terrorism to climate change. Above all, they'll help strengthen the resilience of local communities and drive global economic growth.

Lloyd's 24-month graduate schemes fall into two categories: functional schemes – including HR, IT, Finance and Marketing – and the Insurance scheme.

The Insurance scheme is the first graduate programme in the industry to be accredited by the Chartered Insurance Institute. On it, graduates will complete four different placements across the corporation and the market, giving them a 360° perspective of the specialist insurance industry. Whichever route is chosen, one thing's certain: graduates will gain a wealth of experience and benefit from comprehensive training. On the Insurance Graduate Scheme, graduates will gain the internationally recognised ACII qualification, while those on the functional schemes will work towards relevant postgraduate qualifications.

And all the while, exceptional employee benefits are on offer. These include not just a pension scheme, a competitive salary and 25 days' holiday a year, but also private medical insurance and a flexible benefits package.

With Lloyd's, graduates gain not just experience, technical training and qualifications, but also valuable soft skills like leadership and communication. In short, as they help to empower human progress, they will find that they progress fast too.

STARTING SALARY FOR 2019
£Competitive

UNIVERSITY VISITS IN 2018-19
Please check with your university careers service for full details of local events.

MINIMUM ENTRY REQUIREMENTS
2.2 Degree

APPLICATION DEADLINE
November 2018

FURTHER INFORMATION
www.Top100GraduateEmployers.com
*Register now for the latest news, campus events, work experience and graduate vacancies at **Lloyd's**.*

LLOYD'S

Space tourism.
Get on board.

Space tourism could soon become a reality. And when pioneering organisations need cover for their passengers, they know exactly where to come. At Lloyd's, we develop the complex insurance needed to empower human progress everywhere, whether people are exploring the final frontier, or mitigating the risks of climate change.

As a graduate here, you can help safeguard the future around the world, strengthening the resilience of local communities and driving economic growth. Choose from either our specialist functional schemes, or our rotational Insurance scheme. On the functional schemes you'll be able to achieve a relevant post-graduate qualification, while on the Insurance scheme, you'll gain the full ACII qualification – on the first graduate programme in the industry to be accredited by the CII. Meaning your progress will be assured too.

Empower human progress

www.lloyds.com/graduates

GRADUATE VACANCIES IN 2019

- ACCOUNTANCY
- CONSULTING
- ENGINEERING
- FINANCE
- GENERAL MANAGEMENT
- INVESTMENT BANKING
- MARKETING
- SALES
- TECHNOLOGY

NUMBER OF VACANCIES
250+ graduate jobs

LOCATIONS OF VACANCIES

STARTING SALARY FOR 2019
£Competitive

UNIVERSITY VISITS IN 2018-19
ASTON, BATH, BIRMINGHAM, BRISTOL, CAMBRIDGE, CARDIFF, DURHAM, EAST ANGLIA, EDINBURGH, EXETER, GLASGOW, HERIOT-WATT, IMPERIAL COLLEGE LONDON, KING'S COLLEGE LONDON, LEEDS, LONDON SCHOOL OF ECONOMICS, LOUGHBOROUGH, MANCHESTER, NOTTINGHAM, OXFORD, QUEEN MARY LONDON, SOUTHAMPTON, ST ANDREWS, STRATHCLYDE, SURREY, UNIVERSITY COLLEGE LONDON, WARWICK, YORK
Please check with your university careers service for full details of local events.

MINIMUM ENTRY REQUIREMENTS
2.2 Degree
Relevant degree required for some roles.

APPLICATION DEADLINE
31st December 2018
Early application advised.

FURTHER INFORMATION
www.Top100GraduateEmployers.com
Register now for the latest news, campus events, work experience and graduate vacancies at Lloyds Banking Group.

As the UK's largest retail and digital bank, with over 30 million customers, Lloyds Banking Group offers its employees a wide range of opportunities to make a real impact, through main brands like Lloyds Bank, Halifax, Scottish Widows and Bank of Scotland.

As the Group helps redefine financial services for the digital age, there is a need for a broader range of skills and experiences than ever before – and this means graduates don't necessarily need a business or finance degree to embark on a banking career. Instead, Lloyds Banking Group is looking for passionate, inquisitive graduates who can bring their unique perspective to help drive the business forward. Whether it's building relationships with clients or developing the next generation of digital banking, there is a wide range of opportunities to help the Group build the bank of the future and Help Britain Prosper.

Graduates who share Lloyds Banking Group's vision will be supported and empowered to develop themselves and their career. The graduate and internship opportunities include everything from leading technological innovation, shaping strategy and translating complex financial data, to helping customers, and local and global business clients – all of which will help them learn the basics of the organisation. Through it all, graduates will receive real responsibilities and development opportunities through their roles – all with the support of their mentors and buddies.

Best of all, Lloyds Banking Group offers a friendly working environment where everyone can feel free to be themselves and to openly share their ideas – because people do their best work when they feel valued and are happy in their working environment.

Discover careers with real impact at Lloyds Banking Group.

"THERE ARE SO MANY OPPORTUNITIES HERE. YOU JUST HAVE TO PUT YOURSELF FORWARD."

FELICITY, COMMERCIAL BANKING GRADUATE

As a graduate, Felicity was amazed by the amount of real opportunities available to her, from defining strategy to helping UK businesses thrive, as well as the support she received from her colleagues and mentors. Discover what a Lloyds Banking Group Graduate Programme can offer you, and join us in our vision to help Britain prosper.

DISCOVER CAREERS WITH REAL IMPACT
lloydsbankinggrouptalent.com

8
GRADUATE PROGRAMMES

30+
MILLION CUSTOMERS

UK's
BIGGEST DIGITAL BANK

M&S

EST. 1884

GRADUATE VACANCIES IN 2019

- FINANCE
- GENERAL MANAGEMENT
- HUMAN RESOURCES
- LOGISTICS
- MARKETING
- PROPERTY
- PURCHASING
- RESEARCH & DEVELOPMENT
- RETAILING

NUMBER OF VACANCIES
200 graduate jobs

LOCATIONS OF VACANCIES

M&S always strives for perfection. This passion has led them to create products millions of people love. But they're not standing still. Far from it. From sustainable packaging to ethical supply chains, they're thinking beyond the bottom line – to make a positive impact on communities and the planet.

M&S is a retailer with clear ambitions that are built on the highest standards of integrity. But retail as an industry is becoming tougher and more competitive than ever before, so M&S is preparing for the future by transforming its business, becoming more agile in their mindset and changing their culture. M&S is also adopting a digital-first strategy and embracing smarter working.

For ambitious graduates, this far-reaching transformation means there has never been a more exciting time to join M&S. Everyone who joins will have the opportunity to drive innovation, thinking of new ways to be more responsive to customers, improve performance and grow the business.

They offer a range of specialised programmes including Retail, Buying & Merchandising, Design, Supply Chain and Food Technology. Each offers unique opportunities to learn on the job and build vital skills plus exposure to leadership.

There's also an Enterprise scheme available to the most motivated, entrepreneurial candidates. Graduates on this scheme will benefit from mentoring by top industry experts while developing detailed sector knowledge. It's perfect for those who are proactive and show real leadership potential.

Whichever path they take, graduates will enjoy a competitive salary, great benefits and real opportunities to grow. They'll also be encouraged to demonstrate their ability to put customers at the heart of everything, push the boundaries and think about the bigger picture.

STARTING SALARY FOR 2019
£Competitive

UNIVERSITY VISITS IN 2018-19
ASTON, BIRMINGHAM, BRISTOL, CARDIFF, EAST ANGLIA, EDINBURGH, GLASGOW, LEEDS, LOUGHBOROUGH, MANCHESTER, NORTHUMBRIA, ROYAL HOLLOWAY, UNIVERSITY COLLEGE LONDON, YORK
Please check with your university careers service for full details of local events.

APPLICATION DEADLINE
Mid December 2018

FURTHER INFORMATION
www.Top100GraduateEmployers.com
Register now for the latest news, campus events, work experience and graduate vacancies at M&S.

THE
FUTURE
NEEDS
INNOVATION

And comfortable underpants too, of course

We wouldn't be M&S if we didn't strive for better. Because the future we're headed towards doesn't just need properly fitting bras. Or Colin the Caterpillars. Or underpants you can live in. The future needs well-stocked oceans, ethical supply chains, and communities that stick together. We're setting bolder goals, and we're giving the brightest graduates the space to achieve them. There's never been a more exciting time to be part of M&S. Join us, and you'll not only be shaping the future of our business, you'll be empowering customers to make a positive impact on their communities, and the planet. Let's push forward, together.
Find out more at: **www.marksandspencergrads.com**

THE FUTURE *NEEDS YOU*

mars.co.uk/graduates

facebook.com/MarsGlobalCareers

linkedin.com/company/Mars   twitter.com/MarsGradsUK

instagram.com/Mars.UK   youtube.com/Mars

think. bigger.

GRADUATE VACANCIES IN 2019

ACCOUNTANCY

ENGINEERING

FINANCE

GENERAL MANAGEMENT

HUMAN RESOURCES

LOGISTICS

MARKETING

PURCHASING

RESEARCH & DEVELOPMENT

SALES

TECHNOLOGY

NUMBER OF VACANCIES
25-30 graduate jobs

LOCATIONS OF VACANCIES

Vacancies also available in Europe.

STARTING SALARY FOR 2019
£30,000-£32,000
Plus a £2,000 joining bonus.

UNIVERSITY VISITS IN 2018-19
BATH, BIRMINGHAM, CAMBRIDGE,
DURHAM, EXETER, LANCASTER, LEEDS,
NOTTINGHAM, OXFORD, WARWICK
*Please check with your university careers
service for full details of local events.*

MINIMUM ENTRY REQUIREMENTS
2.1 Degree
Relevant degree required for some roles.

APPLICATION DEADLINE
31st December 2018

FURTHER INFORMATION
www.Top100GraduateEmployers.com
*Register now for the latest news, campus
events, work experience and graduate
vacancies at Mars.*

Think Maltesers®, M&Ms®, Uncle Ben's®, Pedigree®, Whiskas®, Extra® and Orbit®, some of the nation's best-loved and well-known brands. Think the world's third-largest food company with international operations across the world. Know what makes Mars special? Think again.

Sure, Mars is one of the world's leading food companies, but it's more like a community than a corporate – because it's still a private, family-owned business built up of a Mars family of associates. Associates at Mars are united and guided by The Five Principles – Quality, Responsibility, Mutuality, Efficiency and Freedom. These are key to the culture and help associates to make business decisions they are proud of.

The culture at Mars is relationship-driven – and it's how these relationships are built that's most important. Collaborating with others is key to getting things done. Mars encourages open communication as this builds relationships of trust and respect.

Mars want to stretch and challenge associates every day to help them reach their full potential. So they take learning and development seriously – it makes good business sense for Mars to have people performing at the top of their game. With great managers, mentors, coaches and peers, graduates will be supported the whole way. And they will support other associates on their journey too.

At Mars, graduates are offered an unrivalled opportunity to make a difference in their roles from day one. Mars wants everything they do to matter – from the smallest thing to the biggest – and Mars wants their work to make a positive difference to customers, suppliers, associates and the world as a whole. Graduates will have endless support to develop both personally and professionally, creating a start to an exciting and fulfilling career.

The Journey starts here

Explore where our graduate programmes could take you.

For graduates that join us, we can promise you a journey of personal and professional discovery like no other.

You'll be joining one of the biggest family-owned organisations on the planet: 100,000 Associates in 80 countries around the world.

You'll be supported by line managers, mentors and colleagues who will encourage you to develop further and faster than you ever thought possible.

Your relationship building and confidence to lead will grow, as you will be placed in a real role with real responsibility from day one.

We're looking for individuals who can live and breathe our Five Principles: **Quality, Responsibility, Mutuality, Efficiency and Freedom.**

And in return, we offer unparalleled experiences to set you up as a future leader.

Visit **MARS.CO.UK/GRADUATES** to explore the accelerated development programmes we have to offer.

MARS | grow beyond

McDonald's is the biggest family restaurant business in the world and has been a part of the UK since 1974. It has over 1,270 restaurants employing over 120,000 people who work together to deliver great tasting food with service that its customers know and trust.

Training and developing people has been at the heart of the McDonald's business throughout its 44 years in the UK. Each year the company invests over £43 million in developing its people and providing opportunities for progression. Attracting, retaining and engaging the best people is key to their business. It has a proven track record of career progression and prospective managers can create a long-term career with one of the world's most recognised and successful brands.

A graduate job at McDonald's is focused on restaurant management; it involves overseeing the performance and development of an average of 80 employees and identifying ways in which to improve customer service, build sales and profitability. Following the training period, which can last up to six months, Trainee Managers are promoted to Assistant Managers and become part of the core restaurant management team. Successful Trainee Managers can, in future, progress to managing all aspects of a multi-million pound business – opportunities can then arise to progress to area management roles or secondments in support departments. Trainee Managers need to be logical thinkers, have a great attitude, and be committed to delivering a great customer experience.

Working for a progressive company has its perks, including a host of benefits such as a quarterly bonus scheme, six weeks holiday allowance, meal allowance, private healthcare and access to discounts at hundreds of retailers.

GRADUATE VACANCIES IN 2019
GENERAL MANAGEMENT

NUMBER OF VACANCIES
30 graduate jobs

LOCATIONS OF VACANCIES

STARTING SALARY FOR 2019
£22,000

UNIVERSITY VISITS IN 2018-19
Please check with your university careers service for full details of local events.

APPLICATION DEADLINE
Year-round recruitment

FURTHER INFORMATION
www.Top100GraduateEmployers.com
Register now for the latest news, campus events, work experience and graduate vacancies at **McDonald's**.

SETTING MYSELF UP FOR THE FUTURE

With McDonald's, I can.

Our Trainee Manager Programme is the first step to managing a £multi-million restaurant employing over 80 staff.

After six months of training and learning the basics, our Trainee Managers are promoted to Assistant Managers– but if you've got the drive and ambition, there's no limit to how far you can go.

To find out more about working and learning with us visit people.mcdonalds.co.uk

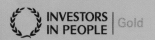

SECURITY SERVICE MI5

MI5 helps safeguard the UK against threats to national security including terrorism and espionage. It investigates suspect individuals and organisations to gather intelligence relating to security threats. MI5 also advises the critical national infrastructure on protective security measures.

Graduates from a range of backgrounds join MI5 for stimulating and rewarding careers, in a supportive environment, whilst enjoying a good work-life balance. Many graduates join the Intelligence Officer Development Programme, which is a structured 3-5 year programme designed to teach new joiners about MI5 investigations and give them the skills to run them. After completing one post of two years, or two posts of one year, in areas which teach aspects of investigative work, and subject to successful completion of a final assessment, graduates will then take up an investigative post as a fully trained Intelligence Officer.

MI5 also deals with vast amounts of data, and interpreting that data is vital to its intelligence work. The Intelligence and Data Analyst Development Programme is a structured two-year programme which prepares graduates to be part of this specialist career stream. It will take them from the basics through to the most advanced data analytical techniques. As they progress, they will work in different teams across the range of MI5's investigations using their analytical expertise.

MI5 also offers a structured Technology Graduate Development Programme, which gives graduates the experience, knowledge and skills they need to be an effective technology professional in the organisation's pioneering IT function.

Graduates who are looking for a rewarding career in corporate services can join MI5 as Business Enablers, where they can develop a breadth of experience undertaking corporate roles across a range of business areas, before having the opportunity to specialise in a particular area.

GRADUATE VACANCIES IN 2019
GENERAL MANAGEMENT
TECHNOLOGY

NUMBER OF VACANCIES
200+ graduate jobs

LOCATIONS OF VACANCIES

STARTING SALARY FOR 2019
£30,000+

UNIVERSITY VISITS IN 2018-19
Please check with your university careers service for full details of local events.

MINIMUM ENTRY REQUIREMENTS
2.2 Degree

APPLICATION DEADLINE
Varies by function

FURTHER INFORMATION
www.Top100GraduateEmployers.com
Register now for the latest news, campus events, work experience and graduate vacancies at MI5.

730 DAYS. DISCOVER HOW TO PROTECT 66 MILLION PEOPLE. NOW THAT'S INTELLIGENT.

INVESTIGATIONS

DIGITAL INTELLIGENCE

POLICY

HM Government

WARRANTRY

ANALYSIS

LEGAL

INTELLIGENCE OFFICER DEVELOPMENT PROGRAMME

Leading investigations is just part of what our Intelligence Officers do. In fact, there's a huge variety of specialisms that they focus on.

On our development programme, you'll learn about every area, from warrantry and policy, to analysis and digital intelligence.

From day one, you'll work on live operational projects, and over the course of two years you'll learn how each of these areas stops the threats our nation faces, and helps to keep the country safe.

To find out more, please visit www.mi5.gov.uk/careers

disability confident LEADER · Stonewall Acceptance without exception · SECURITY SERVICE MI5

Morgan Stanley

facebook.com/MorganStanley

graduaterecruitmenteurope@morganstanley.com

linkedin.com/company/Morgan-Stanley

twitter.com/MorganStanley

instagram.com/Morgan.Stanley

youtube.com/MgStnly

GRADUATE VACANCIES IN 2019

FINANCE

HUMAN RESOURCES

INVESTMENT BANKING

TECHNOLOGY

NUMBER OF VACANCIES
200+ graduate jobs

LOCATIONS OF VACANCIES

STARTING SALARY FOR 2019
£Competitive
Plus benefits and a discretionary bonus.

UNIVERSITY VISITS IN 2018-19
Please check with your university careers service for full details of local events.

MINIMUM ENTRY REQUIREMENTS
2.1 Degree

APPLICATION DEADLINE
Varies by function

FURTHER INFORMATION
www.Top100GraduateEmployers.com
*Register now for the latest news, campus events, work experience and graduate vacancies at **Morgan Stanley**.*

Morgan Stanley is one of the world's leading financial services firms. They generate, manage and distribute capital, helping businesses get the funds they need to develop innovative products and services that benefit millions. Their work is defined by the passion and dedication of their people, and their goals are achieved through hiring, training and rewarding the best possible talent.

At Morgan Stanley attitude is just as important as aptitude, and they want to work with and develop students and graduates who show integrity and commitment to their core values, who share their commitment to providing first-class client service, and who embrace change and innovation. Because the firm values a diversity of perspectives, it encourages people to be themselves and pursue their own interests.

There are numerous opportunities to learn and grow professionally and help put the power of capital to work. All of Morgan Stanley's programmes are designed to provide the knowledge and toolkit graduates need to develop quickly into an effective and successful professional in their chosen area. Training is not limited to the first weeks or months on the job, but continues throughout a graduate's career. Over time, they could become part of the next generation of leaders, and play a part in technological, scientific and cultural advancements that change the world forever.

Morgan Stanley believes that capital can work to benefit all. This success needs financial capital, but its foundation is intellectual capital. The talents and points of view of the diverse individuals working for them helps to build their legacy and shape their future. This is why Morgan Stanley accepts applicants from all degree disciplines who demonstrate academic excellence.

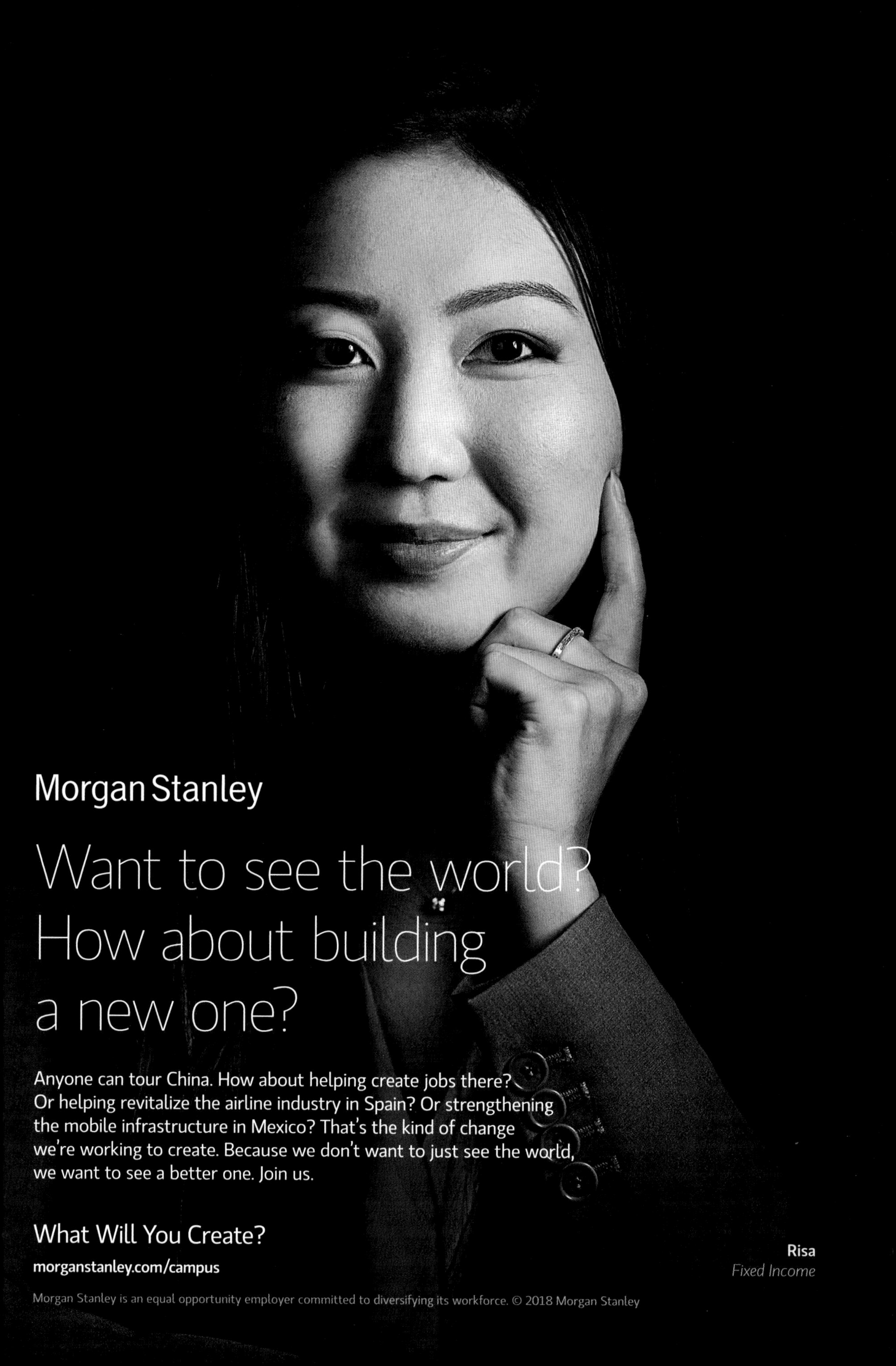

Morgan Stanley
Want to see the world?
How about building
a new one?
Anyone can tour China. How about helping create jobs there?
Or helping revitalize the airline industry in Spain? Or strengthening
the mobile infrastructure in Mexico? That's the kind of change
we're working to create. Because we don't want to just see the world,
we want to see a better one. Join us.
What Will You Create?
morganstanley.com/campus
Risa
Fixed Income
Morgan Stanley is an equal opportunity employer committed to diversifying its workforce. © 2018 Morgan Stanley

NetworkRail

Network Rail own and operate the railway infrastructure in England, Scotland and Wales. Their purpose is to create a better railway for a better Britain. It is the fastest growing and safest rail network in Europe, presenting an abundance of opportunities for ambitious and enthusiastic graduates.

Network Rail have £25bn earmarked to invest in landmark projects and initiatives as part of their Railway Upgrade Plan. They are already making history through some of the largest engineering projects in Europe: Crossrail, Birmingham New Street Station, London Bridge, HS2 and Thameslink.

Although Rail is a huge part of their business, they are also one of the largest land and property owners in Britain. They manage a portfolio that includes 18 of the biggest stations in Britain, the retail outlets inside them and the small businesses that live under their arches.

Network Rail are looking to invest in graduates who are committed to making a difference, to help transform Britain's rail infrastructure, transport network and economy for the 22nd century.

They have supported thousands of graduates through their diverse and challenging programmes. Graduates will have access to Westwood, their state-of-the-art training centre in Coventry, and six other training facilities.

There are two entry routes for graduates. Within Engineering there are three specific schemes: Civil, Electrical & Electronic, and Mechanical Engineering.

In Business Management, applicants can choose from the following schemes: Finance, General Management, Health, Safety and Environment, HR, IT & Business Services, Project Management, Property and Supply Chain Management.

There are also summer and year in industry placements available for those who would like to find out what it is like to work for Network Rail before graduation.

GRADUATE VACANCIES IN 2019

ENGINEERING

FINANCE

GENERAL MANAGEMENT

HUMAN RESOURCES

PROPERTY

NUMBER OF VACANCIES
Around 170 graduate jobs

LOCATIONS OF VACANCIES

STARTING SALARY FOR 2019
£26,500
Plus a £2,000 bonus and a 75% discount on season tickets (up to a maximum of £3,000).

UNIVERSITY VISITS IN 2018-19
BIRMINGHAM, BRUNEL, CARDIFF, DUNDEE, EDINBURGH, GLASGOW, LEEDS, LEICESTER, LIVERPOOL, LOUGHBOROUGH, MANCHESTER, NOTTINGHAM, QUEEN MARY, SHEFFIELD, STRATHCLYDE, UNIVERSITY COLLEGE
Please check with your university careers service for full details of local events.

MINIMUM ENTRY REQUIREMENTS
2.2 Degree

APPLICATION DEADLINE
December 2018

FURTHER INFORMATION
www.Top100GraduateEmployers.com
*Register now for the latest news, campus events, work experience and graduate vacancies at **Network Rail**.*

Newton isn't like most consultancies. Their business model is purposefully disruptive. They hire people with spirit, personality and bravery – and go to extraordinary lengths to build their skills and belief. They also offer unusual levels of responsibility.

In retail, rail, health and social care, fast moving consumer goods, aerospace and defence, Newton's consultants work hands-on with clients to transform organisations that set global agendas, businesses that lead their sectors and services that support entire communities. Fuelling it all is a belief that every organisation can be better. Their approach to solutions is guided by facts, driven by data, and inspired by the insights of every team member involved.

This is a consultancy that stresses the value of deep collaboration and places a premium on personal development. Consultants aren't tied to the office or submerged in paperwork. They're given the means and skills to work closely with client teams and other colleagues; to accelerate their own development from grass roots to management and beyond; and ultimately to get results that are not only sustainable but actually make a difference in the world.

When asked "Why Newton?", the top three reasons people give are: its vibrant culture and strong sense of fellowship; its 'get-stuck-right-in' working style; and its unmatched record of producing up to 50% improvement in six months for their clients, without capital expenditure. In fact, Newton has so much confidence in the quality of their consultants' solutions, they put their fee at risk to deliver guaranteed results.

Newton's philosophy is simple: they demand better – not just for their clients but for their people. It's a place where humility, creativity and versatility thrive. One where, if graduates don't limit themselves, nothing will limit them.

GRADUATE VACANCIES IN 2019
CONSULTING

NUMBER OF VACANCIES
100 graduate jobs

LOCATIONS OF VACANCIES

STARTING SALARY FOR 2019
£45,000-£50,000 package
Including a £5,000 car allowance.
Plus a sign-on bonus.

UNIVERSITY VISITS IN 2018-19
BATH, BRISTOL, CAMBRIDGE, DURHAM,
EXETER, IMPERIAL COLLEGE LONDON,
LONDON SCHOOL OF ECONOMICS,
MANCHESTER, OXFORD,
SOUTHAMPTON, WARWICK
Please check the Newton Europe website
for full details of local events.

MINIMUM ENTRY REQUIREMENTS
2.1 Degree

APPLICATION DEADLINE
14th December 2018
Early application advised.

FURTHER INFORMATION
www.Top100GraduateEmployers.com
Register now for the latest news, campus
events, work experience and graduate
*vacancies at **Newton**.*

www.local.gov.uk/ngdp

ngdp.support@local.gov.uk ✉

facebook.com/ngdpLGA **f**   twitter.com/ngdp_LGA 🐦

The ngdp is a two-year graduate development programme which gives committed graduates the opportunity and training to fast-track their career in local government. Run by the Local Government Association, the ngdp is looking to equip the sector's next generation of high-calibre managers.

Local government is responsible for a range of vital services for people and businesses. They are a diverse and large employer, with more than one million people working in local government, providing more than 800 services to local communities. More than 1,200 graduates have completed the ngdp since 1999 and gained access to rewarding careers in and beyond the sector, with many currently holding influential managerial and policy roles.

The ngdp graduates are positioned to make a real contribution to shaping and implementing new ideas and initiatives in local government. Graduate trainees are employed by a participating council (or group of councils) for a minimum of two years, during which time they rotate between a series of placements in key areas of the council. Trainees can experience a range of roles in strategy, front-line service and support, to expand their perspective of local government's many different capacities and gain a flexible, transferrable skill set.

Ngdp graduates also benefit from being part of a national cohort of like-minded peers. Together they will participate in a national induction event, join an established knowledge-sharing network and gain a post-graduate qualification in Leadership and Management. The learning and development programme gives graduates the chance to learn from established professionals and also each other. The ngdp has been enabling graduates to build varied and rewarding careers for almost twenty years. Join now to start working in an exciting period of opportunity and change for the benefit of local communities.

GRADUATE VACANCIES IN 2019
ACCOUNTANCY
FINANCE
GENERAL MANAGEMENT
HUMAN RESOURCES
LAW
MARKETING
MEDIA
PROPERTY
PURCHASING
RESEARCH & DEVELOPMENT
TECHNOLOGY

NUMBER OF VACANCIES
140 graduate jobs

LOCATIONS OF VACANCIES

STARTING SALARY FOR 2019
£25,295
Plus London weighting where appropriate.

UNIVERSITY VISITS IN 2018-19
ASTON, BIRMINGHAM, BRISTOL, CAMBRIDGE, CARDIFF, CITY, DURHAM, EAST ANGLIA, EXETER, IMPERIAL COLLEGE LONDON, KEELE, KING'S COLLEGE LONDON, KENT, LANCASTER, LEEDS, LEICESTER, LIVERPOOL, LONDON SCHOOL OF ECONOMICS, LOUGHBOROUGH, MANCHESTER, NEWCASTLE, NORTHUMBRIA, NOTTINGHAM, NOTTINGHAM TRENT, OXFORD, PLYMOUTH, QUEEN MARY LONDON, READING, ROYAL HOLLOWAY, SHEFFIELD, SOUTHAMPTON, SURREY, UNIVERSITY COLLEGE LONDON, WARWICK, YORK
Please check with your university careers service for full details of local events.

MINIMUM ENTRY REQUIREMENTS
2.2 Degree

APPLICATION DEADLINE
3rd January 2019

FURTHER INFORMATION
www.Top100GraduateEmployers.com
Register now for the latest news, campus events, work experience and graduate vacancies at Local Government.

NHS Leadership Academy

NHS Leadership Academy
Graduate Management Training Scheme

I'M MAKING AN IMPACT
AND IMPROVING SERVICES
FOR EVERYONE IN THE UK

As Europe's largest employer with an annual budget of over £100 billion, there is no other organisation on Earth quite like the NHS. And with the ability to have a positive impact on over 53 million people, the NHS Graduate Management Training Scheme really is nothing less than a life-defining experience.

It's unquestionably hard work, but this multi-award-winning, fast-track development scheme enables graduates to become the healthcare leaders of the future.

Graduates specialise in one of six areas: Finance, General Management, Human Resources, Health Informatics, Policy & Strategy, and Health Analysis. As they grow personally and professionally they'll gain specialist skills while receiving full support from a dedicated mentor at Executive level.

Everyone joining the scheme will experience a comprehensive learning and development package designed by some of the most experienced and expert learning providers in the UK.

Success is granted only to those who are prepared to give their heart and soul to their profession. The responsibility of the NHS demands that their future leaders have the tenacity, the focus, and the determination to deliver nothing but the best.

Because the scheme offers a fast-track route to a senior-level role, graduates will soon find themselves facing complex problems head on and tackling high profile situations. Working for the NHS means standing up to high levels of public scrutiny and having decisions closely inspected. Graduates who want to succeed will need to be thick-skinned, resilient and able to respond to constant change.

This is a career where the hard work and unfaltering commitment of graduates not only affects the lives of others, but it will ultimately define their own.

GRADUATE VACANCIES IN 2019

ACCOUNTANCY
FINANCE
GENERAL MANAGEMENT
HUMAN RESOURCES
RESEARCH & DEVELOPMENT
TECHNOLOGY

NUMBER OF VACANCIES
500 graduate jobs

LOCATIONS OF VACANCIES

STARTING SALARY FOR 2019
£23,818
Plus a location allowance where appropriate.

UNIVERSITY VISITS IN 2018-19
Please check with your university careers service for full details of local events.

MINIMUM ENTRY REQUIREMENTS
2.2 Degree

APPLICATION DEADLINE
December 2018

FURTHER INFORMATION
www.Top100GraduateEmployers.com
Register now for the latest news, campus events, work experience and graduate vacancies at the NHS.

I WANT TO BE PART OF A
POSITIVE CHANGE
TO IMPROVE
PATIENT CARE AND EXPERIENCE.
THIS IS NO ORDINARY GRADUATE MANAGEMENT TRAINING SCHEME.

The NHS Graduate Management Training Scheme is nothing less than a life defining experience. Whether you join our Finance, General Management, Health Analysis, Health Informatics, Human Resources, or Policy and Strategy scheme, you'll receive everything you need to make a positive impact on the lives of 53 million people across England.

These aren't clinical opportunities, but this is about developing exceptional healthcare leaders. High-calibre management professionals who will lead the NHS through a profound transformation and shape our services around ever-evolving patient needs. Inspirational people who will push up standards, deliver deeper value for money and continue the drive towards a healthier nation.

nhsgraduates.co.uk

70 YEARS OF THE NHS 1948 - 2018

NHS
Leadership Academy

Graduate Management Training Scheme

Life Defining

Penguin Random House UK connects the world with the stories, ideas and writing that matter. As the biggest publisher in the UK, the diversity of its publishing includes brands such as Jamie Oliver, James Patterson and Peppa Pig through to literary prize winners such as Zadie Smith and Richard Flanagan.

Career opportunities range from the creative teams in Editorial, Marketing, Publicity and Design through to teams in Digital, Finance, Technology, Sales and Publishing Operations, to name but a few.

Their flagship entry-level programme, 'The Scheme' focuses on finding new talents for different roles each year – from marketing and publicity, to editorial.

Whether someone is motivated by working on something new, or taking the next step in their career, Penguin Random House is committed to creating an environment, and the opportunities, for their employees to do the best work of their lives.

Penguin Random House has nine publishing houses, each distinct, with their own imprints, markets and identity, including a fast-growing Audio publishing division.

They work with a wide range of talent – from storytellers, animators and developers to entrepreneurs, toy manufacturers, producers and, of course, writers. Just like broadcasters, they find increasingly different ways to bring stories and ideas to life.

Penguin Random House UK has three publishing sites in London – Vauxhall Bridge Road, Strand and Ealing Broadway; distribution centres in Frating, Grantham and Rugby; and a number of regional offices. They employ over 2,000 people in the UK.

GRADUATE VACANCIES IN 2019

MARKETING
MEDIA
SALES

NUMBER OF VACANCIES
200+ entry-level roles

LOCATIONS OF VACANCIES

STARTING SALARY FOR 2019
£23,000

UNIVERSITY VISITS IN 2018-19
Please check with your university careers service for full details of local events.

APPLICATION DEADLINE
Year-round recruitment
Early application advised.

FURTHER INFORMATION
www.Top100GraduateEmployers.com
*Register now for the latest news, campus events, work experience and graduate vacancies at **Penguin Random House**.*

Your Story Starts Here

Finding a great story - editor, publisher, sales director, finance team. Making it look good - designer, copy writer, art director, illustrator. Making the finished book - production controller, product manager, quality controller. Getting it out there - marketing assistant, publicity manager, sales executive, social media manager.

Come and be part of the first of a new kind of publisher that captures the attention of the world through the stories, ideas and writing that matter.

Penguin
Random House
UK

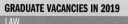

Pinsent Masons is an international law firm with a reputation for delivering high-quality legal advice, rooted in its deep understanding of the sectors and geographies in which their clients operate. The firm employs nearly 3,000 people worldwide, including around 1,500 lawyers and 400 partners.

Pinsent Masons is a global 100 law firm, specialising particularly in the energy, infrastructure, financial services, real estate, advanced manufacturing, and technology sectors.

The firm's international footprint encompasses seven offices across Asia Pacific, two offices in the Middle East, five offices in continental Europe and one in Africa. Pinsent Masons also has comprehensive coverage across each of the UK's three legal jurisdictions.

Penultimate year law students, or final year non-law students, can apply for the Vacation Placement. Over the course of a number of weeks, attendees will be fully immersed in all aspects of working life at Pinsent Masons. Placement students will experience a structured programme of work-based learning, skills training and presentations, as well as plenty of socialising and networking. The programme is available across all of their UK offices.

Pinsent Masons' two-year Training Contract comprises four six-month seats, spent in different Practice Groups, and combines regulatory and skills training. Seat allocations take account of trainees' preferences and aim to strike a balance between their choices and the firm's requirements. In each seat, trainees will be supervised by a senior colleague who will guide them through their learning and development. There is also full support from Pinsent Masons' Graduate Development team, who will meet trainees regularly to discuss their on-going performance.

GRADUATE VACANCIES IN 2019

LAW

NUMBER OF VACANCIES
68 graduate jobs
For training contracts starting in 2021.

LOCATIONS OF VACANCIES

STARTING SALARY FOR 2019
£23,000-£41,000

UNIVERSITY VISITS IN 2018-19
ABERDEEN, ASTON, BIRMINGHAM, BRISTOL, CAMBRIDGE, UNIVERSITY COLLEGE DUBLIN, DUNDEE, DURHAM, EAST ANGLIA, EDINBURGH, EXETER, GLASGOW, KING'S COLLEGE LONDON, LANCASTER, LEEDS, LIVERPOOL, LONDON SCHOOL OF ECONOMICS, MANCHESTER, NEWCASTLE, NOTTINGHAM, OXFORD, SHEFFIELD, STRATHCLYDE, UNIVERSITY COLLEGE LONDON, WARWICK, YORK
Please check with your university careers service for full details of local events.

MINIMUM ENTRY REQUIREMENTS
2.1 Degree
120 UCAS points
300+ UCAS points for those who passed exams before 2017.

APPLICATION DEADLINE
Varies by function

FURTHER INFORMATION
www.Top100GraduateEmployers.com
*Register now for the latest news, campus events, work experience and graduate vacancies at **Pinsent Masons**.*

Take the law into your own hands

with a Pinsent Masons Training Contract

We want people who make the most of every opportunity available to them, so we give them plenty.

If you're prepared to put yourself forward, to have a say, to think commercially, to learn new things and respond to an ever-changing environment, this could be the first opportunity of many. Visit us at **www.pinsentmasons.com/graduate**.

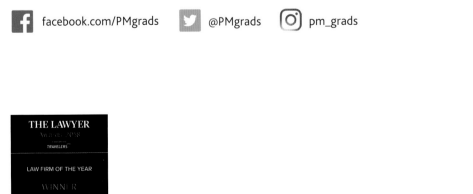

facebook.com/PMgrads　　@PMgrads　　pm_grads

THE LAWYER

TRAVELERS

LAW FIRM OF THE YEAR

WINNER

Pinsent Masons

8894

POLICE:NOW

INFLUENCE FOR GENERATIONS

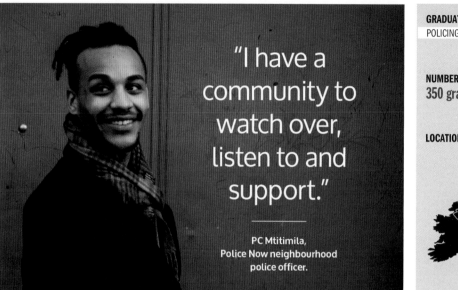

"I have a community to watch over, listen to and support."

PC Mtitimila,
Police Now neighbourhood
police officer.

Police Now's National Graduate Leadership Programme offers outstanding graduates the opportunity to pursue a highly ambitious vision for social change. Its aim? To break the intergenerational cycle of crime in the most challenged areas by creating safe, confident communities in which people can thrive.

This two-year programme operates at pace and intensity. And the challenge is unique. Graduates become fully warranted neighbourhood police officers with responsibility for an area that could be home to as many as 20,000 people. They get to know their communities – the problems, the prominent offenders and the crime hotspots within them. And right from the beginning, they are expected to use innovative ideas and tactics to tackle the toughest problems and deliver high impact results.

The programme is challenging, but graduates are supported by mentors, coaches and line managers. Frontline training is delivered by over 40 different experts and a whole range of operational police officers. Opportunities to undertake prestigious secondments with Police Now's partner organisations give graduates exposure to a wide range of industries and sectors. The skills and experience that graduates gain throughout the Police Now programme ensures that they are highly in demand, whether they choose to stay in policing or pursue a career elsewhere.

This is a challenge that extends beyond the basic mission of the police to prevent crime and disorder. It's the chance to be a leader in society and on the policing frontline.

As Police Now is expanding to work with over 25 forces across England and Wales, there are even more opportunities for outstanding graduates to step forward and change the story, not just today but for generations to come.

GRADUATE VACANCIES IN 2019
POLICING

NUMBER OF VACANCIES
350 graduate jobs

LOCATIONS OF VACANCIES

STARTING SALARY FOR 2019
£29,859
*For London positions –
regional differences apply.*

UNIVERSITY VISITS IN 2018-19
BIRMINGHAM, BRISTOL, CAMBRIDGE, CARDIFF, DURHAM, EXETER, HULL, KING'S COLLEGE LONDON, LANCASTER, LEEDS, LEICESTER, LIVERPOOL, MANCHESTER, NEWCASTLE, NORTHUMBRIA, NOTTINGHAM, OXFORD, SHEFFIELD, SOUTHAMPTON, UNIVERSITY COLLEGE LONDON
Please check with your university careers service for full details of local events.

MINIMUM ENTRY REQUIREMENTS
2.2 Degree
Plus a C grade in English at GCSE.

APPLICATION DEADLINE
1st March 2019
For a July 2019 start date.

FURTHER INFORMATION
www.Top100GraduateEmployers.com
*Register now for the latest news, campus events, work experience and graduate vacancies at **Police Now**.*

If a boy has a father with a criminal conviction, there's a 70% chance he'll end up with one too.

If it's a mother and daughter, the chances are higher.

Join us. Change the story.

National Graduate Leadership Programme

Like mother, like daughter? We've heard it all before; the apple doesn't fall far from the tree, she won't amount to anything. But it doesn't have to be that way, crime doesn't have to 'run in the family'. Police Now neighbourhood officers help to change the story for families like this every day. They continue to break the cycle and transform communities, with young people's confidence in the police having increased by 17% where Police Now neighbourhood officers operate.

Police Now is a two-year programme that offers top graduates the opportunity to become neighbourhood police officers. The challenge is unique and the impact is life changing. Join us to change the lives of people today and for generations to come.

Join us at policenow.org.uk

POLICE:NOW

INFLUENCE FOR GENERATIONS

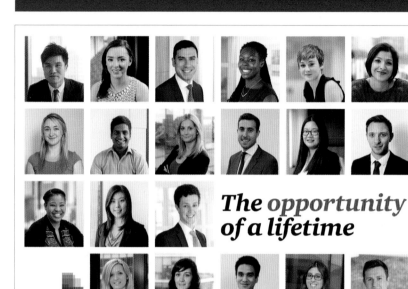

Economics degree

Our training & development is designed to help you excel in your career

Technology degree

Your degree is just the start

Arts degree

History degree

Science degree

50% of our graduate intake studied non-business related subjects

Geography degree

pwc.co.uk/careers

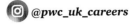 @pwc_uk_careers 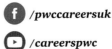 /pwccareersuk @pwc_uk_careers

pwc uk /careerspwc

pwc

Valuing difference. Driving inclusion.

careers.rolls-royce.com

twitter.com/RollsRoyce 🐦 facebook.com/RollsRoyceGroup f
youtube.com/RollsRoyceplc ▶ linkedin.com/company/Rolls-Royce in

From building the world's most efficient large aero-engine to supporting NASA missions on the edge of space, Rolls-Royce transforms the potential of technology. A career with Rolls-Royce means creating cleaner, faster, more competitive power. Looking to the future, and shaping the world we live in.

Rolls-Royce pioneers cutting-edge technologies that deliver the cleanest, safest and most competitive solutions to meet the planet's vital power needs – in the air, on land and at sea. 50,000 people across over 50 international offices make Rolls-Royce one of the world's leading industrial technology companies.

The company invests well over £1 billion each year in research and development, and files for more patents per year than any other company in the UK. At the same time, at Rolls-Royce each and every member of the team is encouraged to be themselves. The company believes firmly that diverse ways of thinking make for ever-better ideas – after all, the next big innovation could come from the smallest element of inspiration.

Opportunities for graduates are available in diverse engineering specialisms, operations, and a wide range of business functions, from HR and Project Management through to Commercial and Procurement. Across every area, Rolls-Royce is looking for people who are logical, analytical, innovative and enthusiastic: individuals who are open-minded and can bring fresh perspectives to enduring challenges.

A career at Rolls-Royce involves learning from a community of brilliant experts and enjoying a breadth of development opportunities – some of which include the chance to gain a professional accreditation. And because graduates across all programmes work on live projects, there's huge scope to make a very big contribution.

GRADUATE VACANCIES IN 2019

ENGINEERING
GENERAL MANAGEMENT
HUMAN RESOURCES
PURCHASING
SALES
TECHNOLOGY

NUMBER OF VACANCIES
300+ graduate jobs

LOCATIONS OF VACANCIES

Vacancies also available in Europe, the USA, and Asia.

STARTING SALARY FOR 2019
£28,500
Plus a £2,000 joining bonus.

UNIVERSITY VISITS IN 2018-19
BATH, BIRMINGHAM, BRISTOL, BRUNEL, CAMBRIDGE, DURHAM, EDINBURGH, EXETER, GLASGOW, IMPERIAL COLLEGE LONDON, LANCASTER, LIVERPOOL, LOUGHBOROUGH, MANCHESTER, NOTTINGHAM, NOTTINGHAM TRENT, OXFORD, SHEFFIELD, SOUTHAMPTON, STRATHCLYDE, WARWICK
Please check with your university careers service for full details of local events.

MINIMUM ENTRY REQUIREMENTS
2.1 Degree

APPLICATION DEADLINE
Year-round recruitment
Early application advised.

FURTHER INFORMATION
www.Top100GraduateEmployers.com
*Register now for the latest news, campus events, work experience and graduate vacancies at **Rolls-Royce**.*

Be bold
& Free the flip flop

Internship and Graduate Opportunities

Whether it's creating cleaner, safer energy or helping people to break out their beach gear via the world's most efficient aero-engines, we pioneer the power that matters. To find out how you could help shape the world we live in, visit **careers.rolls-royce.com**

Beyond tomorrow

www.raf.mod.uk/recruitment

facebook.com/RAFrecruitment
linkedin.com/company/Royal-Air-Force
twitter.com/RAF_recruitment
instagram.com/RAFrecruitment
youtube.com/RoyalAirForce

With cutting-edge technology, hundreds of aircraft and more than 30,000 active personnel, the Royal Air Force (RAF) is a key part of the British Armed Forces, defending the UK and its interests, strengthening international peace and stability, as well as being a force for good in the world.

Its people lie at the heart of the RAF; they're looking for professionalism, dedication and courage to achieve the RAF's vision of being 'an agile, adaptable and capable Air Force that, person for person, is second to none, and that makes a decisive air power contribution in support of the UK Defence Mission'.

The world is continually changing and so the RAF must change in order to meet the challenges of the 21st century. The RAF has become a smaller and more dynamic force, able to deliver capability all over the world; be that in support of combat missions or humanitarian aid and disaster relief. Whilst the exploitation of cutting-edge technologies helps meet these challenges; it is essential that the RAF continues to recruit and select high calibre graduates, for officer roles, to lead the RAF of tomorrow.

Graduates joining the RAF, in an Officer role, have been selected because they have demonstrated that they have the potential to be a leader. As an Officer they will be expected to lead and manage the women and men, for whom they are responsible, to meet the RAF's challenges of today and tomorrow. The world-class training that RAF Officers will receive ensures that they are equipped to do this. There are more than twenty different graduate career opportunities, including Engineering, Aircrew, Logistics and Personnel roles, as well as medical opportunities for qualified doctors, nurses and dentists. In return, the RAF offers a competitive salary, free medical & dental services, travel opportunities and world-class training. It's no ordinary job.

GRADUATE VACANCIES IN 2019
ENGINEERING
HUMAN RESOURCES
LAW
LOGISTICS
TECHNOLOGY

NUMBER OF VACANCIES
500-600 graduate jobs

LOCATIONS OF VACANCIES

STARTING SALARY FOR 2019
£31,232
Starting salary after Initial Officer Training (six months).

UNIVERSITY VISITS IN 2018-19
ABERDEEN, BATH, BELFAST, BIRMINGHAM, BRADFORD, BRISTOL, BRUNEL, CAMBRIDGE, CARDIFF, CITY, DUNDEE, DURHAM, EAST ANGLIA, EDINBURGH, ESSEX, EXETER, GLASGOW, HULL, KENT, LANCASTER, LEEDS, LEICESTER, LIVERPOOL, LOUGHBOROUGH, MANCHESTER, NEWCASTLE, NORTHUMBRIA, NOTTINGHAM, NOTTINGHAM TRENT, OXFORD, PLYMOUTH, READING, SHEFFIELD, SOUTHAMPTON, ST ANDREWS, STIRLING, STRATHCLYDE, SURREY, SUSSEX, SWANSEA, ULSTER, YORK
Please check with your university careers service for full details of local events.

MINIMUM ENTRY REQUIREMENTS
Relevant degree required for some roles.

APPLICATION DEADLINE
Year-round recruitment
Early application advised.

FURTHER INFORMATION
www.Top100GraduateEmployers.com
*Register now for the latest news, campus events, work experience and graduate vacancies at the **Royal Air Force**.*

ROYAL AIR FORCE
REGULAR & RESERVE

"So you think you've got what it takes to be an officer in the RAF"

There are graduate careers and then there are graduate challenges - we'd like to think we're the latter. Our officers don't just have good promotion prospects, they get competitive pay and world-class training, as well as six weeks' paid holiday a year, subsidised food and accommodation, free healthcare, and free access to our sports facilities.

As well as specialist training, you'll learn valuable leadership and management skills; you'll also have the opportunity to take part in adventurous training such as rock climbing, skiing and sailing. As you develop your career, you'll move on to face new challenges and opportunities for promotion - both in the UK and overseas.

Interested? If you think you've got what it takes to be an Officer in the RAF, take a look at the RAF Recruitment website at the roles available, what's required for entry and the 24 week Initial Officer Training Course at RAF College Cranwell. You could also be eligible for sponsorship through your sixth-form or university courses, depending on the role you're interested in. We're currently recruiting Engineers, but have opportunities in Logistics, Medical, Personnel, Intelligence and Aircrew Officer roles. Visit the Education and Funding page of the website to find out about the opportunities available.

Healthcare in action

If you've just completed a relevant medical degree, the RAF can offer you a career filled with variety and adventure, as well as first-class postgraduate and specialist training. Once you've been accepted you'll spend 13 weeks at RAF College Cranwell doing the Specialist Entrants Officer Training Course.

www.raf.mod.uk/recruitment/lifestyle-benefits/education-funding/

ROYAL NAVY

Throughout the course of history, a life at sea has always attracted those with a taste for travel and adventure; but there are plenty of other reasons for graduates and final-year students to consider a challenging and wide-ranging career with the Royal Navy.

The Royal Navy is, first and foremost, a fighting force. Serving alongside Britain's allies in conflicts around the world, it also vitally protects UK ports, fishing grounds and merchant ships, helping to combat international smuggling, terrorism and piracy. Increasingly, its 30,000 personnel are involved in humanitarian and relief missions; situations where their skills, discipline and resourcefulness make a real difference to people's lives.

Graduates are able to join the Royal Navy as Officers – the senior leadership and management team in the various branches, which range from Engineering, Air and Warfare to Medical, the Fleet Air Arm and Logistics. Starting salaries of at least £25,984 – rising to £31,232 in the first year – compare well with those in industry.

Those wanting to join the Royal Navy as an Engineer – with Marine, Weapon or Air Engineer Officer, above or below the water – could work on anything from sensitive electronics to massive gas-turbine engines and nuclear weapons. What's more, the Royal Navy can offer a secure, flexible career and the potential to extend to age 50.

The Royal Navy offers opportunities for early responsibility, career development, sport, recreation and travel which exceed any in civilian life. With its global reach and responsibilities, the Royal Navy still offers plenty of adventure and the chance to see the world, while pursuing one of the most challenging, varied and fulfilling careers available.

GRADUATE VACANCIES IN 2019

ENGINEERING
FINANCE
GENERAL MANAGEMENT
HUMAN RESOURCES
LAW
LOGISTICS
MEDIA
RESEARCH & DEVELOPMENT
TECHNOLOGY

NUMBER OF VACANCIES
No fixed quota

LOCATIONS OF VACANCIES

Vacancies also available elsewhere in the world.

STARTING SALARY FOR 2019
£25,984

UNIVERSITY VISITS IN 2018-19
LIVERPOOL, LOUGHBOROUGH, PLYMOUTH, STRATHCLYDE, SWANSEA
Please check with your university careers service for full details of local events.

MINIMUM ENTRY REQUIREMENTS
Relevant degree required for some roles.

APPLICATION DEADLINE
Year-round recruitment

FURTHER INFORMATION
www.Top100GraduateEmployers.com
*Register now for the latest news, campus events, work experience and graduate vacancies at the **Royal Navy**.*

YOU MAKE A DIFFERENCE NOT MAKE UP THE NUMBERS

ROYAL NAVY OFFICER

Being an officer in the Royal Navy is a career like any other, but the circumstances and places are sometimes extraordinary. With opportunities ranging from Engineer Officer to Medical Officer, it's a responsible, challenging career that will take you further than you've been before. If you want more than just a job, join the Royal Navy and live a life without limits.

LIFE WITHOUT LIMITS
08456 07 55 55
ROYALNAVY.MOD.UK/CAREERS

GRADUATE VACANCIES IN 2019

CONSULTING

FINANCE

HUMAN RESOURCES

INVESTMENT BANKING

TECHNOLOGY

NUMBER OF VACANCIES
100 graduate jobs

LOCATIONS OF VACANCIES

STARTING SALARY FOR 2019
£30,000

UNIVERSITY VISITS IN 2018-19
Please check with your university careers service for full details of local events.

MINIMUM ENTRY REQUIREMENTS
2.1 Degree

APPLICATION DEADLINE
Year-round recruitment
Early application advised.

FURTHER INFORMATION
www.Top100GraduateEmployers.com
Register now for the latest news, campus events, work experience and graduate vacancies at Santander.

Santander is one of the largest and most successful financial groups in the world, and their ambition is to become the best bank for their customers, investors and employees. They recognise technology is changing how customers bank and pay and are working to be at the forefront of that change.

Santander are motivated by having the customer at the heart of what they do. Strong teamwork, an innovative approach to technology, market-leading incentive packages, and a culture of support ensure graduates deliver their personal best, every day. Santander focuses on giving graduates everything they need to be the best they can be in their chosen areas. They are supported in this throughout their programmes, working in an agile and dynamic way within a fast-paced, diverse environment.

Graduate programmes within the business are run across different specialisms and business areas, each designed to give an in-depth understanding of what makes Santander tick. That could mean developing innovative products for their customers, identifying ways to improve processes for colleagues, or building relationships with high-profile clients. In everything that graduates do at Santander, they are continually focused on ensuring that Santander progresses to become a truly digital bank.

What's more, graduates will be part of a structured development scheme split into four learning cycles that usually ends with an industry-recognised qualification in their chosen area.

Through these programmes graduates will have all of the support they need in order to succeed, with a dedicated graduate manager as well as continuous development – there's plenty of benefits and no shortage of opportunities to grow with Santander.

Your future at the heart of our business

Our Emerging Talent schemes provide everything you'll need to realise your future. We're here to help people and businesses prosper and you'll be at the heart of that change, whilst placing the customer at the heart of everything we do.

So, if you're passionate about making our banking products, services and tools simple, personal and fair, whilst helping Santander to become the leading digital bank, we have a scheme for you.

Realise your future, apply today: www.santanderjobs.co.uk/realiseyourfuture

Santander

savills.co.uk/graduates

facebook.com/Savills **f**   gradrecruitment@savills.com ✉

instagram.com/Savills_instagrad 📷   twitter.com/SavillsGraduate **y**

Savills UK is a leading global real estate service provider listed on the London Stock Exchange. The company employs over 35,000 staff and has 600 offices and associates worldwide, providing all trainees with excellent scope for international experience as their careers develop.

Savills passionately believe that their graduates are future leaders, and as such make a huge investment in them. Savills graduates are given responsibility from day one, in teams who highly value their contribution, allowing them to be involved in some of the world's most high-profile property deals and developments. Graduates are surrounded by expert professionals and experienced team members from whom they learn and seek advice. Individual achievement is rewarded, and Savills look for bold graduates with entrepreneurial flair.

Savills are proud to have won *The Times Graduate Recruitment Award: Employer of Choice for Property* for the twelfth year running. A great work-life balance, structured training and a dynamic working environment are amongst the factors which see Savills nominated by final year students as the preferred Property employer year-on-year.

Savills' Graduate Programme offers the chance to gain an internationally-recognised Professional qualification. The company offers roles within Surveying, Planning, Food & Farming and Forestry, and half of the Graduate Programme vacancies are positioned outside of London. The company has offices in exciting locations around the UK, where Fee Earners work with varied and prestigious clients. The diversity of Savills services means there is the flexibility to carve out a fulfilling, individual and self-tailored career path, regardless of the location.

GRADUATE VACANCIES IN 2019
PROPERTY

NUMBER OF VACANCIES
100 graduate jobs

LOCATIONS OF VACANCIES

STARTING SALARY FOR 2019
£23,000-£26,000
Plus a £1,000 sign-on bonus.

UNIVERSITY VISITS IN 2018-19
ABERDEEN, BATH, BIRMINGHAM, BRISTOL, CAMBRIDGE, CARDIFF, CITY, TRINITY COLLEGE DUBLIN, DURHAM, EDINBURGH, EXETER, GLASGOW, HERIOT-WATT, LEEDS, LIVERPOOL, MANCHESTER, NORTHUMBRIA, NOTTINGHAM TRENT, OXFORD BROOKES, PLYMOUTH, READING, SHEFFIELD, SOUTHAMPTON, UNIVERSITY COLLEGE LONDON
Please check with your university careers service for full details of local events.

MINIMUM ENTRY REQUIREMENTS
Relevant degree required for some roles.

APPLICATION DEADLINE
Varies by function

FURTHER INFORMATION
www.Top100GraduateEmployers.com
Register now for the latest news, campus events, work experience and graduate vacancies at Savills.

SHAPE YOUR FUTURE

40% of our board joined us as graduates

Do you have what it takes?

Become the future of Savills

savills.com/graduate

🐦 @savillsgraduate

📷 savills_instagrad

savills

The world needs to find lower carbon ways to produce and consume energy. Shell's purpose is to power progress together with more and cleaner energy solutions. They use advanced technologies and take an innovative approach to help build a sustainable energy future.

Shell offers a wide range of career routes. The scale and global reach of the business means they have a huge range of technical, commercial and corporate roles.

The Shell Graduate Programme is open to graduates and early career professionals. The Programme focuses on leadership development and prepares graduates to tackle the world's growing energy demand. As society moves towards a low carbon energy system, the company and its people will strive towards a cleaner energy future.

The structured Graduate Programme gives graduates immediate immersion in their business with real, high levels of responsibility from day one. The Programme is typically 3 years, although this can depend on the area of the business, and graduates usually complete at least 2 assignments within this time. Throughout they receive comprehensive support from mentors, work buddies, the graduate network (Energie) and access to senior business leaders.

Shell Assessed Internships are open to penultimate year students. They are usually 12 week placements undertaken over the summer. During this time students are supported through delivery of a live project for which they have responsibility. Project topics are determined based on the student's interests and the needs of the business. Shell Internships are very sought-after roles that give a fantastic insight into a fascinating business – one that has an impact on everyone.

GRADUATE VACANCIES IN 2019

ENGINEERING

FINANCE

GENERAL MANAGEMENT

HUMAN RESOURCES

LOGISTICS

MARKETING

RESEARCH & DEVELOPMENT

SALES

NUMBER OF VACANCIES
38+ graduate jobs

LOCATIONS OF VACANCIES

Vacancies also available elsewhere in the world.

STARTING SALARY FOR 2019
£Competitive
Plus a competitive bonus and benefits.

UNIVERSITY VISITS IN 2018-19
ABERDEEN, ASTON, BIRMINGHAM, CAMBRIDGE, HERIOT-WATT, IMPERIAL COLLEGE LONDON, LEEDS, LONDON SCHOOL OF ECONOMICS, MANCHESTER, OXFORD, STRATHCLYDE, UNIVERSITY COLLEGE LONDON
Please check with your university careers service for full details of local events.

MINIMUM ENTRY REQUIREMENTS
No entry requirements.

APPLICATION DEADLINE
Varies by function

FURTHER INFORMATION
www.Top100GraduateEmployers.com
Register now for the latest news, campus events, work experience and graduate vacancies at Shell.

COULD YOU MAKE AN IMPACT THAT MATTERS?

BE PART OF A BETTER FUTURE

www.shell.co.uk/graduates
#makethefuture

SIEMENS
Ingenuity for life

A global technology and engineering powerhouse, Siemens has been an innovative force throughout every major industrial revolution – from the age of steam power to advances in electrification, and then automation. Now, this giant of engineering and international business practices is entering phase four of the revolution – digitalisation.

As a world-class authority on manufacturing, power generation, building technologies, and the infrastructure making up the modern world, Siemens is propelling the UK ahead in this new era, labelled 'Industry 4.0'.

The Chief Executive of Siemens UK, Juergen Maier, believes they have a responsibility to champion projects which make the world a better place. Pioneering new technologies create jobs and improve quality of life. The push towards sustainability is also key, and Siemens leads the way, increasing performance and efficiency simultaneously. They are already developing futuristic technologies such as AI, robotics, driverless cars and MindSphere – a powerful insight into how future cities will connect to the Internet of Things.

Siemens seeks forward-thinking graduates who can launch them to the forefront of just about everything. They have locations across the country, employing the brightest engineers and business minds. New starters can expect to be on the ground, participating in meaningful projects that optimise cutting-edge resources and insights. The culture revolves around ingenuity and inclusion, as well as down-to-earth interaction, preventing hierarchy from obstructing invention. Roles include electrical and mechanical engineering, through to project management and finance. Everyone benefits from a structured two-year Graduate Development Programme, facilitating the essential skills required to succeed in a career at Siemens. This means growing in an environment that's well-known for delivering the very best.

GRADUATE VACANCIES IN 2019

ENGINEERING
FINANCE
GENERAL MANAGEMENT
PURCHASING
RESEARCH & DEVELOPMENT
SALES
TECHNOLOGY

NUMBER OF VACANCIES
70-80 graduate jobs

LOCATIONS OF VACANCIES

STARTING SALARY FOR 2019
£Competitive

UNIVERSITY VISITS IN 2018-19
BIRMINGHAM, CAMBRIDGE, IMPERIAL COLLEGE LONDON, LINCOLN, LOUGHBOROUGH, MANCHESTER, NEWCASTLE, NOTTINGHAM, OXFORD, SHEFFIELD, SOUTHAMPTON, STRATHCLYDE
Please check with your university careers service for full details of local events.

MINIMUM ENTRY REQUIREMENTS
2.2 Degree

APPLICATION DEADLINE
Early January 2019

FURTHER INFORMATION
www.Top100GraduateEmployers.com
Register now for the latest news, campus events, work experience and graduate vacancies at Siemens.

Brave enough to re-imagine the world around you?

Here at Siemens, we're changing the way the world works. Take MindSphere, our ground-breaking open source operating system for the Internet of Things. It helps businesses develop smart new applications, services and business models – while letting our people push their limits and learn new things every day.

Find out more about our graduate programmes and where you fit in by heading to our careers site.

Visit
siemens.co.uk/careers

★ RATEMYPLACEMENT
2018 - 2019
Top 100
Undergraduate
Employers

sky

earlycareers@sky.uk ✉

twitter.com/EarlyCareersSky 🐦   facebook.com/EarlyCareersSky f

GRADUATE VACANCIES IN 2019
FINANCE
MARKETING
TECHNOLOGY

NUMBER OF VACANCIES
90+ graduate jobs

LOCATIONS OF VACANCIES

STARTING SALARY FOR 2019
£26,500-£32,000

UNIVERSITY VISITS IN 2018-19
ASTON, BATH, BIRMINGHAM, BRISTOL, BRUNEL, CARDIFF, DURHAM, EDINBURGH, ESSEX, EXETER, GLASGOW, HERIOT-WATT, HULL, IMPERIAL COLLEGE LONDON, KING'S COLLEGE LONDON, LANCASTER, LEEDS, LEICESTER, LOUGHBOROUGH, MANCHESTER, NEWCASTLE, NOTTINGHAM, QUEEN MARY LONDON, SHEFFIELD, SOUTHAMPTON, STRATHCLYDE, WARWICK, YORK
Please check with your university careers service for full details of local events.

APPLICATION DEADLINE
Varies by function

FURTHER INFORMATION
www.Top100GraduateEmployers.com
Register now for the latest news, campus events, work experience and graduate vacancies at Sky.

29 years of experience. 23 million customers. Seven countries. Sky, Europe's leading entertainment company and communications business, is more than just television, mobile and broadband. With pioneering technology, innovative minds and forward-thinking teams, it makes the future happen.

People drive Sky's success. But the company doesn't look for a certain 'type' of person. And it definitely doesn't look for a certain type of graduate. Instead, with programmes across Software Engineering and Technology, or commercial programmes in areas like Finance or Marketing, Sky looks out for a whole host of different skills. What graduates *do* need to succeed, however, is the drive, passion and ambition to write their own career story – whatever their speciality or degree discipline.

Whether applicants want to develop into business leaders, create cutting-edge products and services, or specialise in an area of their choice, Sky have a programme to fit. For those students who haven't decided on their career route, Sky also offers insight days, work experience programmes and summer internships – giving students the chance to begin their career story.

Sky believes in better. Better roles. Better opportunities. Better work. For graduates based at Sky's state-of-the-art offices in London, Leeds or Edinburgh, that means high levels of responsibility – allowing them to see the impact of their work. And with hands-on training and on-the-job learning, bright new talent can learn everything it takes to keep audiences entertained. Whatever their skills, wherever they join, from day one graduates will be part of a friendly network that stretches right across the business. Add to that flexible working, structured learning plans, competitive rewards and discounts, and graduates have everything they need to flourish.

Introducing

The future stars

Tamera
"The coding guru"

Tristan
"The programming pro"

Phoebe
"The visionary"

Dhiren
"The innovator"

Daisy
"The analytical one"

Sky Early Careers

Doers. Thinkers. Fixers. Innovators. Challengers. All sorts of bright new talent are writing their own stories at Sky – the heart of entertainment and technology. And, with world-class support, a range of graduate, placement, and work experience programmes plus proper responsibility from the start, you could be one of them. So what are you waiting for? Start your story today.

Search 'Sky Early Careers' to find out more.

sky

GRADUATE VACANCIES IN 2019

LAW

NUMBER OF VACANCIES
80-85 graduate jobs
For training contracts starting in 2021.

LOCATIONS OF VACANCIES

Slaughter and May is one of the most prestigious law firms in the world. They advise high-profile and often landmark international transactions. Their excellent and varied client list ranges from governments to entrepreneurs, from retailers to entertainment companies, and from conglomerates to Premier League football clubs.

Slaughter and May has offices in London, Beijing, Brussels and Hong Kong, plus relationship firms in all the major jurisdictions. Slaughter and May has built a reputation for delivering innovative solutions to difficult problems. They are a full service law firm to corporate clients, and have leading practitioners across a wide range of practice areas including Mergers and Acquisitions, Corporate and Commercial, Financing, Tax, Competition, Dispute Resolution, Real Estate, Pensions and Employment, Financial Regulation, Information Technology and Intellectual Property.

Their lawyers are not set billing or time targets, and are therefore free to concentrate on what matters most – expertise, sound judgement, a willingness to help one another and the highest quality of client service.

During the two-year training contract, trainees turn their hand to a broad range of work, taking an active role in four, five or six groups while sharing an office with a partner or experienced associate. All trainees spend at least two six-month seats in the firm's market-leading corporate, commercial and financing groups. Subject to gaining some contentious experience, they choose how to spend the remaining time.

The firm sets great store in drawing strength from diversity. With 111 different degree courses from 83 different universities and 31 nationalities represented among their lawyers, their culture is extremely broad.

STARTING SALARY FOR 2019
£44,000

UNIVERSITY VISITS IN 2018-19
ABERDEEN, BIRMINGHAM, BRISTOL, CARDIFF, CAMBRIDGE, UNIVERSITY COLLEGE DUBLIN, DURHAM, EDINBURGH, EXETER, GLASGOW, KING'S COLLEGE LONDON, LANCASTER, LEEDS, LEICESTER, LONDON SCHOOL OF ECONOMICS, MANCHESTER, NEWCASTLE, NOTTINGHAM, OXFORD, QUEEN MARY LONDON, SHEFFIELD, SCHOOL OF AFRICAN STUDIES, ST ANDREWS, UNIVERSITY COLLEGE LONDON, WARWICK, YORK
Please check with your university careers service for full details of local events.

MINIMUM ENTRY REQUIREMENTS
2.1 Degree

APPLICATION DEADLINE
Please see website for full details.

FURTHER INFORMATION
www.Top100GraduateEmployers.com
*Register now for the latest news, campus events, work experience and graduate vacancies at **Slaughter and May**.*

A world of difference

Laws, international markets, global institutions... all changing every day. So how do we, as an international law firm, create the agility of mind that enables us to guide some of the world's most influential organisations into the future?

By allowing bright people the freedom to grow. By training lawyers in a way that develops a closer understanding of clients through working on a wider range of transactions. By fostering an ethos of knowledge sharing, support and mutual development by promoting from within and leaving the clocks outside when it comes to billing. To learn more about how our key differences not only make a world of difference to our clients, but also to our lawyers and their careers, visit

slaughterandmay.com/careers

SLAUGHTER AND MAY

80
training contracts

300+
workshops
and schemes

Lawyers from
83
universities

TeachFirst

Teach First is a charity working to end educational inequality. Since 2002, they have found and developed over 11,000 talented people to teach and lead in schools facing the greatest challenges. In doing this, they have helped to change the lives of more than a million disadvantaged children.

Young people from disadvantaged backgrounds in this country are being let down by one of the most unfair education systems in the developed world, and the knock-on effect of this injustice lasts a lifetime. It's a cycle that Teach First are determined to break, but they can't do it alone.

On their two-year Leadership Development Programme – based on global best practice and research – Teach First support graduates to become qualified teachers through a fully-funded Postgraduate Diploma in Education and Leadership (PGDE). Participants are placed in a secondary, primary or early years setting, in schools across England and Wales. And by training on the job, they have an immediate impact on the lives of young people who need them the most.

Throughout their time on the Leadership Development Programme, and beyond, participants benefit from Teach First's influential network. There are a wide range of organisations and businesses who share their commitment to ending educational inequality and value the skills and experience their participants gain.

After the two years, more than half of Teach First's trainees continue teaching in schools, many progressing into leadership positions. Others move into positions in government, industry and their own social enterprises, remaining connected to Teach First's goal of ending educational inequality. All participants complete the programme with Qualified Teacher Status, meaning those who move on can return to the profession at any time.

GRADUATE VACANCIES IN 2019
TEACHING

NUMBER OF VACANCIES
1,750 graduate jobs

LOCATIONS OF VACANCIES

STARTING SALARY FOR 2019
£Competitive

UNIVERSITY VISITS IN 2018-19
ABERYSTWYTH, ASTON, BATH, BELFAST, BIRMINGHAM, BRISTOL, BRUNEL, CAMBRIDGE, CARDIFF, CITY, DURHAM, EAST ANGLIA, EDINBURGH, ESSEX, EXETER, GLASGOW, HULL, IMPERIAL COLLEGE LONDON, KING'S COLLEGE LONDON, KENT, LANCASTER, LEEDS, LEICESTER, LIVERPOOL, LONDON SCHOOL OF ECONOMICS, LOUGHBOROUGH, MANCHESTER, NEWCASTLE, NORTHUMBRIA, NOTTINGHAM, NOTTINGHAM TRENT, OXFORD, QUEEN MARY LONDON, READING, ROYAL HOLLOWAY, SHEFFIELD, SOUTHAMPTON, ST ANDREWS, STRATHCLYDE, SURREY, SUSSEX, SWANSEA, ULSTER, UNIVERSITY COLLEGE LONDON, WARWICK, YORK
Please check with your university careers service for full details of local events.

MINIMUM ENTRY REQUIREMENTS
2.1 Degree
However, all applications are assessed on a case-by-case basis.

APPLICATION DEADLINE
Year-round recruitment
Early application advised.

FURTHER INFORMATION
www.Top100GraduateEmployers.com
Register now for the latest news, campus events, work experience and graduate vacancies at Teach First.

FIND THEIR GENIUS.

FIND YOUR PURPOSE.

Help every child believe they can achieve anything. Build skills that could take you anywhere. We find and develop great people to become inspirational leaders in the classroom, in schools and across all sectors of our society. Find your way to lead at **teachfirst.org.uk/recruitment**

Each child. Each future.

TeachFirst

Tesco help their graduates to grow their skills, reach their potential and feel inspired. They believe that the most rewarding way for their graduates to learn is through the responsibility of real-life business experience, which they give them from day one.

Tesco's graduates can apply their knowledge by being innovative, working collaboratively across the business, and being responsive to the business' needs. They want their graduates to feel welcome, so there's always a buddy, mentor or manager on hand to support them. Tesco offer a range of opportunities for graduates through their office, distribution and store programmes.

Tesco was built with a simple mission – to be the champion for customers, helping them to enjoy a better quality of life and an easier way of living. This hasn't changed. Customers want great products at great value which they can buy easily, and it's Tesco's job to deliver this in the right way for them. Tesco's purpose is 'Serving Britain's customers a little better every day'. As a business, serving customers is at the heart of everything they do – from the colleagues in their stores to those in supporting roles within the office and distribution centres.

Earlier this year, the Heart building opened at their Welwyn Garden City campus. It has been designed as a vibrant, colourful and open building, which provides teams with flexible spaces and is a place for colleagues to learn, collaborate and innovate. It's a place to truly experience the Tesco brand. It also offers an Express store, new subsidised gym with treatment facilities, all-weather sports pitch and a coffee shop. Tesco have committed to flexible working to give their colleagues the chance to manage their work around their lifestyles. They want their colleagues to be their best at work and at home. It's important to Tesco that everyone feels welcome, and feels part of the team.

GRADUATE VACANCIES IN 2019
FINANCE
LOGISTICS
MARKETING
PURCHASING
RETAILING
TECHNOLOGY

NUMBER OF VACANCIES
80+ graduate jobs

LOCATIONS OF VACANCIES

STARTING SALARY FOR 2019
£28,000-£32,000

UNIVERSITY VISITS IN 2018-19
Please check with your university careers service for full details of local events.

MINIMUM ENTRY REQUIREMENTS
2.2 Degree

APPLICATION DEADLINE
13th January 2019

FURTHER INFORMATION
www.Top100GraduateEmployers.com
Register now for the latest news, campus events, work experience and graduate vacancies at **Tesco**.

Let's grow together.

We help our graduates to grow their skills, reach their potential and feel inspired. We believe that the most rewarding way for our graduates to learn is through the responsibility of real-life business experience, which we give them from day one. They can apply their knowledge, by being innovative, working collaboratively across the business, and being responsive to the business' needs. We want our graduates to feel welcome so there's always a buddy, mentor or manager on hand to support them.

We offer a range of opportunities for graduates through our office, distribution and store programmes. Find out more at **tesco-careers.com/programmes**

www.thinkahead.org

hello@thinkahead.org ✉

twitter.com/ThinkAheadMH 🐦 facebook.com/ThinkAheadorg f

youtube.com/ThinkAheadMH ▶ linkedin.com/company/Think-Ahead-org in

GRADUATE VACANCIES IN 2019
SOCIAL WORK

NUMBER OF VACANCIES
100-112 graduate jobs

LOCATIONS OF VACANCIES

The Think Ahead programme is a new route into social work for graduates and career-changers remarkable enough to make a real difference to people with mental health problems. The paid, two-year programme combines on-the-job learning, a Masters degree and leadership training.

Mental health social workers use therapy, support, and advocacy to enable people to manage the social factors in their lives – like relationships, housing, and employment – to allow them to get well and stay well.

The Think Ahead programme focuses on adult community mental health teams, supporting people living with a wide variety of illnesses such as bipolar disorder, schizophrenia, and personality disorders. These are multi-disciplinary teams, usually within an NHS Trust, which can include social workers, nurses, support workers, occupational therapists, psychologists and psychiatrists.

Participants on the programme begin their training with an intensive six-week residential over the summer. This prepares them for frontline work by giving them a grounding in approaches to mental health social work.

Following this training, participants work within NHS mental health teams in units of four. Each unit is led by a highly experienced Consultant Social Worker, and participants share responsibility for the care of the individuals they work with. Participants become professionally qualified in the second year of the programme and are then able to work more independently.

Throughout the programme there is regular training and time allocated for academic study. The programme culminates in a Masters degree in social work. Leadership training also takes place throughout the programme, supporting participants to become excellent social workers, and to work towards leading change in the future.

STARTING SALARY FOR 2019
£17,000-£19,000
This is a tax-free bursary.

UNIVERSITY VISITS IN 2018-19
ASTON, BIRMINGHAM, CAMBRIDGE, DURHAM, EAST ANGLIA, EXETER, KING'S COLLEGE LONDON, LEEDS, LIVERPOOL, LONDON SCHOOL OF ECONOMICS, MANCHESTER, NOTTINGHAM, OXFORD, QUEEN MARY LONDON, SHEFFIELD, SOUTHAMPTON, SUSSEX, UNIVERSITY COLLEGE LONDON, WARWICK, YORK
Please check with your university careers service for full details of local events.

MINIMUM ENTRY REQUIREMENTS
2.1 Degree

APPLICATION DEADLINE
Year-round recruitment
Early application advised.

FURTHER INFORMATION
www.Top100GraduateEmployers.com
*Register now for the latest news, campus events, work experience and graduate vacancies at **Think Ahead**.*

Think Ahead has given me a deeper understanding of the impact that mental illness can have on individuals.

Jan, Edinburgh graduate
and Think Ahead participant

thinkahead.org

www.tpptop50.com

facebook.com/TPPcareers **f**   careers@tpp-uk.com ✉

linkedin.com/company/the-phoenix-partnership-TPP- **in**   twitter.com/TPPcareers **𝕏**

instagram.com/TPP_careers **⃝**   youtube.com/TPPsystm1 **▶**

TPP is a global health IT company, working on cutting-edge technology to transform lives across the world. They work on pioneering products, including digital health software, apps, and ground-breaking research. TPP need problem solvers from all disciplines to help them move healthcare forward.

TPP have had great success in the UK, with over 5,500 organisations using their system to support over 48 million patient records. In recent years, TPP has expanded internationally to tackle global health challenges.

The Analyst, Communications and Account teams regularly travel internationally, most recently to China and the Middle East. The technical teams also have the opportunity to travel. During these trips, staff have the time to go sightseeing and sample local cuisine.

It's not just TPP's products that are revolutionary – they've also broken the mould in terms of company culture. TPP recognise the potential that each graduate has from the moment they start, and use that talent to work on exciting projects and challenges. An employee's value at the company isn't based on how long they've been there – TPP operates on a flat hierarchy, so staff can make a difference and work on new projects from the moment they start. TPP listen to their employees and have changed the way they work based on feedback, meaning their staff can be empowered to make a difference. As a result, TPP have been consistently recognised as an outstanding graduate employer.

TPP's hands-on training approach means new employees will have plenty of responsibility from day one, with great support from the team around them, so applicants don't need to have any prior experience – coding or otherwise. A bright graduate who is full of ideas and likes spending time with some of the sharpest minds around will be well suited to a career with TPP.

GRADUATE VACANCIES IN 2019

MARKETING
RESEARCH & DEVELOPMENT
SALES
TECHNOLOGY

NUMBER OF VACANCIES
50+ graduate jobs

LOCATIONS OF VACANCIES

STARTING SALARY FOR 2019
£45,000

UNIVERSITY VISITS IN 2018-19
BATH, BRISTOL, CAMBRIDGE, DURHAM, EDINBURGH, IMPERIAL COLLEGE LONDON, MANCHESTER, OXFORD, SOUTHAMPTON, ST ANDREWS, UNIVERSITY COLLEGE LONDON, WARWICK
Please check with your university careers service for full details of local events.

MINIMUM ENTRY REQUIREMENTS
2.1 Degree

APPLICATION DEADLINE
Year-round recruitment

FURTHER INFORMATION
www.Top100GraduateEmployers.com
Register now for the latest news, campus events, work experience and graduate vacancies at TPP.

Unilever

www.unilever.co.uk/careers/graduates

twitter.com/UnileverGradsUK 🐦   facebook.com/UnileverCareersUK 👤
youtube.com/TheUnileverUFLP ▶   linkedin.com/company/Unilever 💼
@UnileverGradsUK 👤   instagram.com/UnileverGradsUK 📷

Unilever, a leading consumer goods company, makes some of the world's best-loved brands: Dove, Knorr, Magnum, Lynx, Sure, Tresemmé and Hellmann's to name a few. Over two billion consumers use their products every day. Unilever products are sold in 190 countries and they employ 168,000 people globally.

Around the world, Unilever products help people look good, feel good and get more out of life. It's one of the world's greatest businesses, with amazing brands, dynamic people and a sustainable vision. What's Unilever's challenge? To double the size of its business, while reducing its environmental impact and increasing its social impact. Unilever is looking for talented graduates who have the will and the drive to help Unilever achieve this ambition.

Graduates can apply to one of the following areas – Supply Chain Management, Customer Management (Sales), HR Management, Marketing, Technology Management, Research & Development and Financial Management. The UFLP is about making a big impact on business. It is about growing iconic, market-leading brands from the first day and tapping into continuous business mentoring, excellent training, and hands-on responsibility. Whichever area they join, graduates will have the opportunity to make a positive difference.

Graduates will have real responsibility from day one, an opportunity of becoming a manager after three years, and a great support network to see them develop and attain their future goals. Unilever will support them in achieving Chartered status and qualifications such as CIMA, IMechE, IChemE, IEE, APICS, ICS and CIPD.

With such a great ambition lie exciting challenges for the company and its brands, and a fantastic opportunity for graduates to have a great head start in their career, and to make a real difference to Unilever's business and the world!

GRADUATE VACANCIES IN 2019
ENGINEERING
FINANCE
HUMAN RESOURCES
LOGISTICS
MARKETING
RESEARCH & DEVELOPMENT
SALES
TECHNOLOGY

NUMBER OF VACANCIES
40-50 graduate jobs

LOCATIONS OF VACANCIES

STARTING SALARY FOR 2019
£32,000

UNIVERSITY VISITS IN 2018-19
ASTON, BATH, BIRMINGHAM, BRISTOL, CAMBRIDGE, DURHAM, EXETER, IMPERIAL COLLEGE LONDON, KING'S COLLEGE LONDON, LANCASTER, LEEDS, LIVERPOOL, LOUGHBOROUGH, MANCHESTER, NEWCASTLE, NOTTINGHAM, OXFORD, SHEFFIELD, STRATHCLYDE, UNIVERSITY COLLEGE LONDON, WARWICK
Please check with your university careers service for full details of local events.

MINIMUM ENTRY REQUIREMENTS
2.1 Degree

APPLICATION DEADLINE
18th November 2018

FURTHER INFORMATION
www.Top100GraduateEmployers.com
Register now for the latest news, campus events, work experience and graduate vacancies at **Unilever**.

Unilever

CHANGE
LED BY YOU

A BETTER BUSINESS. A BETTER WORLD. A BETTER YOU.

JOIN NOW **UNILEVER.CO.UK/CAREERS/GRADUATES**

Virg.in/graduates

VMGradsandInterns@VirginMedia.co.uk

linkedin.com/company/Virgin-Media   twitter.com/VirginMediaJobs

instagram.com/VMearlycareers   youtube.com/VirginMediaCareers

Virgin Media is part of Liberty Global plc, the world's largest international cable company. Serving 5.9 million cable customers and 3.1 million mobile subscribers across the UK and Ireland, Virgin Media helps to connect people and enable them to experience the endless possibilities of the digital world.

Virgin Media is powering a digital world that makes good things happen. Since the invention of the internet, digital technology has had an increasing impact on the way people live and communicate. But it's not just technology that interests Virgin Media, it's how technology can be used to improve lives and prospects.

Across the UK and Ireland, Virgin Media offers four multi-award winning services – broadband, TV, landline and mobile – and is in the process of growing all aspects of the business so it can connect more of its customers to the things and people they care about.

Virgin Media is looking for the future leaders and experts who can help them stay ahead of the game. In return, its graduates will be put right at the heart of the business – dialling up their strengths, stretching and challenging the norm and broadening their knowledge of the company and the telecoms industry.

Whether a candidate sees their future in finance, marketing or another exciting area of Virgin Media, every graduate will gain the relevant knowledge, skills and experience they need to supercharge a successful career. Virgin Media believes that anything is possible and encourages its graduates to grab new opportunities, get involved and gain invaluable experience through exposure and education.

So, why not join Virgin Media – one of the world's most exciting companies – kick start your career, and make good things happen.

GRADUATE VACANCIES IN 2019
ENGINEERING
FINANCE
GENERAL MANAGEMENT
HUMAN RESOURCES
MARKETING
SALES

NUMBER OF VACANCIES
60+ graduate jobs

LOCATIONS OF VACANCIES

STARTING SALARY FOR 2019
£30,000+
Varies by function.

UNIVERSITY VISITS IN 2018-19
ASTON, BATH, BIRMINGHAM, CAMBRIDGE, DURHAM, IMPERIAL COLLEGE LONDON, LEEDS, LOUGHBOROUGH, MANCHESTER, OXFORD, READING, SOUTHAMPTON, SURREY, UNIVERSITY COLLEGE LONDON, WARWICK
Please check with your university careers service for full details of local events.

MINIMUM ENTRY REQUIREMENTS
Varies by function

APPLICATION DEADLINE
Varies by function

FURTHER INFORMATION
www.Top100GraduateEmployers.com
*Register now for the latest news, campus events, work experience and graduate vacancies at **Virgin Media**.*

Wellcome exists to improve health for everyone by helping great ideas to thrive. Wellcome is a global charitable foundation, both politically and financially independent. It supports scientists and researchers, takes on big problems, fuels imaginations and sparks debate.

Wellcome's independence allows it to support transformative work, such as co-funding the development of a new Ebola vaccine, leading policy and campaign work to promote change in mitochondrial donation, and opening Wellcome Collection – a museum and library that explores medicine, life and art.

Wellcome is well known for funding scientific and medical research, but more broadly it is interested in the intersection of health and society, and so is looking for graduates from all backgrounds. For recent graduates, Wellcome offers a two-year graduate development programme. During the programme, graduates try out four different jobs for six months at a time. These could involve working with Wellcome's Africa and Asia Programmes, writing parliamentary briefings, or identifying new ways to engage the public. No matter which rotations graduates choose, they'll be valued members of the team, with support from mentors, line managers and peers. They'll also benefit from training, real responsibilities, and the knowledge that they're contributing to Wellcome's overall purpose.

With a focus on development, the programme encourages graduates to select rotations outside of their comfort zone, to expand their career potential. At the end of the programme many graduates go on to more senior roles at Wellcome, while others move to other charities, further study, cultural venues or even set up their own businesses. Whatever graduates choose, Wellcome values ongoing relationships with their alumni so they can continue to make a difference in global health.

GRADUATE VACANCIES IN 2019

ACCOUNTANCY
FINANCE
GENERAL MANAGEMENT
HUMAN RESOURCES
INVESTMENT BANKING
MARKETING
MEDIA
RESEARCH & DEVELOPMENT
TECHNOLOGY

NUMBER OF VACANCIES
12 graduate jobs

LOCATIONS OF VACANCIES

STARTING SALARY FOR 2019
£26,000

UNIVERSITY VISITS IN 2018-19
BATH, BIRMINGHAM, BRISTOL, BRUNEL, CAMBRIDGE, CITY, EAST ANGLIA, EXETER, IMPERIAL COLLEGE LONDON, KING'S COLLEGE LONDON, KENT, LEICESTER, LONDON SCHOOL OF ECONOMICS, QUEEN MARY LONDON, READING, SHEFFIELD, UNIVERSITY COLLEGE LONDON, YORK
Please check with your university careers service for full details of local events.

MINIMUM ENTRY REQUIREMENTS
2.2 Degree

APPLICATION DEADLINE
November 2018

FURTHER INFORMATION
www.Top100GraduateEmployers.com
Register now for the latest news, campus events, work experience and graduate vacancies at Wellcome.

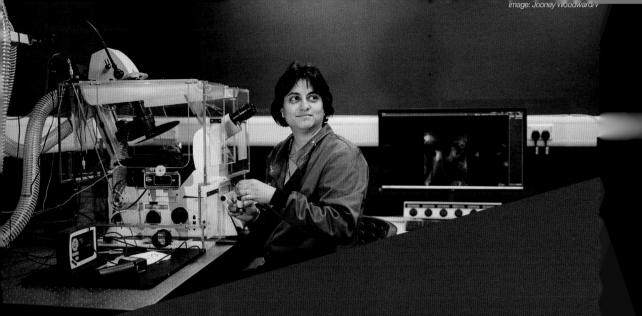

—

"It's two years of learning and discovery in an inspiring and supportive working environment"

Robyn, joined Wellcome in 2017

—

wellcome

WHITE & CASE

White & Case is a global law firm with nearly 2,000 lawyers worldwide. They've built an enviable network of 44 offices in 30 countries. That investment is the foundation for their client work in 160 countries today. Many White & Case clients are multinational organisations with complex needs that require the involvement of multiple offices.

White & Case trainees will work on fast-paced, cutting-edge, cross-border projects from the outset of their career. In London, the key areas of work include: bank finance (including regulatory compliance); financial restructuring and insolvency; capital markets (high yield and securitisation); dispute resolution (including antitrust, commercial litigation, intellectual property, international arbitration, trade, white collar and construction and engineering); energy, infrastructure, project and asset finance (EIPAF); corporate (including M&A, private equity, employment, compensation and benefits, investment funds, real estate and tax).

White & Case is looking to recruit ambitious trainees who have a desire to gain hands-on practical experience from day one and a willingness to take charge of their own career. They value globally-minded citizens of the world who are eager to work across borders and cultures, and who are intrigued by solving problems within multiple legal systems.

The training contract consists of four six-month seats, one of which is guaranteed to be spent in one of their overseas offices, including Abu Dhabi, Beijing, Dubai, Frankfurt, Geneva, Hong Kong, Moscow, New York, Paris, Prague, Singapore, Stockholm, and Tokyo. The remaining three seats can be spent in any one of the firm's practice groups in London. Receiving a high level of partner and senior associate contact from day one, trainees can be confident that they will receive high-quality, stimulating and rewarding work.

GRADUATE VACANCIES IN 2019

LAW

NUMBER OF VACANCIES
50 graduate jobs
For training contracts starting in 2021.

LOCATIONS OF VACANCIES

STARTING SALARY FOR 2019
£46,000

UNIVERSITY VISITS IN 2018-19
BIRMINGHAM, BRISTOL, CAMBRIDGE, DURHAM, EDINBURGH, EXETER, KING'S COLLEGE LONDON, LEEDS, LONDON SCHOOL OF ECONOMICS, MANCHESTER, NOTTINGHAM, OXFORD, QUEEN MARY LONDON, SCHOOL OF AFRICAN STUDIES, SOUTHAMPTON, ST ANDREWS, TRINITY COLLEGE DUBLIN, UNIVERSITY COLLEGE DUBLIN, UNIVERSITY COLLEGE LONDON, WARWICK, YORK
Please check with your university careers service for full details of local events.

MINIMUM ENTRY REQUIREMENTS
2.1 Degree

APPLICATION DEADLINE
Please see website for full details.

FURTHER INFORMATION
www.Top100GraduateEmployers.com
*Register now for the latest news, campus events, work experience and graduate vacancies at **White & Case**.*

Together we
make a mark

The future of law is global. If you'd like to
join a firm that guarantees all trainees an
overseas seat, we'd like to hear from you.
whitecase.com/careers

WHITE & CASE

WPP

www.wpp.com

GRADUATE VACANCIES IN 2019
MARKETING
MEDIA

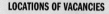

NUMBER OF VACANCIES
To be confirmed

LOCATIONS OF VACANCIES

WPP is the world leader in communications services - including digital, ecommerce and shopper marketing; advertising & media investment management; data investment management; public relations & public affairs; brand consulting; health & wellness communications; and specialist communications.

WPP's companies set industry standards and work with many of the world's leading brands, creating communications ideas that help to build growth for their clients. Collectively, over 203,000 people (including associates and investments) work for WPP companies, in over 3,000 offices across 112 countries.

WPP Fellowships develop high-calibre management talent with unique experience across a range of marketing disciplines. Over three years, Fellows work in three different WPP operating companies, each representing a different marketing communications discipline and geography. Fellows are likely to work in a client management or planning role, although some work on the creative side of an agency. Each rotation is chosen on the basis of the individual's interests and the Group's needs.

Fellowships will be awarded to applicants who are intellectually curious and motivated by the prospect of delivering high-quality communications services to their clients. WPP wants people who are committed to marketing communications, take a rigorous and creative approach to problem-solving, and will function well in a flexible, loosely structured work environment. WPP is offering several three-year Fellowships, with competitive remuneration and excellent long term career prospects with WPP. Many former Fellows now occupy senior management positions in WPP companies.

STARTING SALARY FOR 2019
Dependent on scheme

UNIVERSITY VISITS IN 2018-19
Please check with your university careers service for full details of local events.

APPLICATION DEADLINE
Please see website for full details.

FURTHER INFORMATION
www.Top100GraduateEmployers.com
Register now for the latest news, campus events, work experience and graduate vacancies at **WPP**.

WPP

Ambidextrous brains required

For more information,
visit our website at

www.wpp.com

Useful Information

EMPLOYER	GRADUATE RECRUITMENT WEBSITE	EMPLOYER	GRADUATE RECRUITMENT WEBSITE
AECOM	aecom.com/amazing	HSBC	www.hsbc.com/earlycareers
AIRBUS	www.jobs.airbus.com	IBM	ibm.biz/uk-graduates
ALDI	www.aldirecruitment.co.uk/graduate	IRWIN MITCHELL	graduaterecruitment.irwinmitchell.com
ALLEN & OVERY	aograduate.com	JAGUAR LAND ROVER	www.jaguarlandrovercareers.com
AMAZON	www.amazon.jobs	JOHNSON & JOHNSON	www.jnjuniversityrecruitment.com
AON	www.aonearlycareers.co.uk	J.P. MORGAN	careers.jpmorgan.com/careers
APPLE	www.apple.com/jobs/uk	KPMG	www.kpmgcareers.co.uk/graduates
ARMY	apply.army.mod.uk/what-we-offer/regular-officer	L'ORÉAL	careers.loreal.com/global/en
ARUP	www.arup.com/careers	LIDL	www.lidlgraduatecareers.co.uk
ASOS	asoscareers.asos.com	LINKLATERS	careers.linklaters.com
ASTRAZENECA	careers.astrazeneca.com/students	LLOYD'S	www.lloyds.com/graduate
ATKINS	careers.atkinsglobal.com/graduates	LLOYDS BANKING GROUP	www.lloydsbankinggrouptalent.com
BAE SYSTEMS	www.baesystems.com/graduates	MARKS & SPENCER	marksandspencergrads.com
BAKER MCKENZIE	uk-graduates.bakermckenzie.com	MARS	mars.co.uk/graduates
BANK OF ENGLNAD	www.bankofenglandearlycareers.co.uk	MCDONALD'S	people.mcdonalds.co.uk
BARCLAYS	joinus.barclays/eme	MI5 - THE SECURITY SERVICE	www.mi5.gov.uk/careers
BBC	www.bbc.co.uk/careers/trainee-schemes	MORGAN STANLEY	www.morganstanley.com/campus
BLACKROCK	careers.blackrock.com	NETWORK RAIL	www.networkrail.co.uk/careers/graduates
BLOOMBERG	bloomberg.com/careers	NEWTON	newtoneurope.com/graduate
BMW GROUP	www.bmwgroup.jobs/uk	NGDP	www.local.gov.uk/national-graduate-development-programme
BOOTS	www.boots.jobs/graduate-schemes	NHS	www.nhsgraduates.co.uk
BOSTON CONSULTING GROUP	careers.bcg.com	PENGUIN RANDOM HOUSE	www.penguinrandomhousecareers.co.uk
BP	www.bp.com/grads/uk	PINSENT MASONS	www.pinsentmasons.com/graduate
BRITISH AIRWAYS	www.britishairwaysgraduates.co.uk	POLICE NOW	www.policenow.org.uk
BT	www.btplc.com/careercentre/earlycareers	PWC	pwc.co.uk/careers
CANCER RESEARCH UK	graduates.cancerresearchuk.org	ROLLS-ROYCE	careers.rolls-royce.com
CHARITYWORK	www.charity-works.co.uk	ROYAL AIR FORCE	www.raf.mod.uk/recruitment
CIVIL SERVICE	www.faststream.gov.uk	ROYAL NAVY	www.royalnavy.mod.uk/careers
CLIFFORD CHANCE	careers.cliffordchance.com/london	SANTANDER	www.santanderjobs.co.uk/realiseyourfuture
CMS	graduates.cms-cmno.com	SAVILLS	savills.co.uk/graduates
DANONE	www.danonegraduates.co.uk	SHELL	www.shell.co.uk/graduates
DELOITTE	deloitte.co.uk/careers	SIEMENS	siemens.co.uk/careers
DLA PIPER	www.dlapipergraduates.com/uk/apply	SKY	skyearlycareers.com
DYSON	careers.dyson.com/early-careers	SLAUGHTER AND MAY	www.slaughterandmay.com
EXXONMOBIL	careers.exxonmobil.com	TEACH FIRST	teachfirst.org.uk/recruitment
FRESHFIELDS	www.freshfields.com/ukgraduates	TESCO	tesco-careers.com/programmes
FRONTLINE	thefrontline.org.uk	THINK AHEAD	www.thinkahead.org
GOLDMAN SACHS	goldmansachs.com/careers	TPP	www.tpptop50.com
GOOGLE	www.google.com/students	UNILEVER	www.unilever.co.uk/careers/graduates
GRANT THORNTON	trainees.grant-thornton.co.uk	VIRGIN MEDIA	virg.in/graduates
GSK	www.gsk.com/careers	WELLCOME	www.wellcome.ac.uk/graduates
HERBERT SMITH FREEHILLS	careers.herbertsmithfreehills.com/uk/grads	WHITE & CASE	www.whitecasetrainee.com
HOGAN LOVELLS	hoganlovells.com/graduates	WPP	www.wpp.com